VICTORIAN COLONIAL WARFARE

Other published titles by Donald Featherstone
All for a Shilling a Day
MacDonald of the 42nd
Captain Carey's Blunder
At Them with the Bayonet!
Colonial Small Wars 1837–1901
Conflict in Hampshire
The Bowmen of England
Weapons and Equipment of the Victorian Soldier
Victoria's Enemies
Featherstone's Complete Wargaming
Wargames
Naval Wargames
Air Wargames
Advanced Wargames
Wargames Campaign
Battles with Model Soldiers
Wargames through the Ages
Vol. 1 3000 BC–AD 1500
Vol. 2 1420–1783
Vol. 3 1792–1859
Vol. 4 1861–1945
Poitiers 1356 – Battles for Wargamers
Battle Notes for Wargames
Solo Wargaming
Tank Battles in Miniature: The Western Desert Campaign
Tank Battles in Miniature: The Mediterranean Theatre
Skirmish Wargames
Wargaming the Ancient and Medieval Periods
Wargaming the Pike and Shot Period
The Wargamers Handbook of the American Revolution
Wargaming Airborne Operations
Battles with Model Tanks (with Keith Robinson)
Tackle Model Soldiers this Way
Handbook for Model Soldier Collectors
Military Modelling
Better Military Modelling

VICTORIAN COLONIAL WARFARE

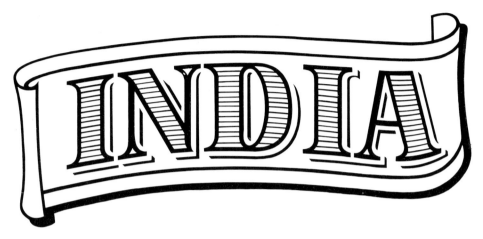

**from the conquest of Sind
to the Indian Mutiny**

Donald Featherstone

BLANDFORD

First published in the UK 1992
by Blandford, a Cassell imprint
Villiers House, 41/47 Strand
LONDON WC2N 5JE

This edition 1993

Distributed in the United States
by Sterling Publishing Co., Inc.,
387 Park Avenue South, New York, NY 10016-8810

Distributed in Australia
by Capricorn Link (Australia) Pty Ltd,
PO Box 665, Lane Cove, NSW 2066

British Library Cataloguing-in-Publication Data
Featherstone, Donald, 1918-
  Victorian colonial warfare from the conquest of
Sind to the Indian mutiny.
  I. Title
325.3410954

ISBN 0-7137-2255-X

Typeset by Litho Link Limited, Welshpool, Powys

Printed in Great Britain by
Hillmans Ltd, Frome, Somerset

Contents

Preface

The aim of this book is to transport its reader back in time – in effect to become the eyes and mind of his or her great-great grandfather and see, by means of words and pictures, 'How our boys are doing in India.' This transformation of the reader into 'a fly on the wall of history' is made possible by the revelation, through contemporary quotations and illustrations, of the way these wars were experienced and viewed at the time they were taking place.

This 'view' was created by three distinct groups. *The participants* – the military personnel, the soldiers – British and otherwise – and their commanders fighting the wars; *the onlookers* – the ever-present war correspondents and military artists describing them in words and pictures; and the *newspapers* and *magazines* of the day – whose reports, publications of official despatches, illustrations and general contemporary presentations shaped the way in which events were seen by the public.

Thus transported back in time, the reader will understand the shaped contemporary view, so that he or she considers the events of that day and era without the sanitising distortion of historical awareness and hindsight.

Since these colonial wars took place, historians and journalists have written millions of words in their attempts to analyse, assess, condemn, praise, recriminate or debunk – but none of us was actually *there* on the day, and so we cannot capture the real feel of those events as experienced at first hand by the troops who fought them or the journalists who were privileged to witness them. Only by scrutiny of the actual contemporary writings and illustrations – for this was before the camera appeared on the battlefield – can one acquire a really 'truthful' version of these Victorian small wars and the men who fought them.

Anything other than first-hand accounts are an abridged, often academic, collection of latterday conclusions, culled from other literature and adulterated as much as enlightened by each writer's personal bias and opinion. In no way can this reflect the human aspects of

both friend and foe, nor can it do justice to their courage and fears, their noble or ignoble reactions.

In Britain during the nineteenth century as in America and Europe – there was a vast public interest in the seemingly perpetual colonial wars, and all classes eagerly devoured first-hand accounts of victories and defeats, written 'on the spot' by a plethora of war correspondents, whose names became household words – William Russell, G. A. Henty, Archibald Forbes, H. M. Stanley. And there were many others who accompanied the expeditions, exposing themselves to the same dangers and hardships as the soldiers. Alongside these men worked talented artists, sketching pictures of the violence taking place around them. Returned to Britain with all possible speed, these sketches were carved onto boxwood printing blocks to emerge within weeks of their birth as graphic woodcuts in illustrated journals, such as the *Illustrated London News*, *Black and White*, *The Graphic* and *Penny Illustrated*.

The extraordinary commercial expansion of the nineteenth century was accompanied by a spread of literacy, which created a new buying public avid for the details that a new popular press was always ready to print. And most popular were the stories and reports of the heroic deeds – in defeat as well as victory – of British soldiers fighting on the far-flung battlefields of the Empire. Lacking radio, television or the cinema, all that the general public really knew of these stirring events was gleaned from the pages of the journals and accounts in contemporary books.

By means of extensive quotes from such sources, this book is an attempt to place its readers in the same position as those earlier readers who followed the unfolding of events in chronological order.

With some justification it might be asked of this book, 'But where are all those numerous other minor campaigns and expeditions fought in India during the Victorian era?' And there were many – Sikkim, 1861, Ambela, 1863, Bhutan, 1865, Lushai, 1871, Manipur,

1891, Chilas, 1892, Chitral, 1895 and Tirah, 1897–8. Perhaps even better known was the North-West Frontier – that ready-made battle-school for every Victorian soldier, where rarely a year passed without Afridis, Mahsuds, Mohmands, Orakzais or Wazirs rising up to bring a bloody upsurge of ferocious border fighting.

However, despite being unquestionably hard-fought and ruthless, the importance of minor wars in the general picture of the British in India, pales to insignificance when compared with the historic and military importance of five major wars

The Conquest of Sind
The Gwalior War
The First Sikh War
The Second Sikh War
The Indian Mutiny

Their story only has to be read to understand the justification for allowing them to take up the entire book. (In fact, each is fully entitled to fill a book of its own!) However, this concentration on five major and significant campaigns does not diminish the other mentioned lesser campaigns and expeditions, nor the colourful tapestry of the North-West Frontier.

To prevent possible misunderstanding, it must be explained why some place-names are spelt differently, sometimes within the space of a few lines or a paragraph. When contained in contemporary Victorian reports and quotations, they are left in the Victorian style of spelling – *Beloochee, Moodkee* and *Scinde,* for example – when they form part of the author's text they are presented in modern style thus, Baluchi, Mudki and Sind.

Introduction

In the beginning . . . this Indian Empire, governed by a curiously complicated bargain between a sovereign and a company, has been growing for a hundred years, and still continues growing. In fits of national anger or international generosity, we inveigh against the Czar of Russia for processes of aggression and plans of annexation in regions around and between the Caspian and Black Seas, and we compassionate and assist his weak neighbours under the pressure of his ambition; but it is only in times of excitement or peril that we consider the extraordinary way in which our own Indian Empire has been built up – by conquest, by purchase, by forfeiture – and in some cases by means which, called robbery by our enemies, do at any rate demand a little compunction from us as a Christian people.

THE HISTORY OF THE REVOLT IN INDIA, *1859*

During the Victorian era, in the numerous far-flung corners of the Empire, most colonial campaigns fought by British soldiers presented diverse features, and drastically different styles of fighting were encountered from the varied enemies. In sharp contrast to such foes as Ashantis, the Dervishes and Hadendowah tribesmen of the Sudan, or the militant hillmen of the North-West Frontier of India, some Victorian small wars were against enemies trained and organised like regular troops, formed into battalions, squadrons and batteries, with efficient weapons comparable to those of such British forces as the armies of the East India Company. When, as in the case of the Khalsa – the Sikh army of the Punjab – they had been trained by instructors with knowledge and experience of European methods, the subsequent operations resembled the regular warfare of the day. Their undoubted fighting capacity and considerable courage necessitated hard fighting before they could be defeated.

The five major wars fought in India during the 15 years between 1843 and 1858 were all against these organised armies. Beginning with the Baluchis in Sind, then the Mahrattas in Gwalior, followed by two wars in the Punjab against the Sikhs, the British faced the best trained, best organised and most courageous of all enemies in India. The rebel sepoys of the Indian Mutiny could put British-trained armies in the field, and the operations against them were of a most definite and stirring character. How victory was finally achieved was discussed in 1906 by C. E. Callwell in *Small Wars: Their Principles and Practice*:

'The records of small wars show unmistakably how great is the impression made . . . by a bold and resolute procedure. The military history of our Indian Empire affords proof of this on every page. From the days of Clive down to the present time victory has been achieved by vigour and by dash rather than by force of numbers. The spirit of attack inspiring leaders and subordinates alike has won the day for us. Arcot, Plassey, and Meani may be cited as examples; their story is familiar to all. And in no campaign has this spirit been more constantly evinced, and has its influence been demonstrated with such irresistible force, as in that where the enemy was from strength of numbers and from the peculiar conditions which prevailed the most formidable – the Indian Mutiny.

'During this great struggle the operations in the field consisted, almost to a monotonous extent, of a succession of combats in which small British columns always attacked the very superior forces of the enemy, and always beat them. Blow upon blow was delivered, and the rebels were never allowed to strike back. It was not that there was no resistance – far from it; the mutineers in the earlier stages always fought with courage, at times they fought with desperation. Nor was it that the

11

enemy was crushed by force of armament; relatively to the British troops the rebels were supplied with efficient weapons. It was the spirit of the offensive animating the British leaders and their men throughout the vicissitudes of a singularly active campaign, which led to their long succession of victories.'

Indeed, in those lines probably lies the formula that brought British success in all these wars – resolute, breathtakingly courageous, all-out infantry attacks, in which cold steel prevailed without a shot being fired during the approach, although invariably with incredible numerical inferiority. Read the awed testimony of Sikh soldier Hookhum Singh, describing the advance of the 10th Regiment of Foot at Sobraon, or Napier's nonchalant acceptance of odds of eight-to-one at Miani. Note the persistent Sikh numerical superiority in both Sikh Wars, and remember that the Indian Mutiny abounds with such occasions, with few more astonishing than the puny force on the ridge besieging Delhi.

Decisive battles such as Arcot, 1751, Plassey, 1757, Pondicherry, 1760, and Assaye and Laswari, both in 1803, had played a major part in establishing British rule in India. Their effects were coalesced in the five wars fought between 1843 and 1858, and India was thus moulded into the form it was to retain until 1948. Characteristic in their form and style for the place and the time, these battles and wars were archetypal Victorian colonial conflicts.

A notable feature of the period was the extraordinary collection of commanders it threw up, some perhaps whose charisma veiled perceptible tactical failings but who, without exception, possessed in abundance that greatest of all virtues, courage, together with a blind and unquestioning patriotism and belief in their cause. What visions are conjured up by their names – Sir Charles Napier, Sir Hugh Gough, Sir Harry Smith, Sir Henry Lawrence, Sir John Lawrence, William Hodson, John Nicholson, Sir Herbert Edwardes, Sir Henry Havelock, Sir James Outram, Sir Colin Campbell (Lord Clyde) and Sir Hugh Rose. It is interesting to speculate on what these men of action would have made of this panegyric from E. H. Nolan's *The Illustrated History of the British Empire in India and the East*, which was published in the mid-1860s:

'The story of English power and progress in India, and of the wars waged with Persia, China, and other contiguous countries, is probably the most romantic and curious ever unfolded. What deeds of heroism! what unforeseen and unexpected conquests! what striking and singular providences! over what variety and extent of realm the flag of Britain has been unfurled! through what remote glens, and passes, and defiles, her sound of bugle and tap of drum have echoed! on what historic, and yet far-off, fields and mountains the sheen of her bayonets has gleamed in the blazing light of the Eastern sun! even when progressing only by her commerce and her law, and the reverberation of her cannon ceased among the hills and valleys of the vanquished, how largely she has entered into what Sir Archibald Alison has designated the everlasting war between East and West! how the opinions and feeling of Britain have percolated the moral soil of Asia, to spring up again in renewing and fertilising streams! The people of England must become better acquainted with all this if they will impress their own image upon the Eastern world, and leave it for posterity to recognise. They must study these records of their own fame, as well as of earlier times, if they perform the still nobler task of impressing the image of their God and Saviour upon the oriental heart. If we rise to the greatness of our opportunities and apparent destinies, we need have no fears for our work or for ourselves.'

1 · The Conquest of Sind
1843

Another glorious achievement has been added to the long line of our Indian triumphs. The conquest of Scinde has been completed by a victory equal, in all respects, to that of the 17th February, which gained us a footing in the country, and still more decisive in its results: 19 standards, 11 pieces of cannon, and some thousands of killed and wounded are the trophies of an engagement in which the victors were one to five, as in the former they had been only one to eight. Meeanee and Hyderabud will long be remembered as worthy to rank with Plassey and Assaye, or any other of those memorable battles which laid the foundation or consolidated the edifice of our Indian power. If any one ever doubted the bravery of our native Indian troops, when commanded by generals who treat them with fairness, and respect their opinions and prejudices, that doubt must have been dispelled by the events of the last three months. They have proved themselves superior to the bravest enemy whom they could encounter in Asia, and capable of meeting a European army, should any continental power be found possessed of ambition, daring, and resources sufficient to instigate it to dispute with us the empire of India. They have shown by their steady bravery, their cool discipline, their physical powers of endurance, that they are worthy to stand in battle by the side of Britons, and to contend for the palm of valour with those who have ever been foremost in the strife, whether in Europe or Asia, at Badajoz and Salamanca, or on the blood-stained ramparts of Bhurtpore, and at the blazing gate of Ghuznee.

The selection of Sir Charles Napier by Lord Ellenborough for the command-in-chief of the army of Scinde, and for the government of the conquered province has been most fortunate. Well has he justified the confidence reposed in him, and upheld the great interests intrusted to his charge. His campaign has demonstrated that he possesses military genius of the highest order, for in no quality of a great commander has he shown himself deficient. The promptitude and vigour of his operations, the decision with which, on hearing of the treacherous attack on the British residency at Hyderabud, he pushed forward, without losing a moment, avenged the outrage, and overwhelmed his opponents in a great battle – the celerity of his advance from his entrenched camp to the scene of the recent action, where the Scindian chiefs had again collected their shattered forces, and resolved to risk a fresh contest – his energy in battle, now exercising the careful and vigilant superintendence of a cautious commander, now exposing his person to the storm of shot like the meanest soldier in his army, and leading his gallant followers to the charge which swept the foe from his path, are all that could be wished in the ideal of a leader. A sign yet more sure of his talents for war is the enthusiastic confidence with which he has inspired his troops, and which, we are told by those who write from the information of eye-witnesses, was such, that 'his army might have been cut to pieces, but could never have been defeated.' It is in securing the attachment of their men that many commanders, otherwise great, have failed, and in this object, so difficult of attainment, Napier has been successful.

Doubts have been cast, by some of our daily contemporaries, on the justice of the course which the Governor-General of India has pursued in the Scindian war. The invasion of that country has been represented in the light of an unprovoked aggression; and we are told that at no distant day we shall be driven out from Scinde in disgrace, and that the disasters of Affghanistan will be acted over again. Those who hold this language forget that the Ameers drew upon themselves the retribution which has fallen upon them; that, after intriguing with our enemies, and being in consequence compelled to sign a treaty, acceding to certain demands of the British Government, they violated that treaty when the wax of its seal was scarcely cooled, and made an attack on the life of our envoy from which although he escaped uninjured, the British residency was destroyed. Is no punishment to be awarded for a gross breach of faith, and a flagrant insult to the Majesty of England in the shape of its ambassador?

ILLUSTRATED LONDON NEWS, *10 June 1843*

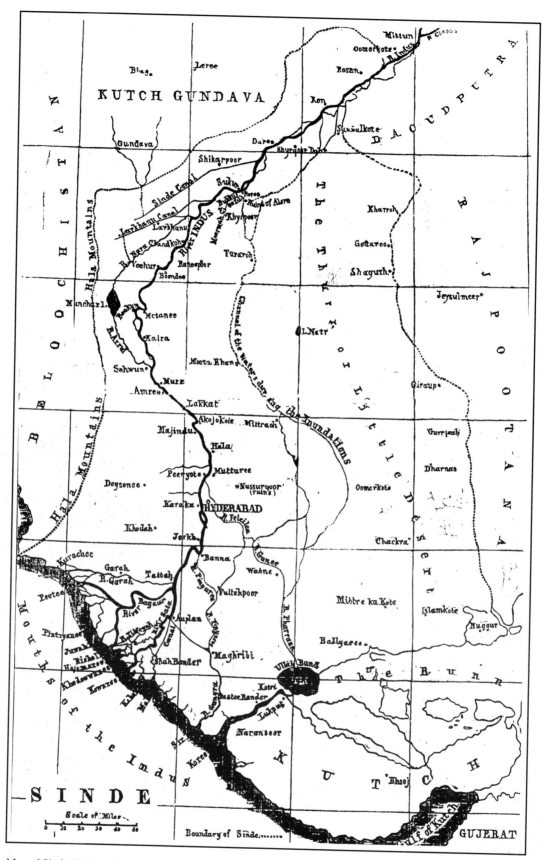

Map of Sind, 13 May 1843.

The sword was barely in the sheath and the last shots scarcely fired in the Afghan and China wars than the Governor-General, Lord Ellenborough, found himself involved in troubles in Sind that were described by the conquering Napier as 'the tail of the Afghan storm'. Lying in the valley of the Indus between India and Afghanistan in what today is Pakistan, in 1843 Sind was a native kingdom whose chieftainship was divided among the Amirs of Khyrpur (Upper Sind), Hyderabad (Lower Sind) and Mirpur on the borders of the eastern desert. Its population of slightly more than a million was composed of four distinct elements – Sindians proper, Hindus, Baluchis of the plains and Baluchis of the mountains. Contemporary reports provide an outline of the situation as it was seen at the time:

'The Government of India was most anxious to obtain control of the Indus for commercial and strategic reasons, and it was evident that while the Amirs of Sind held the banks of the river they could interfere with traffic on its waters. The Amirs of Sind – a class little less rapacious than the Pindari chiefs – has been most unfriendly and suspicious since Lord Auckland, the previous Governor-General, had forced them to allow the Army of the Indus to traverse their country on its journey to Afghanistan in 1838, and since the disastrous retreat from Cabul had assumed a hostile and defiant attitude. So determined was Lord Ellenborough to gain the Indus that he seems to have deliberately provoked a war against the Amirs and [it was reported] to have been discovered by the Indian Government that the Amirs were in league with the Sikh chief of Multan and other powerful leaders [in the Punjab] and were gradually weaving a scheme by which our Indian empire was indisputably in danger; and they were only waiting an opportunity to take us by surprise. Nothing remained to us now but the usual recourse to arms, yet it was not taken precipitately, and the Amirs received a warning letter from the Governor-General.'

There were those who disagreed with the policy of the Indian Government, as other reports of the day reveal:

'Various treaties had been forced already on these free and independent chiefs; and now Britain treats their country as if it were a province taken in war. When Lieutenant Eastwick, on behalf of the Bombay Government, laid before the Amirs the draft-treaty, Noor Mohamad, one of the most powerful, took from a box all the treaties currently in force and, with some sarcasm, asked what was to become all of these? Before he could be replied to, he added indignantly: "Here is another annoyance! Since the days that the Sind has been connected with Britain there has always been something new; your Government is never satisifed. We are anxious for your friendship, but we cannot be continually persecuted. We have given a road to your troops through our territories, and now you wish to remain!" Later, the death of this patriotic chief facilitated the designs of Britain, which were carried out with as little sense of scruple as of justice.'

Lord Ellenborough's choice of what was by way of

being a military 'dictator' was Sir Charles Napier to whom, at the time of placing him in civil and military command, Ellenborough said:

'Should any Amir or chief with whom we have a treaty of alliance or friendship, have evinced hostile intentions against us during the late events, which may have induced them to doubt the continuance of our power, it is the present intention of the Governor-General to inflict upon the treachery of such ally and friend so signal a punishment as shall effectually deter others from similar conduct.' (Reported in 'Parliamentary Papers referring to Sind')

Napier was a remarkable man, whose nature was to a certain extent akin to his appearance. He was said to be 'aggressive, dictatorial and, at times, merciless . . . as brave as a lion, a good tactician, sound administrator, and popular with his men'. Military historian Sir John Fortescue described him thus:

'His appearance was so strange that the Baluchis might well have mistaken him for a demon. Beneath a huge helmet of his own contrivance there issued a fringe of long hair at the back, and in front a large pair of round spectacles, an immense hooked nose and a mane

Sir Charles Napier, from the Illustrated London News, *6 April 1843.*

of moustache and whisker reaching to the waist.'

An entry in his journal, written in India on 10 August 1842, says much for the man:

'This day 60 years old. Well, patriotism is no chimera; it is the resolution to be honest, carried into effect where our country requires us to act contrary to our wishes, comforts and happiness. Perhaps few trials are more severe than sending a man of 60 away from his family to a distant country and a bad climate. Well, Lord Collingwood did not flinch, nor will I, if I know myself. I am too old for glory now . . . if a man cannot catch glory when his knees are supple he had better not try when they grow stiff!'

These views did not prevent Napier taking up the sword and writing: 'We have no right to seize Scinde, yet we shall do so; and a very advantageous, useful humane piece of rascality it will be!' In expressing such a view, Napier was merely reflecting the beliefs of his age, for most Victorians were convinced that the benefits of British rule justified all interference with existing rights, particularly when exercised by such as the corrupt and tyrannical confederation of Amirs who governed Sind so poorly. It was a sincere conviction of the age that nothing but improvement could result from British government in Sind, although idealistic administrators such as Henry Lawrence and James Outram did not share this view, both believing the Amirs to have been forcibly dispossessed of hereditary rights. The chivalrous aspects of Outram's character aroused within him a deep sympathy with the Amirs, and he strove unceasingly to avert their approaching downfall. At his own request, Outram went to Hyderabad with Napier's words echoing in his ears: 'I am sure the Amirs will not resist by force of arms, but I would omit no step that you think can avert that chance.' The time for signing the treaty was extended time and time again, but Outram, unwilling to believe reports of warlike preparations by the Amirs, told Napier that not a man in arms could be seen in Hyderabad and suggested that he should come alone to the city. 'This,' said Outram, 'will remove all difficulties,' to which the General replied: 'Yes, and my head from my shoulders!', a remark uttered in the knowledge that spies had reported 25,000 men gathering within a few miles of Hyderabad and a further 25,000 converging on the general rendezvous.

However, on 12 February 1843, 'in full durbar, with all formalities,' wrote Napier, the Amirs signed the treaty. As soon as this was known, noted Outram in a letter to Napier, 'the spirit of the people rose and they execrated the Amirs for their dastardly submission to what they [the people] called robbery'. Outram and his suite were assaulted as they left the durbar and reached the residency in safety only with the aid of Baluchi cavalry sent by the Amirs. On the following two days, according to Outram, the hostile spirit of the people increased. The treaty was stolen and torn to pieces and trampled upon by the mob, and more than 4,000 Baluchis, under the leadership of Amirs Shahdad and Sobdar, planned to attack the residency. Napier, 'disre-

garding the signature of the treaty, which he looked upon as a mockery', had continued his advance, and, anticipating that the residency might be attacked, he sent an armed steamer, with ammunition and reinforcements, to join Major Outram.

'From one of those incidents so frequent in war,' said Napier's biographer, Sir William Napier, 'the steamer proceeded without the men or the supplies, and Major Outram had therefore to resist the assault of 8,000 men with 6 guns, with two steamers, a stone house, and 100 men, each with but 40 rounds of ammunition.'

Fighting his way out of his dilemma, Outram came up with the main army at Muttari, a town on the Indus, one march north of Miani, and immediately reported to Napier, to whom he persisted in declaring that 'the innocent Amirs desired peace . . . [and] pressing the General to halt another day'. Sir Charles Napier, aware that the enemy outnumbered him by at least eight to one, refused to listen to his representations. Buoyed by the belief that 'the great recipe for quieting a country is a good thrashing first and a great kindness afterwards; the wildest chaps are thus tamed,' Napier fell in his army of 2,800 men, of whom only 500 were British, and prepared for war. Against him were massed an estimated 25,000 Baluchis.

His daring he revealed characteristically by an astonishing demonstration in early January 1843, at a time when the Amirs were seeking to harass him by petty incursions against his communications and base. Napier had heard of the fortress of Emaum Ghur, which lay 100 miles out in the great eastern desert, and knew that the Amirs considered it invulnerable and beyond the reach of a hostile force. Now Napier announced his resolution of reducing and destroying Emaum Ghur because it was known as 'the Gibraltar of Upper Sind', and he was determined to show the Amirs that 'neither the deserts nor their negotiations could intercept the progress of a British army'. The fort's location was unknown to Napier, although he believed it to be about eight long marches from Khyrpur, over vague and ill-defined tracks. Scouts brought in such dismal accounts of arid sands and dried-up wells that he determined to take only a picked body of men. His force consisted of 350 men of the Queen's 22nd Regiment, two men to a camel, two 24-pounder howitzers with double teams of camels, and 200 troopers of the Sind horse. They took provisions for 15 days and water for five days.

Leaving Dejee on the night of 5 January 1843, two marches brought the little force to the springs of Dom, where they saw trees and found water; Choonka was reached on 7 January, and 150 troopers were sent back. The rest pressed on for eight days, with the forces of the Amirs constantly in evidence but not offering any opposition, and on 12 January they were before Emaum Ghur, where Napier stood on a sandy eminence looking down at the square fort that had been built of burned brick, with round towers about 50 feet high. There was a weird and deathly silence about the place, the clatter of Napier's horse's hoofs in the courtyard awakening the

Sir Charles Napier's cavalry chasing a Baluchi force in Sind, 1843.

echoes. Completely deserted by the garrison, loaded cannon crouched on the battlements with priming freshly laid. It was effectively destroyed, using 10,000lb of Baluchi powder, in sight of clouds of angry enemy horsemen hovering in the distance. The astonishing event was reported in a journal of the day:

'Thus the impregnable refuge of the Ameers, the fortress which no European had ever before seen, fell into British hands without the loss of a single man. During the three days of rest twenty-four mines were loaded with gunpowder; and just before the departure the fortress was blown up. "Emaum Ghur [wrote Napier] is shattered to atoms with 10,000 lb of powder. The explosion was grand and hellish beyond description; the volumes of smoke, fire, and embers flying up were a throne fit for the devil!"'

The force then withdrew and on 21 January reached Peer Abubeker, on the road from Khyrpur to Hyderabad. Without a single casualty, they returned to the vicinity of Dejee to await the arrival of the rest of Napier's army. Of this desert expedition, the Duke of Wellington wrote:

'Sir Charles Napier's march on Emaum Ghur is one of the most curious military feats I have ever known to be performed, or have ever read an account of, in my life. He moved his troops through the desert against hostile forces; he had his guns transported under conditions of extreme difficulty, and in a manner the most extraordinary; and he cut off a retreat of the enemy which rendered it impossible for them ever to regain their position.'

True to his creed of never retreating before a barbarian army, Napier moved rapidly towards the Baluchi encampment on the plain before Miani, six miles north of Hyderabad, in the district of Tutta, where the Indus is a mile wide and 18 feet deep. On the night before the battle, Napier wrote to John Kennedy, a friend:

'Not to be anxious about attacking such immensely superior numbers is impossible, but it is a delightful anxiety. . . . It is my first battle as a commander, it may be my last. At sixty that makes little difference, but as my feelings are it will be do or die. . . . God bless my wife and precious girls. My hope is to live or die worthy of them: no Cabul for me to make them blush.'

Napier's official account of the action, sent to Lord Ellenborough on 18 February, appeared in the *Illustrated London News* on 13 May 1843:

'From Major-General Sir C. J. Napier, KCB., commanding in Scinde and Beloochistan, to Lord Ellenborough, Governor-General, &c.

Meanee, six miles from Hyderabad. 18 February

'My Lord, the forces under my command have gained a decisive victory over the army of the Ameers of Upper and Lower Scinde. A detailed account of the various circumstances which led to this action does not belong to the limited space of a hasty despatch. I therefore begin with the transactions belonging to the battle. On the 14 inst., the whole body of the Ameers, assembled in full durbar, formally affixed their seals to the draft treaty. On leaving the durbar, Major Outram and his companions were in great peril – a plot had been laid to murder them all. They were saved by the guards of the Ameers; but the next day (the 15th) the residence of Major Outram was attacked by 8,000 of the Ameer's men headed by one or more of the Ameers. The report of this nefarious transaction I have the honour to enclose. I heard of it at Hala, at which place the fearless and distinguished Major Outram joined me with his brave companions in the stern and extraordinary defence of his residency against so overwhelming a force, accompanied by six pieces of artillery. On the 16th I marched to Muttaree, having there ascertained that the Ameers were in position at Meanee (10 miles distant) to the number of 22,000 men, and well knowing how a delay for reinforcements would both strengthen their confidence and add to their numbers, already seven times that which I commanded, I resolved to attack them, and we marched at four a.m. on the morning of the 17th. At six o'clock the advanced guard discovered their camp; and at nine o'clock we formed in order of battle, about 2,800 men of all arms, with 12 pieces of artillery. We were now within range of the enemy's guns, and 15 pieces of artillery opened upon us, and were answered by our cannon. The enemy were very strongly posted – woods were on their flanks, which I did not think could be turned. The two woods were joined by the dry bed of the river Fulaillee, which had a high bank. The bed of the river was nearly straight and about 1,200 yards in length. Behind this and in both woods the enemy were posted. In front of their extreme right, and on the edge of the wood, was a village. Having made the best examination of their position which the time permitted, the artillery was posted on the right of the line, and some skirmishes of infantry with the Scinde Irregular Horse were sent in front to try and make the enemy reveal his force more distinctly.'

In *England's Battles by Sea and Land*, William Cooke Stafford recorded: 'He had twelve small guns, under Major Lloyd, which were placed on the right; the Scinde irregular horsemen, led by Captain Lamb, covered the left; and the centre was formed of the 22nd, under Colonel Pennefather; the Bombay sepoys; the 25th, under Major Teesdale; the 12th, under Major Reid; and the 1st sepoy grenadiers, under Major Clibborne.'

Napier's despatch continues: 'we then advanced from the right in echelon of battalions, refusing the left to save it from the fire of the village. The 9th Bengal Light Cavalry formed the reserve in rear of the left wing; and the Poonah Horse, together with four companies of infantry, guarded the baggage. In this order of battle we advanced, as though at a review, across a fine plain, swept by the cannon of the enemy. The artillery and Her Majesty's 22nd Regiment in line formed the leading echelon, the 25th Native Infantry the second; the 12th Native Infantry the third, and the 1st Grenadiers (Native Infantry) the fourth.'

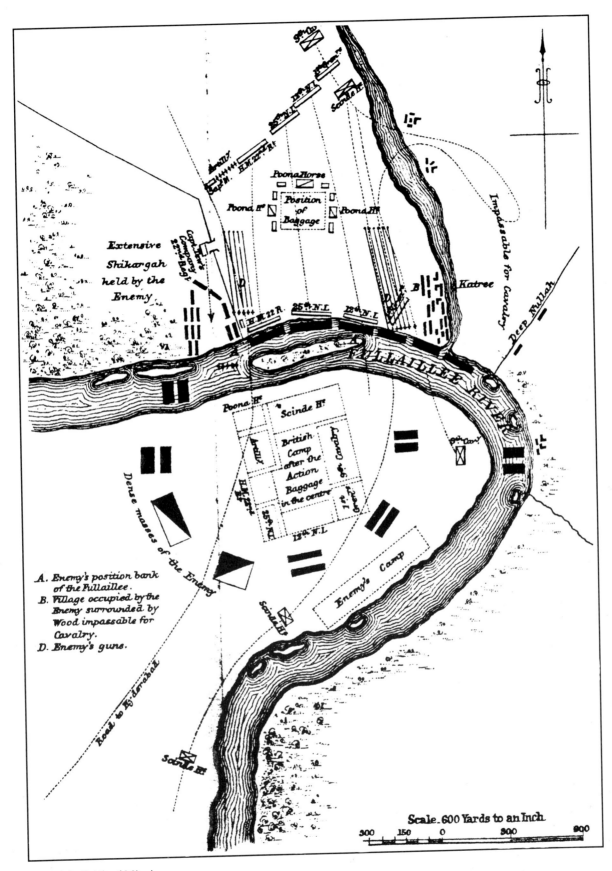

Plan of the Battle of Miani.

are the paragraphs mentioning by name the officers who had particularly distinguished themselves, for Napier gave credit to individual officers for valour and energy. He also did something never before known in the history of the British Army when he mentioned by name non-commissioned officers, privates and even a drummer who had performed exceptionally on the field of battle. More than that, Napier also listed the names of Indian soldiers whose conduct had been brought to his notice; thus, for the very first time, Havildar Thackur Ram and Sowar Motee Singh were honoured by a 'mention in despatches'.

It is also interesting to consider that Napier's comments on the leading of sepoys in action seemingly received little attention, as the same faults manifested themselves two years later, in Gough's army during the First Sikh War.

Napier's tactics of attacking in echelon were designed to protect his refused left flank from possible threat by the village on its flank and, at the same time, to bring as quickly as possible into action his best troops, the 22nd Regiment. These troops, with their high morale, would then pierce the weaker Baluchi centre by their bayonets rather than by sheer fire power. In his book *Defects, Civil and Military, of the Indian Government*, which was written in 1853. Sir Charles Napier claimed that: 'no troops in the world will stand the assault of British troops, if made with the bayonet and without firing.' In addition, he believed that: 'The short range and very uncertain flight of shot from the musket begets the necessity of closing with the enemy, which the British soldier's confidence in superior bodily strength, due to climate, pushes him to do.'

In the event, at Miani it did not work out in that manner, and a letter of John Jacob (who was present at the battle in command of the Sind Horse) reveals that Napier and other regimental commanders vainly entreated the 22nd to charge. For this regiment, on coming upon the dense mass of Baluchis in the river bed, withdrew to the edge of the bank from where they poured in successive volleys, while the guns enfiladed the position. Lieutenant Montague McMurdo of the 22nd Regiment is said to have been told by a man of his own regiment that he would shoot him if he did not cease in his efforts to lead an assault. McMurdo later testified that it was, in fact, disciplined fire power rather than the bayonet that carried the day. Another officer of the 22nd, Major Waddington (or Warrington), said

Hyderabad.

much the same thing: 'the bayonet was but little used except in defence, and it shortly became evident that the fire of the [Baluchi] matchlock and the glancing of the keen sabre were less and less frequent, while the continued and destructive roll of musketry, delivered from the edge nearly of the river bank, levelled every living being before it.'

As soon as he received Napier's report, Lord Ellenborough, not waiting to ascertain the result of the campaign in Sind and the occupation of its capital city, issued on 5 March a proclamation annexing Sind to the British possessions and ordering the Amirs to be sent to Bombay as prisoners. Napier's first thought was to reinforce his army, and Stafford tells of his efforts:

'He . . . sent to Kurrachee and Sukkur, to order every detachment that could be spared to be sent to him; and Lord Ellenborough, who heard rumours of the battle of Meeanee before the general's despatch reached him, ordered three regiments of infantry, 350 of Chamberlain's irregular horse, and a camel battery, to be dispatched immediately to Sukkur, and from thence to Hyderabad. Captain Leslie's and Blood's batteries of horse artillery, the 3rd Bombay cavalry, and 800 sepoy infantry, under Major Stack, were also detached from General Nott's force after it passed the Sutledj, and forwarded to Hyderabad. Whilst waiting for the arrival of troops, the general formed an intrenched camp on the banks of the Indus, where he placed his hospitals and stores; and by his other arrangements for the security of his position, "manifested all the discretion and ability of an officer familiar with the most difficult operations of war."'

These last words were spoken by the Duke of Wellington, in his speech moving the thanks of the House.

Stafford continues the story:

'Communications above and below Hyderabad were cut off by the Beloochees at Shah Ghur, under Roostum's nephew Mohammed Ali on the one side and by Shere Mohammed on the other. The latter also was gathering a force with which he meant to attack and retake Hyderabad. In March, having considerably reinforced his already considerable army, Shere Mohammed advanced upon Hyderabad. He took up a strong position at Dubba, four miles from the city.'

Sir William Napier wrote of him 'openly boasting' that he would 'Cabool the British' and how he sent a message to the General on 18 March, saying: 'Quit this land and your life shall be spared, providing you restore all you have taken.' Seemingly the evening gun was firing as the message was delivered, causing Sir Charles Napier to say: 'You hear that sound? It is my answer to your chief. Begone!'

Napier's subsequent actions were reported at length in the *Illustrated London News* on 13 May 1843:

'The Overland Mail from Bombay, express from Marseilles, brings the important details of the victory

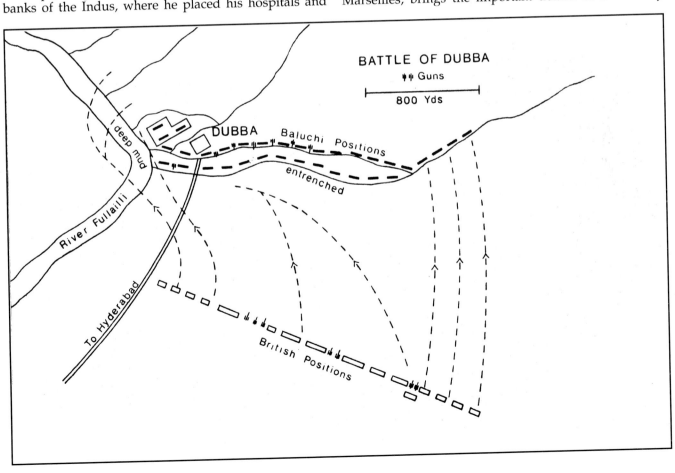

gained by Sir Charles Napier, on 24th March. It will be remembered that a rumour of this second splendid victory had reached Bombay on the morning of the last despatch, but the particulars of the actions were jumbled together in such a confused manner that it was impossible to render it intelligible. The following, however, is a narrative of this brilliant affair.

'At daybreak on the morning of the 24th, Sir C. Napier with a force of 3,000 set out in pursuit of the enemy. He came up with them about eight o'clock the same morning and found them amounting to 20,000 under the personal command of Shere Mohammed Khan of Meerpoor, occupying a position much stronger than that taken up at the battle of Meanee. They were drawn up almost in a straight line, having the village of Dubba in rear, with two parallel ditches cut out in one of those huge nullahs which traverse their country – one eight feet by twenty wide, the other seventeen by forty-two feet wide; these ditches appear to have been recently formed and the earth being heaped up behind the original embankment, thus forming two considerable barriers. On the right lay their favourite stream, the Fullalie; and at a short distance from its opposite bank, a dense shikergah, or jungle. Indeed, from the nicety shown in the selection of their position and the ingenuity displayed in rendering it so formidable, their assailants were impressed with no mean idea of their acquaintance at least with the arts of war; and found that they had profited in no slight degree by former reverses. The enemy having opened fire on our approach, Major Leslie with a troop of horse artillery, moved forward and attempted to rake the nullah; while the 9th Light Cavalry and Poonah Horse, on his left, advanced in lines, his right being supported by Her Majesty's 22nd Regiment. The latter, however, being too far forward to allow of the oblique range of Leslie's guns, a partial stop was put to operations; but on this being remedied, the artillery opened a terrific fire, and the troops advanced in echelons of regiments, the 22nd leading the attack. Her Majesty's 22nd Regiment attacked the nullah on the left; but being desired to reserve their fire until within forty paces of the entrenchment, and being completely exposed in this manner to the fire of the enemy's match-lockmen,

The 22nd Foot advance into the nullah at Dubba.

suffered exceedingly in consequence, having 23 men killed and 131 wounded; and ultimately succeeded in carrying the entrenchment in the most gallant style. Lieut. Cooke, who was the first to mount the rampart, succeeded in seizing one of the enemy's standards and while waving it and cheering the men onward, was severely wounded. The Poonah Horse under Captain Tait, and Major Storey in command of the 9th Cavalry, turned the enemy's right flank and pursued them for a considerable distance. Major Woodburn, at the head of the 2nd Brigade, consisting of the 25th, 21st and 12th Regiments . . . and protected by the fire from Major Whitley's battery, bore down all before them; and on the right of these again the 8th and 1st Regiments . . . and who, while advancing towards the entrenchments, observed a portion of the Scinde Horse and the 3rd Cavalry who had, while charging the enemy, got directly in front of the 2nd Brigade and within range of our own fire. Not a moment was lost in checking the firing, and when all was adjusted, they carried on in the most gallant manner, driving off the enemy at every point.

'The Horse Artillery and Her Majesty's 22nd Regiment completed the work by scouring the villages and jungles. No quarter was asked or given and, as a proof of the deadly nature of the strife, only five prisoners were taken.'

The British had lost 20 officers and 250 men (39 killed and 231 wounded), more than half these casualties occurring in the ranks of the long-suffering 22nd Regiment. The Baluchis were said to have lost as many as 6,000 men, and reports tell of between 500 and 600 counted dead on the field of battle and as many more in the village and jungles. Writing of the battle in later years, Napier said:

'God knows I was very miserable when I rode over the fields, and saw the heaps of slain: then all my own soldiers stark and stiff as we laid them in a row for burial next day.'

In his book *The Conquest of Scinde*, Sir William Napier talks of 'eight hundred dead bodies laying in the nullahs and at Dubba . . . all the villages and lanes beyond the latter place were so filled with dead and dying that, to avoid them, the army was forced to encamp on the ground it occupied before the action commenced. All the fallen Beloochees were of mature age – grim-visaged men of athletic forms; the carcase of a youth was not to be found.'

The trophies of this battle, which has been called by three names – Dubba, Naraja and Hyderabad – were 17 standards and 15 guns; 11 taken on the field and four next day. The Duke of Wellington, addressing the House, said that the Battle of Dubba was 'a brilliant victory, in which he [Sir Charles Napier] showed all the qualities of a general officer, and in which the army displayed all the best qualities of the bravest troops'.

Three of the Baluchi chiefs fell in the action, but Shere Mohammed had escaped in the direction of the desert. Napier personally led a small detachment of cavalry some 80 miles into the desert, to the fort of Omerkote, supposedly garrisoned by 4,000 troops but found to be abandoned. Napier attached great importance to this capture, writing: 'Omerkote is ours . . . this completes the conquest of Scinde; every place is in my possession; and, thank God I have done with war. Never again am I likely to see a shot fired in anger.'

However, the account of the conclusion of the war in Sind given in Stafford's *England's Battles by Sea and Land* suggests that he was a little premature:

'Shere Mohammed remained in the desert till the close of April, when he removed to Khoonhera; and as the robber bands joined him, he was soon surrounded by 8,000 or 10,000 men, with four guns. His brother, Shah Mohammed, also collected a considerable force at Sehwan, a town situate at the verge of a swamp on the right or south-west bank of the Arul, which flows from Lake Monchur to the Indus. The object of Sir Charles Napier was to prevent the junction of the two brothers; and dividing his force into three bodies, one of which he commanded himself – the other two being under the orders of Colonel (late Major) Jacob and Colonel Roberts – he succeeded, by his skilful dispositions, in keeping the two Beloochee armies in an isolated position. On the 7th of June, it was ascertained that Shah Mohammed had encamped at Peer-Arres, near the Lukkee hills, fourteen miles from Sehwan. Here he was attacked, on the 8th, by Colonel Roberts, his troops dispersed, himself and seventeen attendants taken prisoners, and his matchlocks, swords, and shields captured. Shere Mohammed was pursued by the divisions under Sir Charles Napier and Colonel Jacob; and finding that he had little or no hopes of escape, and learning that Jacob had the weakest force, he determined once more, with him, to try the fortune of war. Of his 10,000 men and four guns, so many had left him, that when, on the morning of the 14th of June, he came up with Jacob's division, he had not more than 4,000 men and three guns. He took his post behind a deep nullah, commanding the left wing himself, and giving the right, which was composed of cavalry, to Mohammed Khan. The British were now slow in accepting what looked like a challenge. The ground was so rugged, that they had great difficulty in coming into action; and after a brief cannonade on both sides, the Beloochee infantry dispersed; and the following is the account which Mohammed Khan gave to Sir Charles Napier of the cavalry: –

'"I commanded the right wing; the Ameer commanded the left; he had the guns, and I nearly all the cavalry. It was hardly light when I heard the Lion's guns. I thought that Jacob was upon him, as there was nothing I could distinguish in my front: I therefore rode full gallop, expecting to charge Jacob's flank. You know our horrible dust; it was in vain to look for a man. I thought I was followed. I reached the Ameer; he was alone almost. On halting, the dust cleared off, and behold! only twenty-five men were with me. I was lucky; for had Jacob been there, I should have been killed. But all had run under cover of the dust, and so the Lion and I ran also; and this is all I know of the battle."

'That battle completed the conquest of Scinde. Shere Mohammed (the Lion) escaped across the Indus, and degenerated into a mere robber-chief, being joined by Mohammed Ali, the nephew of Roostum. Mohammed Khan surrendered to the British general, to whom, soon afterwards, 400 minor chieftains came in and gave up their swords, all of which, though very valuable, Sir Charles returned.'

Revealing himself as a true prophet, Sir Charles Napier wrote at the time: 'We have taught the Belooch that neither his sun, nor his deserts, nor his jungles, nor his nullahs can stop us. He will never face us more.'

Although feeling a deep sympathy for the poor people of Sind, Napier agreed with the Governor-General that there could be no question of returning the country to the Baluchis. His conquest of their country he justified by maintaining that the common people would be better off under British rule than under the Amirs. In June, treaties were forgotten, and Sind was annexed to become part of the Bombay presidency, adding nearly 50,000 square miles to the British Empire; Napier was appointed its first governor.

BATTLE HONOURS FOR SIND, 1843

MIANI

22nd (Cheshire) Regt. of Foot

Indian Army

Poona Auxiliary Horse
1st Regt. Scinde Irregular Horse
2nd Regt. Scinde Irregular Horse
Corps of Madras Sappers & Miners
12th Regt. Bombay Native Infantry
25th Regt. Bombay Native Infantry

DUBBA

22nd (Cheshire) Regt. of Foot

Indian Army

3rd Regt. Bombay Light Cavalry
Poona Auxiliary Horse
1st Regt. Scinde Irregular Horse
2nd Regt. Scinde Irregular Horse
Corps of Madras Sappers & Miners
1st or Grenadier Regt. Bombay Native Infantry
8th Regt. Bombay Native Infantry
12th Regt. Bombay Native Infantry
21st Regt. Bombay Native Infantry (The Marine Battalion)
25th Regt. Bombay Native Infantry

SIND

22nd (Cheshire) Regt. of Foot

2· The Gwalior War
1843

The Indian Mail of the 1st February announces two victories which have been fought at Gwalior, vis., Maharajpoor and Punniar; our loss has been severe: 141 killed, and 866 wounded. Nine officers have been killed or died of their wounds, viz., Major-General Churchill, Col. Sanders, Major Crommelin, Captains Stewart, Magrath, and Cobban; Lieutenants Newton and Leaths; and Ensign Bray. The loss of the enemy is estimated at between 3,000 and 4,000 killed and wounded, with the loss of 56 pieces of artillery. The army under the Commander-in-Chief was about 14,000 strong, of which 3,000 was cavalry, and 40 pieces of artillery. The force opposed to this – 15,000 infantry, 3,000 cavalry, and 100 guns. The wing under General Grey, including the Sippree Contingent, 7,000 strong, including 1,800 cavalry, and 28 guns; the Mahrattas mustered about 12,000, with from 20 to 30 guns.

ILLUSTRATED LONDON NEWS, 9 March 1844

Written in 1840, Macaulay's 'Essay on Lord Clive' recalled the ancient terror of the Mahratta name, and, in a memorable paragraph, Macaulay wrote:

'The highlands which bordered on the western sea-coast of India poured forth . . . a race which was long the terror of every native power and which, after many desperate and doubtful struggles, yielded only to the fortune and genius of England. It was under the reign of Aurungzebe (1658-1707) that this wild clan of plunderers first descended from their mountains; and soon after his death, every corner of his wide empire learned to tremble at the mighty name of the Mahrattas. Many fertile viceroyalties were entirely subdued by them. Their dominions stretched across the peninsula from sea to sea. Mahratta captains reigned at Poonah, at Gwalior, in Guzerat, in Berar, and in Tanjore. Nor did they, though they had become great sovereigns, therefore cease to be freebooters . . . Every region which was not subject to their rule was wasted by their incursions. Wherever their kettledrums were heard, the peasant threw his bag of rice on his shoulder, hid his small savings in his girdle, and fled with his wife and children to the mountains or the jungles, to the milder neighbourhood of the hyaena and the tiger . . . Even the European factors trembled for their magazines. Less than a hundred years ago it was thought necessary to fortify Calcutta against the horsemen of Berar, and the name of the Mahratta ditch still preserves the memory of the danger.'

In the crowded century of conquest that marked the career of the East India Company, the Mahrattas displayed the stoutest and most prolonged resistance to the expansion of British rule. Four times in a space of 65 years, these warriors of the Deccan faced the Company's armies in the field, and on every occasion acquitted themselves as staunch and worthy foes. In 1778, a 2,500-strong East India Company army, despatched to attack Poona, was compelled to retreat after abandoning its guns. In 1803 the victories of Lake and Wellesley at Laswari and Assaye brought considerable territorial acquisitions. Fifteen years later, during the administration of the Marquess of Hastings, war broke out again, and the brilliant campaigns of 1817 and 1818 once more reduced the turbulent area to order. The year 1843 was full of uneasiness and anxiety to those responsible for British rule in India. The annihilation of British-led forces in Afghanistan in the previous year had sadly affected Britain's prestige as the paramount power in the country. The memories of the disaster suffered in the Khyber Pass suggested highly dangerous possibilities to British dominion and was vivid in the minds of the independent Indian princes whose tone became haughty

Gwalior, from the Illustrated London News, *9 March 1844.*

Kasgeewhala, 'the Usurper of Gwalior'.

and insolent. This defiant attitude was especially notice-able in the Punjab and in Sind. In the former a magnifi-cently trained army of 80,000 men and 300 guns crouched on the British northwestern frontier, awaiting its opportunity. Within easy political touch with the Sikhs of the Punjab stretched the territory of Sind, which was garrisoned by a military force of 30,000 disciplined infantry, 10,000 cavalry and 200 guns. The real power in both these countries lay in the hands of these two stand-ing armies, which completely overawed and controlled the governments of Lahore and Gwalior, the capitals of the two countries. A combination of the Sikhs and the Mahrattas would have brought 120,000 men and 500 guns into the field against the East India Company, a force strong enough to make success extremely doubt-ful, unless it could be comprehensively defeated.

In Gwalior a boy of nine years of age was on the throne. He ruled through the agency of a powerful minister, but Gwalior was a hotbed of intrigue, and rival factions and internal jealousies raged and reduced the capital to a state of tumult and anarchy. The chief element antagonistic to the British was the military, whose hostility was based on the well-grounded convic-tion that Britain's aim was to secure the disbandment of the standing army. These fears were justifed, for large and powerful native armies were inconsistent with the civilisation the East India Company was spreading over India, and, wherever British power reached, standing armies were stamped out. The Mahratta military was the first to insist on resistance to the advance of British power in Sind. Discovering that secret negotiations were going on with the Sikhs, Lord Ellenborough, the Governor-General, decided to take the initiative and order the assembly of an army on the frontiers of Sind. It was divided into two wings, the right being collected in the north under command of Sir Hugh Gough, the Commander-in-Chief, and the left, on the eastern boundary, under General Grey. After addressing an explanatory letter to the Maharajah of Gwalior, Lord Ellenborough ordered the armies in motion on 17 December 1843, with orders to converge on Gwalior for the purpose, as he stated in a public proclamation, of effecting the establishment of complete order in that city.

The *Illustrated London News* of 9 March 1844 published extracts from this proclamation to 'explain the course of policy adopted by the noble lord'.

OFFICIAL DESPATCHES

CAMP HINOGONA, *27th Dec., 1843.*

'The British armies have entered the dominions of Scindia as the friends and allies of Maharaja, whose person and whose rights the British Government is bound by treaty to protect.

'The British Government desires only to establish the just authority of the Maharaja over all his subjects, and to place upon firmer and permanent foundations that friendship between the two states which, for their mutual benefit, has existed so long, and which, not the British Government, but the evil disposed advisers of the Maharanee, have now interrupted.

'The British Government knows only as enemies those who oppose its armies, and are obedient to the Maharaja, and disturbers of peace.

'The armies, will regard and treat as friends all peaceful cultivators and traders; they will pay for all supplies brought to the camp; give compensation for all injury unintentionally done to property, and injure no one but such as act hostilely.

'A strong government having been established at Gwalior, capable of maintaining the Maharaja's authority over all, and willing, as well as able, to preserve tranquillity on the common frontier, the British armies will return to their territory.

'By order of the Right Hon. the Governor General of India,

F. CURRIE, *Secretary to the Government of India,*
with the Right Hon. the Governor-General.
(True Copies).
J. P. WILLOUGHBY, *Secretary to the Governor.'*

Lord Ellenborough had joined Sir Hugh Gough's staff,

Lord Ellenborough.

hoping that his presence would aid in the maintenance of peace and that this demonstration of the effective power of the British Army might be sufficient to secure all he desired at Gwalior. Being imperfectly informed of the spirit and determination of the Mahratta army, he considered himself justified in insisting upon the extinction of that force. In a letter to the Queen, included in *The Indian Administration of Lord Ellenborough,* he explained his motives:

'It is a matter of great moment . . . to reduce the strength of the army maintained by the Gwalior State. It has long been the real master of the State. It is in amount wholly disproportioned to its revenues and wants; and it never can be otherwise than a subject of disquietude to have an army of thirty thousand men within a few days' march of Agras. The existence of an army of such strength in that position must very seriously embarrass the disposition of troops we might be desirous of making to meet a coming danger from the Sutlej.'

In order to avoid creating undue alarm at Gwalior, he requested the Commander-in-Chief to leave behind at

Agra his battering train, with the exception of 10 guns. But the Mahratta army, rightly suspecting Ellenborough's intention of disarming and disbanding them, threw off all vestiges of control, crying out that they were being betrayed and that they would resort to the test of battle. In the highest spirits, they marched out of Gwalior on 25 December 1844 and by the evening of the following day were in a strong defensive position at Chonda on the river Asun. Sir Hugh Gough was aware of this, as Robert S. Rait, his biographer reveals:

'The British army remained at Hingonah (six miles distant), and Sir Hugh had the Mahratta position carefully reconnoitred. He found that the enemy had wisely chosen their ground, which was protected on both sides by dangerous ravines, but that their flank could be turned by a march on a point where the Asun bends circuitously. On the evening of the 28th of December, Sir Hugh issued his instructions to officers commanding divisions and brigades. The difficulty of the ground involved the separation of the army into three columns; not only was it necessary to arrange for a speedy passage of the Kohari, but the country was very rough and intersected by deep ravines, only made practicable by the labours of the sappers. The routes for each column had been carefully chosen, and an officer of the Quartermaster-General's Department accompanied each column.'

Rait reveals that the three columns were formed as follows:

'*Right Column*: Cureton's Cavalry Brigade, H.M.'s 16th Lancers, Governor-General's Bodyguard, 1st Regiment of Light Cavalry, 4th Irregular Cavalry; supported by Major Lane's and Major Alexander's troops of horse artillery under Brigadier Gowan. The whole under Thackwell. *Central Column*: H.M.'s 40th Foot, 2nd and 16th Native Grenadiers; the whole under Valiant. *Left Column*: 2nd Division of infantry, under Dennis; 14th and 31st Native Infantry, and 43rd Light Infantry, under Brigadier Stacey, supported by Captain Browne's Light Field Battery. 3rd Division of infantry, under Littler. H.M.'s 39th Foot, and 56th Native Infantry, under Brigadier Wright, supported by Major Sander's Light Field Battery. Scott's Brigade of Cavalry. 4th and 10th Bengal Light Cavalry, supported by Captain Grant's troop of horse artillery.'

A second force under Sir John Grey had been assembled at Jhansi, and this was to march when ordered and advance on Gwalior from the south; this force consisted of: *1st Brigade*: 3rd Foot (The Buffs), 39th Native Infantry, 51st Native Infantry, 58th Native Infantry; *2nd Brigade*: 50th Foot; 38th Native Infantry, 50th Native Infantry, Sappers and Miners, *Cavalry Brigade*: 9th Lancers, 6th P.W.O. Cavalry, 8th Light Cavalry, 8th Irregular Cavalry. 1st and 3rd Troops 3rd Brigade Royal Horse Artillery.

Rait asserts: 'It was the intention of Sir Hugh to turn the enemy's left flank with Cureton's Cavalry Brigade, co-operating with Valiant's infantry, to threaten their right flank with Scott's Cavalry Brigade, and to attack their centre with Dennis's Division, supported by Littler.'

Gough had sent 'final instructions' to Grey on 25 December, when, as, Rait states, becoming aware of the Mahratta movements:

'He desired, if possible, to secure the co-operation of the two columns, and indicated to Grey the point selected for that purpose. The most direct route from Grey's position to Gwalior lay through the Antri Ghat, a narrow rocky ravine which it was quite evident the Mahrattas would defend: Sir Hugh therefore directed General Grey to leave this pass on his right and "to cut in on the high road from Nurwur [in Bhopal] to Gwalior." This road led to a strong hill fort called Himutgarh, which stood at the entrance of a narrow pass leading to Punniar, and Grey was instructed to leave this fort either to his right or to his left, and so make his way to Punniar. He was expected to reach Punniar on the 30th, by which time he would find a reinforcement, consisting of a contingent which had been stationed at Sipri to prevent any unrest there. These orders were, as we shall see, carried out by General Grey, but a movement on the part of the enemy prevented any attempt at co-operation, and the two wings fought separate battles with different bodies of the enemy.'

On 29 December, in three columns, the army marched out before daybreak without hindrance, eventually coming within a mile or so of the village of Maharajpore, about a mile and half nearer to them than Chondra, where the enemy was known to be posted. Possibly relying on his reconnaissance of the previous day or perhaps believing that the enemy would withdraw at the sight of British redcoats, Gough apparently had no scouts out, and the force was marching at ease and in column. Lord Ellenborough, the Governor-General, was riding on an elephant besides the advancing columns, accompanied by other elephants bearing Lady Gough, Harry Smith's wife Juanita, Miss F. Gough (the commander's youngest daughter) and Mrs Curtis (wife of the Commissary-General). Reportedly to avoid the dust raised by the advancing columns, this group of elephants were plodding along near the front of the army, and its adventures are related in a memorandum left by Sir Patrick and Lady Grant (the Major Grant and Miss Gough of the story):

'Their presence, mounted as they were on elephants, and so towering over the low roofs of the village, early attracted the notice of the enemy, and they came, almost at once, under fire. With their small escort they went to meet the troops as they marched up to Maharajpore, and kept behind them until they were actually engaged, when they looked out for any other regiment coming up, and followed them until they also were under fire. Towards the close of the day, their elephants, frightened by the explosion of a powder-magazine, ran away with them; and their ignorance of the fortunes of the battle added to the anxiety of their position. Major Grant was the first to reassure them with tidings of victory, and he conducted them back to Sir Hugh's camp.'

Lady Gough and the wives of several officers upon their elephants.

Their presence and adventures are confirmed by Sir Harry Smith, who wrote in a letter: 'Juana was under a heavy cannonade with Lady G., Miss G., and a Mrs Curtis on their elephants. Juana had this command of Amazons, and as she was experienced and they young, her command was anything but satisfactory.'

Sir Charles Napier, writing to Harry Smith early in 1844, treats humorously of the presence of these ladies under fire at this battle: 'I congratulate you on your feats of arms. You had a tough job of it: these Asiatics hit hard, methinks. How came all the ladies to be in the fight? I suppose you all wanted to be gloriously rid of your wives? Well, there is something in that; but I wonder the women stand so atrocious an attempt. Poor things! I dare say they too had their hopes. They talk of our immoral conduct in Scinde! I am sure there never was any so bad as this. God forgive you all. Read your Bible, and wear your laurels.'

Not unnaturally, it was later claimed that Gough had been surprised at Maharajpore, a claim indignantly repudiated by his biographer Rait, who wrote that there was no surprise in the ordinary sense of the term and that the legend owed its existence to two incidents in the battle:

'Littler's division, it will be remembered, had been drawn up a little beyond the point prescribed, and they had been under a harmless fire, just within distant range, while the Chief made his reconnaissance. Vague reports of this trivial incident gave rise, not unnaturally, to an impression of a surprise. In the second place, the presence in the field of the Governor-General and a party of ladies had a similar effect. Lord Ellenborough had been asked by Sir Hugh Gough to take up a position in the rear of the reserve battery, whence he might watch the fighting. When the Commander-in-Chief suddenly altered his plans for the battle, he omitted to send fresh information to the Governor-General; the reserve battery was that attached to Littler's force, and, as Littler now made the frontal attack, it came at once into action. It was suggested to Lord Ellenborough that he should retire to a safer position, a suggestion which, as Sir Henry Durand mentions, originated with a staff officer. He did so, but found himself exposed to the fire of a Mahratta battery, whose gunners observed that he was a person of importance. "Once in it [said Durand] he thoroughly enjoyed it, and seemed utterly regardless as to danger." . . . We have seen that the Commander-in-Chief knew that Maharajpore was held by the enemy the day previous to the battle, and that he made a personal reconnaissance for over half an hour before the action commenced. He expected to find it held as an outpost, but he had not anticipated that the enemy would play into his hands so far as to occupy it in force. It was this fact, and not the mere occupation of the village, that caused the change in his plans, a change whose object was to take full advantage of the enemy's error in diverting the fighting from their strong position at Chonda. To do so involved the necessity of precipitating the action, a necessity which carried with it some disadvantages; but this precipitation was the result of Sir Hugh Gough's personal inspection of the ground, not of an unexpected assault by the enemy. The Commander-in-Chief was not surprised at Maharajpore.'

So far as Gough is concerned, many of the details of the battle of Maharajpore are derived from private letters he wrote to his son after the action, complemented by a contemporary account written by General Sir J. Luther Vaughan, acting ADC to General Littler, who

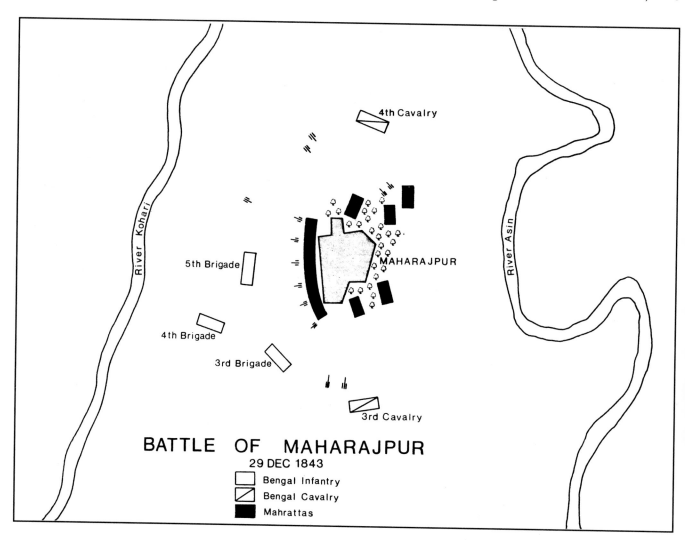

BATTLE OF MAHARAJPUR
29 DEC 1843

☐ Bengal Infantry
▨ Bengal Cavalry
■ Mahrattas

llowed Rait to print them in his biography of Gough:

'As they approached, they found the village strongly occupied by the enemy, who opened guns upon them. This was no surprise; Sir Hugh had never doubted that the enemy would have to occupy Maharajpore as an outpost, and, in point of fact, Major-General Churchill, the Quartermaster-General of Her Majesty's troops, had been fired at from Maharajpore on the previous day. Nor did the preliminary cannonade disconcert the British troops. Most of them, in fact, had not come up; Littler's Division, which had arrived, advanced about 500 yards beyond its appointed station at Jowra and so came within distant range; but so distant that the 39th Regiment piled arms, and sat down and breakfasted while the firing was going on. For an hour before either Valiant or the cavalry arrived, the Commander-in-Chief reconnoitred the position, walking within 300 paces of the enemy's sentries, allowing only one of his staff to approach him at a time, in order to avoid drawing the enemy's fire.

'The result of these investigations was to alter considerably Sir Hugh Gough's plan of attack. "I was surprised . . . and most agreeably surprised to see that they had pushed forward, into a plain open for all arms, so large a body of their force". His intention, in these circumstances, was to destroy the force at Maharajpore, and so to divert the fighting, as far as possible, from the strong position of Chonda. Accordingly, he gave orders to Littler to make a direct attack upon Maharajpore, while Valiant's Brigade took it in reverse, Major-General Dennis's Division acting as a support to both Littler and Valiant, along with Thackwell's Cavalry Division, which was specially directed to follow up any advantage secured by the infantry. When the army came up, Sir Hugh at once brought the field-guns (thirty in all) into action, to cover the advance of the divisions to which they were attached; and he sent orders to Colonel Tennant to bring up four 8-inch howitzers. As the enemy had opened fire, it would have been disastrous to withdraw, and the artillery responded to the enemy's challenge.'

The work of the artillery in this opening of the contest was described by eyewitness Sir C. A. Gordon KCB in his book *Recollections of Thirty Nine Years in the Army*:

'Horse Artillery commanded by Captain Grant, at full gallop, rode directly at the Gwalior Battery, opened fire upon it with crushing effect, and within the space of a few minutes reduced it to silence. Having done so, away again at full gallop, Captain Grant led his battery against one on the left of the former, that had meanwhile opened upon us, our infantry columns plodding their way, slowly but steadily against its line of fire. Very soon that battery also was silenced.'

As the full line of Mahratta batteries opened fire, their position, hitherto concealed by trees and the villages, was seen to extend in the shape of a horseshoe and to dominate their entire front. Between them and the British force stretched what appeared to be a lovely, level, green plain, with the tender crops just sprouting from the soil, but on advancing, the ground was found to be intersected with countless ravines, and on the smoother stretches between them there was not a stone or shrub to afford shelter. Aiming low and serving their guns with well-drilled rapidity, the enemy swept the ground from end to end with a murderous and withering fire. The broken surface of the plain made it impossible for the cavalry and artillery to act with effect, and the British line halted in uncertainty and inaction. They were about 1,500 yards from the village, well out of musketry range, and the British artillery had failed to silence the enemy batteries. The unslackening enemy fire filled the air with shot and chain and grape and canister, and in the British lines men were falling fast on all sides. Gough's plan of attack under the altered conditions was impracticable, and the old general's abiding faith in the British bayonet and the infantry who handled it came to the fore. He gave but one laconic order: 'On and at them!'

Exposed to an artillery fire that could not be returned by their own guns, the infantry struggled forward over the long and trying distance with only shouts and cheers, which soon died away as their breath was saved for the advance. Soon the difficulties of the ground obstructed their progress: ravines yawned before the advancing line and broke it up as the companies clambered down and up their sides. On the left, the 39th soon outstripped all others, outdistancing the 56th Native Infantry with which they were brigaded so that they were perilously isolated in advance. Noting this Gough grew anxious: 'Will no one get that native regiment along?'

Henry Havelock heard the appeal. At the time a comparatively unknown man, he had, after 28 years' service, only within the last few months obtained his regimental majority and was disappointed because his recent splendid services in Afghanistan had been overlooked. But he was a soldier before all things, and he spurred his horse forward to reach the native infantry regiment. He asked them their native name and was told they were Lambourne's Regiment. He placed himself at their head and, taking off his cap, called out to them to uphold the honour of their name. The appeal to their traditions had an almost magical effect and their demeanour changed; the laggards became eager warriors and, with Havelock at their head, they rushed forward to overtake the 29th.

Rait mentions this incident but in less detail:

'Littler now made his frontal attack. When Wright's Brigade (Her Majesty's 39th Foot and the 56th Native Infantry) came within three or four hundred yards of the village, the order was given to deploy into line. While this was being done, a round shot fell among the 56th Native Infantry and killed three men, causing the regiment to hang back for a moment. This was at once perceived by the Chief himself, who rode up and said: "For shame, men; look at your gallant comrades [the 39th]." The formation was at once completed and both regiments advanced upon the enemy's guns. The Mah-

Mahrattas at the Battle of Maharajpore, 1843.

ratta gunners now commenced firing grape, canister-shot, and even old horseshoes, anything, in short, that could be crammed in; but the brigade persevered.

'The plain was crossed with heavy loss, men falling by scores as they pushed on to the mouth of the Mahratta batteries. Not until Gough's infantry were within sixty yards of the enemy position was the order given to fire a volley and then charge. With a wild cheer, the infantry obeyed and dashed forward upon the guns, which were about twelve or fifteen yards apart and manned by ten or twelve men each. With a final rush, they captured them, bayoneting the gunners, who stuck nobly to their posts. Behind the guns stood the Mahratta Infantry, armed with matchlock and sword. After the matchlocks had been discharged, they engaged in a hand-to-hand conflict. In so sternly contested a field, there could not but be considerable

losses, especially in the British regiment which led the brigade, but, ere long, Valiant made his presence felt on the enemy's left and rear, and Scott's Brigade, with Grant's troop of horse artillery, operated on their right and dispersed a body of cavalry. Valiant, like Littler, met with a determined resistance; the conflict raged mercilessly, and very few of the enemy escaped from among the defenders of the position. All their guns (thirty in number) were captured. So quickly was this result achieved that Tennant was unable (in spite of two further messages from the Chief) to bring up the howitzers. Within half an hour after the first shot was fired into Valiant's column, the village of Maharajpore was in flames, its guns were taken, and the four regiments which had defended it were cut to pieces. Difficulties of ground made it impossible for Scott's Cavalry to prevent some of the enemy from escaping to the village of Shirkapore, which lay to the east of the direct route from Maharajpore to Chonda. The escape of these men necessitated Valiant's crossing by the rear of Littler to pursue them, and his instructions were, after taking Shirkapore, to attack the right of the enemy's position at Chonda, on which Littler was ordered to advance. Littler's Infantry Brigade was supported by the 1st Regiment of Light Cavalry and by the never-failing troop of horse artillery under Grant. As they approached, the enemy opened fire, to which our guns replied. The position was carried as before, by a rush of Wright's Brigade, in which the leader of the 39th Foot was very severely wounded; a number of men were killed by shots from Mahratta soldiers concealed by the stacks of corn through which the division was advancing, and it became necessary to leave no stack in the rear without putting the bayonet in first. The Mahrattas made a last stand in defence of a small work of four guns on their left, which was finally carried by Captain Campbell and the grenadiers of the 39th. Here the enemy did not await the final charge, but took refuge in the ravines behind their batteries, abandoning their camp. Not less severe fighting fell to the lot of Valiant's column. Near Shirkapore, Valiant had to take (in the words of the dispatch) "three strong entrenched positions, where the enemy defended their guns with frantic desperation; Her Majesty's 40th Regiment losing two successive commanding officers (Major Stopford and Captain Coddington, who fell wounded at the very muzzles of the guns) and capturing four regimental standards." The 40th Regiment was supported by the 2nd and the 16th Native Grenadiers, and ere long the enemy were driven back in headlong flight, having lost all their guns and making no attempt to defend the strong position afforded by the ravines at Chonda.

'The simultaneous success of Valiant and Littler had now resulted in the capture of the whole of the Mahratta artillery, and they had been driven from every position with enormous loss. Complete as was the victory, it would have been even more overwhelming, had not Thackwell's Cavalry Brigade, which had charged in support of the infantry, as occasion offered, been led too far to the right in its pursuit of the enemy when they finally broke and fled. It was, in consequence, stopped by a ravine, which prevented further pursuit. The Chief had ordered this brigade to form up close to Valiant, and had they done so, they would have "been one mile clear of any ravine, with a level country in their front, and might have swept that country in line between Maharajpore and Chonda." '

On 9 March 1844 the *Illustrated London News* published a very full report of the battle, detailing numbers of casualties that included even horses:

'GWALIOR – VICTORIES OF MAHARAJPOOR AND PUNNIAR.

'The disturbances which have so long been maturing in Gwalior, have at length come to a crisis, and, in a manner, as creditable to our Government as to our brave and valorous troops.

'The confederates of the now incarcerated Khasgeewallah, having, since his surrender, been supreme in the Court, every means have been used by them to ween the Maharanee from the confidence which she has begun to place in our professions. Having some to the determination of visiting the Governor-General in the camp, at Dholepore, and having gone a part of the way, she was advised, from the reports circulated by the Vakeels, then in our camp, on no account to visit it, as our professions of friendship were counterfeit, seeing that a large portion of the army were on their way to the capital, and had already crossed the river. This intelligence, combined with that brought by others, tending to the same effect, overturned all the resolutions which she had lately come to. Her first step on returning to Court, was to assemble all the chiefs and officers, and the resolution was come to of opposing the further advance of our troops. With this view, Colonels Baptiste and Jacob, were directed to oppose the advance of the right wing of our army, while Colonel Secunder was deputed to oppose our left. The first appearance of hostility was shown on the part of the enemy, by firing on the baggage party of Colonel Sleeman, and again on a reconnoitring party under Colonel Garden. This, of course, decided the course to be pursued, and General Sir J. Thackwell, with the troops under his command, was directed to make an immediate attack on the enemy's left flank, supported by those under Major General Valiant. The enemy's centre was ordered to be attacked by the troops under the command of Major-General Dennis, supported by those under Brigadier Wright. To the left of this, with the view of threatening the right flank of the enemy, was the 4th brigade of cavalry, under Colonel Scott. The whole of this force, numbering 3,000 cavalry, 12,000 infantry, artillery and sappers, with forty pieces of artillery, ten of which were howitzers and heavy guns, was about a mile in front of Maharajpoor, by eight o'clock on the morning of the 29th of December. It was found that the enemy had taken possession of the village the previous evening; some little alteration was requisite from the original disposition of the force, and General Littler's column was directed to advance from the village, while General Valiant took it in reverse. These being supported by General Dennis's column, with the two light field-batteries. When these columns arrived in front of the village of Jourah, the enemy opened their fire from Maharajpoor, where several regiments, with twenty-eight guns, had taken up their position. The brigade have deployed into line, was ordered to advance on Maharajpoor, from which issued a galling fire. Her Majesty's 39th, supported by the 56th Native Infantry, under General Littler, then advanced on the fort with the view of taking it in front, and having made a charge, cheering as they went, pushed forward, bearing down every obstacle. So severe was this struggle, that the enemy's artillerymen stood fighting at their guns until cut down in great numbers. Within the village, where numbers of the enemy had taken refuge, a severe hand-to-hand encounter occurred when the enemy, throwing down their matchlocks, resorted to the sword. Gen. Valiant, having at this time pressed upon, in order to take it in reverse, had to pass over six hundred yards of ground. In doing this he was assailed with rounds of grape and shot, and having stormed the battery he entered the village, carrying everything before him. Twenty-eight guns were here taken, and so desperately was this position defended that very few of the enemy escaped. Having finished this work at Maharajpoor, her Majesty's 39th, with the 56th Native Infantry, pushed forward towards the next position – Chonda. This was taken likewise, after a short but severe conflict. Here one of the enemy's tumbrils blew up, wounding Major Bragg. A small work, mounting four guns on the left of this position, was assailed by the 39th Grenadiers, under Captain Campbell, supported by a wing of the 56th Native Infantry. This was taken possession of and the guns captured. The action lasted about three hours, and no less than fifty-six pieces of artillery, with nearly the whole of their baggage and camp equipage, fell into our hands. The Governor-General, with Lady Gough and daughter, and several other ladies, were on the field – his lordship at times in the heat of action, distributing money and oranges among the wounded.

'The following is an abstract of the casualties sustained by the right wing of our army at the attack on Maharajpoor:-

'Staff – officers and 16 horses killed, 2 officers and 3 rank and file wounded.

'Artillery Division – 1 officer, 1 sergeant, 1 rank and file, 3 grooms, and 27 horses killed; 1 sergeant, 25 rank and file, 9 grooms, 1 ordnance driver, and 12 horses wounded; 1 groom and 7 horses missing.

'Cavalry Division – 1 European and 1 native officer, 1 trumpeter, 9 troopers, and 79 horses killed; 5 European and 4 native officers, 5 sergeants, 3 trumpeters, 37 troopers, and 48 horses wounded; 1 trooper, 3 grooms, and 10 horses missing.

'3rd Infantry Division – 1 European and 1 native officer, 1 sergeant, 2 drummers, 43 rank and file, and 1 horse killed; 15 European and 7 native officers, 32 sergeants, 4 drummers, 304 rank and file, and 2 horses wounded; 1 rank and file missing.

'3rd Infantry Division – 1 officer, 2 sergeants, 1 drummer, 32 rank and file, and 3 horses killed, 12 officers, 21 sergeants, 1 drummer, and 190 rank and file wounded; 1 rank and file missing.

'7th Company of Sappers and Miners – 2 rank and file wounded.

'Kelat-i-Ghilzie Regiment – 1 rank and file killed, and 1 rank and file wounded.

'Escort to Governor-General's Agent – 1 groom and 1 horse killed, and 1 horse wounded.

'Total killed – 6 European and 2 native officers, 4 sergeants, 4 trumpeters and drummers, 86 rank and file, 4 grooms, and 117 horses. Wounded – 34 European and 11 native officers, 39 sergeants, 8 trumpeters and drum-mers, 562 rank and file, 9 grooms, 1 ordnance driver, and 63 horses. Missing – 3 rank and file, 4 grooms, and 17 horses.

'Killed – European officers, 6; Native officers, 2; non-commissioned officers, drummers, rank and file, 94; grooms, 4 – Total, 106.

'Wounded – European officers 34; native officers, 11; non-commissioned officers, drummers, rank and file 629; syces and ordnance drivers, 10 – Total, 684.

'Missing – Rank and file, 3; syces, 4: total, 7.

'Grand total of all ranks killed, wounded, and missing, 797.

'A certain amount of the loss was incurred after the fighting was over, for, until nightfall, mines which the enemy had made all over the ground occupied by their guns continued to explode and seriously wounded many men and some officers.'

'RETURN OF ORDNANCE CAPTURED FROM THE ENEMY BY THE RIGHT WING OF THE ARMY OF GWALIOR, ON THE 29th DECEMBER, 1849.

CAMP CHOUNDAH, *1st Jan., 1844.*

'Two 12- and one 18-pounder brass howitzers: one 4, four 4½, six 4¼, three 5, fourteen 6, four 6¼, two 6½, three 7, two 8, and one 8½ pr. brass guns. – Destroyed, two 12 pr. iron howitzers; three 3, three 3¼, three 6, and two 12 pr. iron guns. Total 56.

'Several tumbrils of ammunition have been destroyed. In one of them cash to the amount of 2,141 Gwalior rupees was discovered, which will be paid into the military chest.'

Meanwhile, the success of General Grey was equally satisfactory and is described by Rait:

'While Grey marched from Himutgarh to Punniar, a large body of Mahrattas, who had been ready to dispute with him the Antri Ghat, made a march parallel to that of Grey himself, and when the British army reached Punniar they found that the enemy had occupied a strong position at Mangore, on a neighbouring hill. They opened fire upon his baggage, and Grey sent a force of cavalry and horse artillery to defend it. Brigadier Harriott, who was in command of the cavalry, found that the nature of the ground prohibited his attacking the enemy, and he was forced to return to Grey, who was preparing to take the offensive. Grey detached Her Majesty's 3rd Buffs, and five companies of the 39th Native Infantry with a company of sappers and miners, to take up a position on an opposite ridge and attack the enemy. The Buffs and sappers charged the enemy's centre and captured their guns, while the wing of the 39th Native Infantry gained the crest of a hill commanding the enemy's left, and after pouring on him a severe fire, charged and carried the battery opposed to them. These regiments were well led by Colonel Clunie of the Buffs and Brigadier Yates who commanded the 39th Native Infantry, but they were exposed to a heavy fire and suffered severely. The remainder of Grey's force

Her Majesty's 50th Foot and the 50th and 58th Native Infantry) now came up and attacked the enemy's left, and put an end to the action, totally defeating the Mahrattas and forcing them to abandon their guns, in number. The losses in General Grey's force were 35 killed and 182 wounded.'

In the same issue of the *Illustrated London News* that carried the report on Maharajpore – that is, 9 March 1844 – was a similar story of Punniar

'The left wing of our army, under the command of General Grey, were equally successful at Punniar, which lies about twelve miles from Gwalior. He had been directed to march direct on Punniar, for the purpose of hemming in the enemy, in conjunction with the right-wing of our force. This, however, was frustrated, the enemy having sub-divided their force so as to meet both divisions of ours, and a portion having taken up a position at some miles distance from our right, completely screened by lofty hills, near the village of Mangor, a short distance from Punniar, where they began firing on our baggage. Brigadier Harriott, with a troop of Horse Artillery under Captain Brind, took up a position beyond the baggage, where they returned the enemy's fire; but unable, from the impassable nature of the ground to bring them to close quarters, they returned to the rear under a heavy cannonade. The enemy, however, having changed their position to one four miles on

the east of General Grey's camp, it was resolved immediately to attack them. This was done by her Majesty's 3rd Buffs, with a company of Sappers and Miners, followed shortly afterwards by five companies of the 39th Native Infantry, some delay being occasioned, it getting dark before the remaining force, amounting to 2,000, could be brought up. The Buffs and Sappers then attacked the enemy's centre, exposed to a galling fire; they drove the Mahratta from the post to post, and captured a standard with eleven guns. Brigadier Anderson, with the 2nd brigade, arrived only in time to finish the action. Having formed on the west of the hill, they attacked and routed the enemy, capturing the remainder of their guns.

'*Return of Casualties in the Left Wing of the Army of Gwalior, under the Command of Major-General J. Grey, CB, in action near Punniar, December 29, 1843.*

Camp, Punniar, *December 29, 1843*

'Staff – 1 officer wounded.

'1st and 3rd Troops, 3rd Brigade Horse Artillery. – 1 rank and file and 1 horse killed.

'1st Company Sappers and Miners – 3 rank and file wounded.

'8th Light Cavalry – 1 trooper and 2 horses killed; 3 rank and file wounded.

'8th Irregular Cavalry – 4 horses killed; 1 trooper and 3 horses wounded.

'Her Majesty's 3d Buffs – 1 officer, 4 sergeants, 6 rank and file, and 1 horse killed; 3 officers, 2 sergeants, and 56 rank and file wounded.

'Her Majesty's 50th Foot – 1 officer, and 8 rank and file killed; 1 officer, 3 sergeants, 1 drummer, and 28 rank and file wounded.

'39th Native Infantry – 1 sergeant and 12 rank and file killed; 2 European and 3 native officers, 5 sergeants and 39 rank and file wounded.

'50th Native Infantry – 3 rank and file wounded.

'51st Native Infantry – 1 rank and file wounded.

'58th Native Infantry – 1 rank and file wounded.

'Sippree Contingent – 2 sergeants, and 24 rank and file wounded.

'Total Killed – 2 officers, 5 sergeants, 28 rank and file, and 8 horses. Wounded – 7 European and 8 native officers, 12 sergeants, 1 drummer, 159 rank and file, and 3 horses.

'Grand Total Casualties – 217 men and 11 horses.

The Gwalior Campaign was of only 48 hours duration, the double victory putting an end to all resistance. It had been purchased at considerable cost; the enemy had shown gallantry and devotion, and they had great advantages in numbers and artillery and in the nature of the ground. The British forces at Maharajpore numbered 4,810 infantry, with 350 artillerymen and 30 field guns, supported by 1,340 cavalry. These figures represent the numbers actually brought into the field and are taken from a letter written by Sir Hugh Gough. On paper, the full strength of the two European and six native infantry regiments was 8,800. This explains the discrepancy

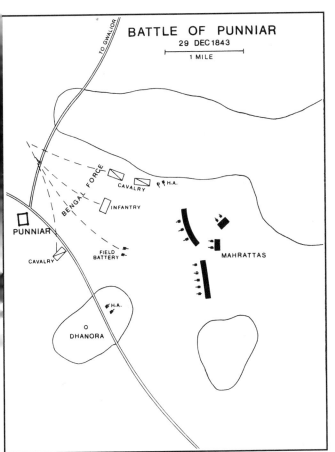

BATTLE OF PUNNIAR
29 DEC 1843
1 MILE

between this statement and the ordinary estimate of the whole army as being at about 20,000 men (including both Gough's and Grey's forces). The actual numbers of men present in the field must be kept in mind when estimating proportions of casualties, which were six officers and 100 men killed, and 34 officers and 650 men wounded. The stress of fighting fell, as always in Indian warfare of this period, upon the European troops, who therefore suffered highest casualties. As Rait notes:

'The army defeated at Maharajpore amounted, according to Sir Hugh Gough's estimate, to fourteen regiments of about 800 men each, a total infantry force of 11,200 men. Four of these regiments defended the battery at Maharajpore, three the position between that village and Skirkapore, and the remaining seven the main position in front of Chonda. Fifty-six guns were captured, and it was calculated that the Mahratta cavalry numbered about 3,000. The proportion of combatants was thus very much greater on the Mahratta side; their guns were also more numerous and more powerful, for among the captured ordnance were an 18-pounder and two 12-pounder howitzers, and a 12-pounder gun.'

The Mahratta casualties at Maharajpore were said to have been in the nature of over 3,000 killed and wounded, with 56 guns falling into British hands. At Punniar their losses were said to have approached 1,000 killed and wounded, but they managed to take 16 guns with them from the field.

When the news of the victory and the conquest of Gwalior reached Britain it received scant popular applause, the nation's attention being taken up with the Corn Law struggles and the trial of Daniel O'Connell. However, the praise of the media meant far less to Sir Hugh Gough than a letter received from his old master and mentor, the Duke of Wellington, whose disdain for laudatory expressions was sufficiently well known for Gough to be much gratified by his words: 'I sincerely congratulate you on the Battle of Maharajpore. I have perused the details thereof with the greatest satisfaction, they are highly creditable to the officers and troops engaged as well as to yourself.

A General Order dated 4 January 1844 sanctioned the award of bronze stars, to be known as the Gwalior Campaign Stars, instead of the usual silver medals. They were 2 inches high and 1.7 inches wide, with a six-pointed silver star in the centre, carrying a circular disc with either the name Maharajpore or Punniar 1843, enclosing the date '29th Decr'. Obviously only one star could be awarded to each man as both battles were

fought on the same day. The star presented to Gough bore a small silver elephant instead of the date. The reverse of the stars were flat, with the recipient's name and regiment engraved in script. The stars were directly attached to the uniform by broad brass hooks fitted to the reverse side; most were later converted by having wide straight bar suspenders attached to the topmost point of the star and the early rainbow type of India medal ribbon used. Four special gold stars of similar design with an enamelled riband were presented to the ladies who were present at the battle of Maharajpore; their arms were elaborately faceted with Queen Victoria's head on the obverse and the inscription 'Maharajpore 29 December 1843' on the reverse. These unofficial awards were given by Lord Ellenborough 'to show his admiration of the spirit and courage displayed by the four ladies who, for some time were under severe enemy fire'. Their hectic day did not end when their elephants were brought back from running away, as was related in a memorandum by Sir Patrick and Lady Grant: 'The excitement of the day was not yet over, for no sooner had they gained a much-needed rest in a tent on the ground held by the enemy at the beginning of the day, than (just as tea was being prepared) they were suddenly seized by British soldiers and carried out. Immediately afterwards a mine exploded, and the tent was blown to pieces.'

BATTLE HONOURS

MAHARAJPORE

16th (The Queen's) Regt. of Light Dragoons (Lancers)
39th (Dorsetshire) Regt. of Foot
40th (2nd Somersetshire) Regt. of Foot

Indian Army

Governor General's Body Guard
4th Regt. Bengal Irregular Cavalry
31st Regt. Bengal Native Infantry
43rd Regt. Bengal Native (Light) Infantry
The Regiment of Kelat-i-Ghilzie

PUNNIAR

9th (The Queen's) Regt. of Light Dragoons (Lancers)
3rd (East Kent) Regt. of Foot (The Buffs)
50th (The Queen's Own) Regt. of Foot

Indian Army

8th Regt. Bengal Irregular Cavalry

3 · The First Sikh War
1845–1846

THE VICTORIES IN INDIA

'On Friday morning (the 27th ult.) the 2nd Battalion of the Grenadier Guards, stationed at the Wellington Barracks, were formed into square by the Adjutant, who read the despatches of the Governor-General of India, containing the account of the glorious victory of the British arms under Sir Harry Smith. On the battalion being dismissed from the square, they gave three hearty ch~ers for their brothers in arms in India' – Globe.

The news arrives! the glorious news!
  Recalling England's pristine fame;
With honest pride the land reviews
  Both Wellington's and Marlborough's name.
But Waterloo and Ramillies
  Cannot excel the trophies bright,
Won from the ruthless enemies
  Who wildly dared the Briton's might.
Behold Old England's Grenadiers!
  The hoary chief and drummer-boy
Welcome alike, with triumph cheers,

The news that fills their hearts with joy.
How eagerly their ears they feast:
  Smith, Gough and Hardinge – household words!
Recount the glories of the East,
  Achieved by Britain's stainless swords.

Ay! stainless; and therein consists
  Our greatest fame – there rests no blot
Upon the banners where the lists
  Of warfare peal the shell and shot.

ILLUSTRATED LONDON NEWS, *18 March 1846*

During the first third of the nineteenth century, the ruler of the Punjab, Ranjit Singh – the Old Lion – had increased and encouraged the natural fighting ability of the Sikhs by importing foreign instructors with experienced military backgrounds. These instructors transformed the Sikhs into a disciplined regular army, with a superb artillery arm and backed by innumerable irregular forces. By revolutionising the Sikh infantry arm, enlarging it into a well-trained force of about 40,000 men, by forming and training a cavalry arm and, above all, by providing a practised artillery arm of 400 guns, these foreigners presented the British with opponents of an incomparably higher standard than any others encountered on the Indian continent. By the early 1840s, the Sikh army – the Khalsa – was well-trained, equipped and numerous. Dedicated and stimulated by religious zeal, its manoeuvres and firing had been raised almost to the standards of the Company's British troops and were infinitely superior to the Company's Indian regiments. The British soon found out that this was true in 1845 when, from the battle of Mudki on, the Sikhs competently handled their heavy guns, and their infantry fought efficiently and stubbornly.

In July 1844 Sir Henry Hardinge arrived in India to succeed Lord Ellenborough as Governor-General. Two years earlier he had refused the appointment of Commander-in-Chief in India, a post now held by Sir Hugh Gough, who rejoiced at the appointment of a soldier and old comrade-in-arms. After serving with distinction in the Peninsular and Waterloo Campaigns, Hardinge had seen no fighting – he had been Secretary of State for War in 1828 and again in 1841–4. Together, he and Gough considered the threat posed by the Sikhs, Gough revealing in a letter to the Governor-General in

Ranjit Singh.

Ghulab Singh, one of the Sikh leaders in 1845.

A Sikh light horseman.

Hugh, First Viscount Gough, from a painting by Sir Francis Grant PRA.

autumn 1844 that he did not underestimate their strength:

'The Sikh Artillery are good; they are bringing into the field a much larger force than we are, even as aggressors; if on the defensive, they will treble ours, with much heavier metal. Our advantage will, and ever must be Manoeuvre, and the irresistible rush of British soldiers.'

Then, in words that form either the vindication or the condemnation of his whole military policy, Gough added: 'Cavalry and Artillery are excellent arms in aid, but it is infantry alone can in India decide the fate of every battle.' This was also the view of Sir Henry Lawrence, who said: 'Our infantry must ever be our mainstay; if it is indifferent, the utmost efficiency in other branches will little avail.'

Gough's letter to Hardinge continues:

'Our six pounders are pop-guns, very well and effective against Infantry, but unequal to cope with the heavy Metal of the Native States, when outnumbered as we shall be. I do not mean by any means to throw a slur on our Artillery; I know them to be almost invariably the élite of the Bengal Army, and that they will ever nobly do their duty; but if we have to go into the Punjab, we may look forward to being opposed by from 250 to 300 Guns in position, many of them of large Calibre. The Governor-General, in his letter of September 8, had estimated our available artillery at 8 companies of European artillery and 5 Native companies, 78 guns in all; "and we have [he said] no possibility of using the European portion of it, in consequence of the scanty accommodation beyond Meerut".'

The autumn crept on with alterations of hope and fear, and 1845 arrived without war, although the Sikh court at Lahore continued in a dangerous state of flux throughout the early months. Throughout, Hardinge remained on the defensive.

At this stage, the British force on the frontier numbered over 30,000 men – 7,000 at Ferozepore, 5,000 at Ludhiana, 10,000 at Umballa, Kassauli and Subathu, and 9,000 at Meerut – formed as follows:

'*At Ferozepore*: – European Infantry: H.M.'s 62nd Foot; Native Infantry: 12th, 14th, 27th, 33rd, 44th, 54th, and 63rd Regts.; 8th Native Light Cavalry; 3rd Native Irregular Horse; two troops of Horse Artillery and two light batteries of six guns each.

'*At Ludhiana*: – European Infantry: H.M.'s 50th Foot; Native Infantry: 11th, 26th, 42nd, 48th, and 73rd Regts.; Native Cavalry; two troops of Horse Artillery.

'*At Umballa*: – European Infantry: H.M.s 9th, 31st, and 80th Foot; Native Infantry: 16th, 24th, 41st, 45th, and 47th Regts.; Cavalry: 3rd Light Dragoons; Native Cavalry: 4th and 5th Regts. H.M.'s 29th Foot at Kassauli, and 1st Bengal Eur. Regt. at Subathu.

'*At Meerut*: – Cavalry: 9th and 16th Lancers, 3rd Light Cavalry; Infantry: H.M.'s 10th Foot (except one company) and some regiments of Native Infantry; Artillery: 26 guns, with sappers and miners.'

The events of the last few days of peace, in December 1845, are adequately covered in Sir Henry's despatch to the secret committee at India House:

'In common with the most experienced officers of the Indian Government, I was not of the opinion that the Sikh Army would cross the Sutlej with its infantry and artillery. I considered it probable that some sort of aggression would be committed by parties of plunderers. Up to the morning of the 12th [of December] the information received from Lahore had not materially varied; but the reports received on that day showed that the general aspect of affairs appeared more warlike. Still no Sikh aggression had been committed, and no artillery had moved down to the river. On the 13th December, I received precise information that the Sikh Army had crossed the Sutlej, and was concentrating in great force on the left bank of the river.'

The Sikhs had crossed the river on 11 December, hoping to cut off Ferozepore from other British forces and then to deal separately with the Ludhiana and Ambala forces. The Governor-General had sent final orders to the Commander-in-Chief on 10 December, and

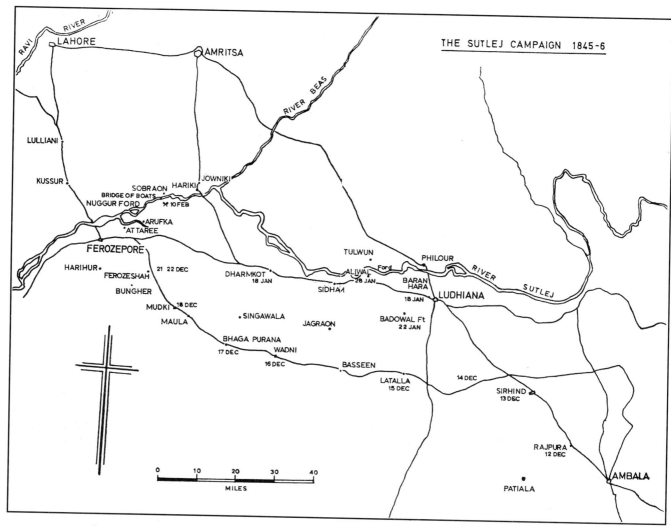

on the same day Gough gave orders for the cavalry to move next day, and for the infantry to march on the 12th. Everything was seemingly in readiness for immediate action. On 10 December, Gough wrote to Hardinge: 'I shall remain here to see the troops march the day after tomorrow, and will then push on and join the advance. I greatly fear the troops from the hills will not get down as soon as you wish.'

The target of the marching columns was Ferozepore, 160 miles from Gough's starting place at Ambala, and the principal station in support of the advanced posts, apart from the 8,000- or 9,000-strong force at Meerut, nearly 120 miles from Ambala and about 280 miles from Ferozepore. To ensure adequate water supplies, the only road suitable for an army marching from Basian to Ferozepore passed through the village of Mudki, 20 miles from Ferozepore.

The transport situation was relatively unorganised. A scanty amount was kept ready for immediate use, but beyond that, transport animals, mostly camels, had to be requisitioned by the civil authorities. Writing on the 12 December, Gough noted that the great fault is Corps not having their camels . . . sooner . . . we have been

obliged to substitute Hackerries [bullock-carts] for camels.' The Commissariat Department was reasonably efficient, and supplies of all sorts were generally obtained in full without delay, Broadfoot (at the urgent request of Lord Hardinge) had arranged for supply depots for 10,000 men at 20-mile intervals between Meerut and Ferozepore.

The country between Ambala and Mudki was dead flat, overgrown with camel-thorn and low jungle trees without any undergrowth. It was very sandy and dusty, and the roads were mere tracks, extremely heavy for both foot and wheeled transport, being better suited for camels. The sand and jungle alternated with ploughed land, where thick dust obscured the air, and the hot sun beat mercilessly down upon the heavily burdened soldiers. The nights were cold and chill. There were very few villages and little or no water except from the wells dug by the villagers, while food was scarce until they reached Wadni, where grain was available. There was neither the time nor the means to cook rations of meat. The force marched 16 miles to Rajpura on 12 December, 18 miles to Sirhind on the 13th, 20 miles on the 14th to Isru, 30 miles on the 14th to Lattala and another 30 miles to Wadni on the 16th, where they overtook Wheeler's Ludhiana force, which, accompanied by the Governor-General, had marched from Basian.

On 17 December the rest of the men from Ambala joined the force. A short march westward to Charrak took place on this day, giving the weary men and beasts some rest. The whole march up from Ambala had been exceptionally rapid and through an exceedingly trying country – so far they had marched over 100 miles in five days. At dawn on the 18th the camp came to life, shivering camp-followers congregating around the expiring fires, the roaring of the camels, the babel of tongues and the heavy tramp of the troops as they marched off. The dark forms of the elephant contingent added a mysterious character to this moving mass, causing it to resemble a stirred-up antheap. The long lines of camels, the troops in column of route, the grey-headed subahdar and the ligh-hearted ensign, all pointed to the unmistakable fact that it was an Indian army on the march. The whole force totalled between 11,000 and 12,000 men, formed of five regiments of cavalry (grouped in one cavalry division) and three infantry divisions under Generals Smith, Gilbert and McCaskill. Only one division was complete, the other two being practically no more than strong brigades. There were five troops of horse artillery, and two field batteries, altogether 42 guns. Of the 13 battalions of infantry, only four were British.

This day's march was most harassing, at one time over heavy ploughed land, then through low, thorny jungle, which broke up all order, then again over heavy sand, the most fatiguing of all ground for an army on the march. The rising dust was blinding and clogged the throats and nostrils of the soldiers. When Mudki was reached at about 1.00 pm it was found to be abandoned by the Sikhs, so the force halted and occupied the place.

Eating a meal sitting on the ground in the shelter of a small tent, the Commander-in-Chief, the Governor-General, Broadfoot and Havelock were interrupted by an orderly riding rapidly in and handing a note to Broadfoot, who leapt to his feet, crying out: 'The enemy are upon us!' Jumping on his horse, he disappeared as the air echoed with the notes of bugles. Incredulously, weary men rose stiffly from the ground and scrambled into their equipment. Horses were quickly saddled and discipline gradually asserted itself as the men, reluctantly abandoning half-cooked rations, came to arms. To their front they could see a distant dust-cloud rising, to spread ominously across the countryside. Broadfoot came galloping back, and Havelock heard him cry excitedly to Gough: 'There, your Excellency, is the Sikh Army!'

There has been some controversy as to whether the army was actually surprised by the Sikhs at Mudki, but it would certainly seem that they were aware that the enemy was in the vicinity, although not a great deal was done to prepare for any offensive action. The advance was covered by Irregular Horse, accompanied by Broadfoot, who reached Mudki before the main body and found the village in the possession of some parties of Sikh horse. He sent this information back to Gough, who changed his formation from column of route to order to battle and marched on. Nevertheless, the fact remains that the troops formed up in a great hurry, without finishing their hard-earned meal and under fire from the Sikh artillery. If he did know that the Sikh Army was approaching, it is astounding that Gough took so few pains to ensure that his force prepared to meet them in the best heart and under the most propitious conditions.

THE BATTLE OF MUDKI – 18 DECEMBER 1845

Now began the last of the wars in which the army, still geared to Waterloo and the Napoleonic wars, went into battle with an order of battle and the old-style dress, and Peninsular veterans as their leaders. It was fought in the cold climate of a north Indian winter, where the army dressed as it did in Europe, with uniforms and accoutrements that had not greatly changed since Waterloo in 1815. The Indian battalions, like the Europeans, had scarlet coatees and white cross-belts, with white, drill-covered shakos, which some brigades discarded as the weather grew cold. The order of battle *was* an order of battle, and the troops formed up and fought accordingly, each unit in line or column, the cavalry on the flanks, the artillery in the intervals.

Seeing the British force moving to meet them, the Sikhs halted and took up a position in the dense, low jungle, among a maze of copses and sand-hills, with their numerous guns positioned in the intervals between the infantry, and strong bodies of cavalry on the flanks.

The scene was vividly described in a letter to a brother officer, written by Lieutenant J. P. Robertson of the 31st Foot:

'We were regularly done up when we got into camp at Moodkee, and lay down on the ground to sleep as the tents were not up. I was just dozing off when I heard a running of men and the order to "fall-in sharp". We formed a quarter-distance column and went forward immediately, some of the officers with their swords drawn, without their belts, and the men with their jackets off. Old Quigley of the Grenadiers was dressed this way. You may remember him as one of the oldest 31st men. Forward we went, no one knew where to, but all the other regiments were doing the same. Presently the artillery began to blaze away ahead of us, and we saw the shells bursting in the air. We all forgot sore feet then and went on at a kind of run for about three miles, the men calling out, "Come on boys, or they will be away before we get at them". Old Willes was riding his white charger, as he was quite done up and couldn't walk. Tritton and I were his subs. We deployed into line, a short distance from a low, thick jungle, on the other side of which there lots of dust, smoke, and what the men called "A — row going on". Just as No. 1 was formed something hit the dust in front of us and went whiz over my head. One of the men called out, "Holy Jesus! that was a bullet!" It was the first I had heard, and sounded very nasty.

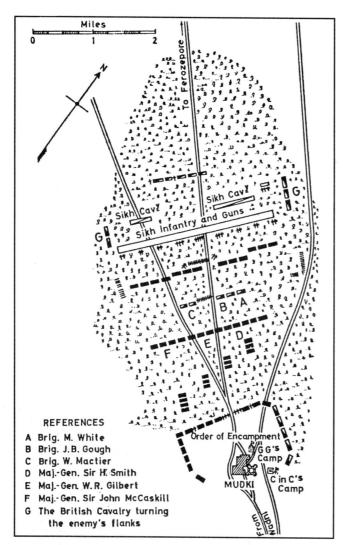

Battle of Mudki, 18 December 1845.

'We moved forward with lots of sepoy regiments behind us and the 80th on our left. Presently I saw them form square and some cavalry came out of the dust. This proved to be some stragglers from [our cavalry]. Two or three of them halted close behind me, and one called out, "Go on, boys, there are lots of them before you. We were through them from right to left". The man was plastered with dirt, and his sword blood-stained. On we went into the jungle, with a tremendous fire of musketry and guns in front of us. Of course we were much broken by the bushes, which would have done well for Light Infantry, but for nothing else, and the men were beginning to get hit. The first person I saw on the ground was Bulkeley, who looked quite dead, and just then there was a sort of rush to the rear of a chief and his followers on horseback, who had been with us all the morning to show us the shortest way. How he got into the fight I know not, but he made the best of his way out again. A beast with two tom-toms, who had been tormenting us all the day with his thumping, nearly rode over us. He was followed by the Hooka Burda,

A European officer of the 7th Bengal Light Cavalry 1845.

standard-bearer, and the "Bhai-log" in a terrible hurry. The sepoys were doing the same, and one was shot by our men for running away. I saw a batch of them behind a big tree, firing straight up in the air, and shouting to us "Barrow, Broders, Barrow". But no "Barrow" in them!'

The Governor-General and his son, together with Broadfoot and Cuist, the assistant political agent, noted with dismay that the sepoys were panic-stricken and firing their muskets into the air and to their right and left, while their officers belaboured them with the flats of their swords and seemed to have lost all control over them. One native regiment turned suddenly towards the rear and began to retire. Gough sent Havelock to bring them back, and he cantered round to face them, crying out 'the enemy are in front of you and not behind you!'

Lieutenant Robertson's regiment, the 31st, was in Colonel Samuel Bolton's Brigade of Sir Harry Smith's Division. Bolton, a Peninsular War veteran of the 31st, rode forward on his grey charger, his bugler by his side. Robertson takes up the story:

'The last words I heard Bolton say were "Steady, 31st, steady, and fire low for your lives!" Cockins, the bugler, was trying to hold the grey horse, when they were all three hit and went down together. This was from the first volley by the enemy. Shortly after Willes was hit, and I took command of No. 1 (which I had all through the campaign). The ball entered his right arm, below the shoulder, and went into his chest, making only one wound. He said he was hit from behind by the sepoys. Young was hit in the back of the neck, and the buckle of his stock saved him, as the ball ran round and came out in front. Hart and Brenchley were both hit in the body, and did not live long.'

Bolton died a few days later. Hardly had the 31st begun to advance when their commander, Lieutenant-Colonel John Byrne, was severely wounded, and the two officers carrying the colours and the rest of the colour party were killed. The colours were immediately raised by Quartermaster-Sergeant Jones, who carried them throughout the rest of the battle and was later rewarded by being granted a field commission as ensign. The 31st, reeling under the heavy and continuous fire, were in danger of annihilation.

Lieutenant Robertson graphically describes the confusion of battle:

'We soon got into a regular mob, blazing away at everything in front of us, and nearly as many shots coming from behind us as in front. I saw Napier, the Umballa "Wattle and dab" man, in a blue pea-coat and black sailor's hat, laying about him, and Sir H. Hardinge in a black coat and "tile" with his "star on". Sir Hugh Gough rode up to us and called out, "We must take those guns". Law was standing near us with his legs wide, shouting out, "Charge! Charge!" and hitting the ground with his sword, and sometimes the men's toes (just as he used to set Growler on Shaw's dog). I called out to Sir Hugh Gough: "Where are the guns, and we will soon take them?" and Somerset put his hat on his sword and called out, "Thirty-first, follow me!" We rushed after him through the smoke and had the guns in a moment. On we went and came upon two light guns which the enemy were trying to take off the field; but some of our shots hit the horses and brought them to a standstill. They then took a shot at us, not twenty yards off; down we went on our noses at the flash, and the grape went over our heads in a shower. I felt it warm; then a rush, and the guns were ours, the gunners not attempting to run away, but cutting at us with their tulwars. I think those two guns were taken away by the Sikhs later on that night, as I never saw them afterwards. Pollard was shot in the leg at Moodkee, and the sergeant-major, old Mulligan, was cut all to pieces. After it was quite dark the firing was kept up, the men blazing away at nothing, or at each other, and the bugles sounding "cease firing" in all directions. At last they left off firing, and we got something like a regiment formed at quarter distance, but no colours or bugler to sound the Regimental Call, so we got a nigger bugler to try it, and just as he got out a squeak someone nearly knocked the bugle down his throat; this was Sir Harry Smith, who asked what on earth we were making such a row for. We were a long time collecting the men, and then marched back towards camp, but were halted some way in front of it, and had to sleep on the sand till morning. So much for my first battle.'

Lieutenant Robertson was to see many more battles, eventually rising to become a colonel, and he was believed to be the last survivor of the battle of Mudki when he died in 1916.

Finally, the Sikhs gave way, the cavalry and infantry,

The colours of the 31st Regiment of Foot, which were carried throughout the Sikh War, from the Illustrated London News, *19 December 1846.*

45

Sepoy of the British East India Company.

buglers all along the line sounded the cease fire. Minutes later the silence was shattered by three thunderous cheers wrung from parched throats, and cheering with the rest of them was white-coated, white-haired Sir Hugh Gough, their Commander-in-Chief.

Everyone was worn out by their arduous day's work and the severe fighting, which foreshadowed the nature of the coming struggle with the Khalsa. The indecisive victory convinced the British leaders that they had to effect a junction with General Littler before attempting anything further. John Lawrence's biographer observes that in this war it was to become a commonplace that, if the issue depended upon the sepoys, who fought only for pay, Mudki would have been a defeat.

By the light of torches, Gough and what was left of his staff picked their way across the scene, where the wounded and dying of both sides were lying in scores. Heaped around the captured cannon lay the stalwart forms of the Sikh gunners. Over the field itself was the usual mingling of the dead – the Khalsa soldiery, the European linesman, the young officer, groups of horses and camels, all lay in one shapeless mass. It was midnight before the troops were back at the camp. 'Our faces and hands,' as one private wrote, 'covered with blood mingled with dust and filth from all kinds of smoke, our clothes from head to foot painted all over and our once white belts, now sable, besmeared with it.' Gough did not leave the field until two o'clock in the morning of 19 December, and four hours later he was back upon the scene.

'MOODKEE

'From General Sir Hugh Gough, Bart., G.C.B., the Commander-in-Chief of the Army in India, to the Governor-General of India.

HEAD QUARTERS, ARMY OF THE SUTLEJ, CAMP MOODKEE,
December 19th, 1845

'RIGHT HONOURABLE SIR,

'It would be a superfluous form in me to address to you a narrative of the campaign which has opened against the Sikhs, and the successful action of yesterday, since you have in person shared the dangers and fatigues of our army, and witnessed its efforts and privations, but that my position at its head renders this my duty; and it is necessary, from that position, I should place these events on record, for the information of all Europe as well as of all India.

'You, Sir, know, but others have to be told, that the sudden and unprovoked aggression of the Sikhs, by crossing the Sutlej with the great proportion of their army, with the avowed intention of attacking Ferozepore in time of profound peace, rendered indispensable, on our side, a series of difficult combinations for the protection of our frontier station, so unjustifiably and so unexpectedly menaced. . . . When their march had been further prolonged to this place, they had moved over a distance of upwards of 150 miles in six days, along roads of heavy sand; their perpetual labour

eventually fleeing in great disorder, and taking with them their commander, Lal Singh, who was reported to have been slightly wounded. The darkness of the night and the ever-increasing risk of the troops firing into each other, together with their extreme fatigue, made prolonged pursuit impossible, and in the inky blackness of the Indian jungle the roar of battle faded as the allowing them scarcely time to cook their food, even when they received it, and hardly an hour for repose, before they were called upon for renewed exertions.

'Soon after mid-day, the division under Major-General Sir Harry Smith, a brigade of that under Major-General Sir John M'Caskill, and another of that under Major-General Gilbert, with five troops of horse artillery, and two light field batteries, under Lieut.-Col. Brooke, of the horse artillery (Brigadier in command of the artillery force), and the cavalry division, consisting of Her Majesty's 3rd Light Dragoons, the body guard, 4th and 5th Light Cavalry, and 9th Irregular Cavalry, took up their encamping ground in front of Moodkee.

'The troops were in a state of great exhaustion, principally from the want of water, which was not procurable on the road; when, about three p.m. information was received that the Sikh army was advancing; and the troops had scarcely time to get under arms, and move to their positions, when the fact was ascertained.

'I immediately pushed forward the horse artillery and cavalry, directing the infantry, accompanied by the field batteries, to move forward in support. We had not proceeded beyond two miles, when we found the enemy in position. They were said to consist of from fifteen to twenty thousand infantry, about the same force of cavalry, and forty guns. They evidently had either just taken up this position, or were advancing in order of battle against us.

'To resist their attack, and to cover the formation of the infantry, I advanced the cavalry under Brigadiers

White, Gough, and Mactier, rapidly to the front, in columns of squadrons, and occupied the plain. They were speedily followed by the five troops of horse artillery, under Brigadier Brooke, who took up a forward position, having the cavalry then on his flanks.

'The country is a dead flat, covered at short intervals with a low, but, in some places, thick jhow jungle, and dotted with sandy hillocks. The enemy screened their infantry and artillery behind this jungle, and such undulations as the ground afforded; and, whilst our twelve battalions formed from échellon of brigades into line, opened a very severe cannonade upon our advancing troops, which was vigorously replied to by the battery of horse artillery under Brigadier Brooke, which was soon joined by the two field batteries. The rapid and well-directed fire of our artillery appeared soon to paralyze that of the enemy; and, as it was necessary to complete our infantry dispositions without advancing the artillery too near to the jungle, I directed the cavalry under Brigadiers White and Gough to make a flank movement on the enemy's left, with a view of threatening and turning that flank, if possible. With praiseworthy gallantry, the 3rd Light Dragoons, with the 2nd brigade of cavalry, consisting of the body guard and 5th Light Cavalry, with a portion of the 4th Lancers, turned the left of the Sikh army, and, sweeping along the whole rear of its infantry and guns, silenced for a time the latter, and put their numerous cavalry to flight. Whilst this movement of the 4th Lancers, the 9th Irregular Cavalry, under Brigadier Mactier, with a light field

The charge of the 3rd Light Dragoons at Mudki.

battery, to threaten their right. This manœuvre was also successful. Had not the infantry and guns of the enemy been screened by the jungle, these brilliant charges of the cavalry would have been productive of greater effect.

'When the infantry advanced to the attack, Brigadier Brooke rapidly pushed on his horse artillery close to the jungle, and the cannonade was resumed on both sides. The infantry under Major-Generals Sir Harry Smith, Gilbert, and Sir John M'Caskill, attached in échellon of lines the enemy's infantry, almost invisible amongst wood and the approaching darkness of night. The opposition of the enemy was such as might have been expected from troops who had everything at stake, and who had long vaunted of being irresistible. Their ample and extended line, from their great superiority of numbers, far outflanked ours; but this was counteracted by the flank movements of our cavalry. The attack of the infantry now commenced; and the roll of fire from this powerful arm soon convinced the Sikh army, that they had met with a foe they little expected; and their whole force was driven from position after position with great slaughter, and the loss of seventeen pieces of artillery, some of them of heavy calibre; our infantry using that never-failing weapon, the bayonet, whenever they stood. Night only saved them from worse disaster, for this stout conflict was maintained during an hour and a

The charge of the King's Own Dragoons at Mudki.

half of dim starlight, amidst a cloud of dust from the sandy plain, which yet more obscured every object.

'I regret to say, this gallant and successful attack was attended with considerable loss; the force bivouacked upon the field for some hours, and only returned to its encampment after ascertaining that it had no enemy before it, and that night prevented the possibility of a regular advance in pursuit.'

'Return of the Killed and Wounded of the Army of the Sutlej, under the command of His Excellency General Sir Hugh Gough, G.C.B. Commander-in-Chief, in the Action fought at Moodkee, on the 18th of December, 1845.

CAMP, SULTAN KHAN WALLAH, *Dec. 26, 1845.*

'*Personal Staff* – 2 officers killed; 2 officers wounded.
'*General Staff* – 1 officer killed; 1 officer wounded.
'*Artillery Division*' – 2 officers, 4 sergeants, 13 rank and file, 5 syces and grasscutters, 3 syce drivers, 45 horses – killed; 4 officers, 1 native officer, 2 sergeants, 22 syces and grasscutters, 11 lascars, 2 syce drivers, 7 syces, 25 horses – wounded.
'*Cavalry Division* – 3 officers, 6 sergeants or havildars, 1 trumpeter, 71 rank and file, 164 horses – killed; 9 officers, 1 native officer, 6 sergeants or havildars, 1 trumpeter, 70 rank and file, 63 horses – wounded.
'*1st Infantry Division* – 4 officers, 1 native officer, 4

sergeants or havildars, 69 rank and file – killed; 18 officers, 2 native officers, 20 sergeants or havildars, 299 rank and file, 4 horses – wounded.

'*2nd Infantry Division* – 1 native officer, 17 rank and file, 1 horse – killed; 4 officers, 5 native officers, 10 sergeants or havildars, 81 rank and file – wounded.

'*3rd Infantry Division* – 1 officer, 1 sergeant or havildar, 6 rank and file – killed; 1 officer, 4 sergeants or havildars, 73 rank, and 1 lascar – wounded. – Total – 13 officers, 2 native officers, 15 sergeants or havildars, 1 trumpeter, 176 rank and file, 5 syces and grasscutters, 3 syce drivers, 210 horses – killed; 39 officers, 9 native officers, 42 sergeants or havildars, 1 trumpeter, 545 rank and file, 12 lascars, 2 syce drivers, 7 syces, 92 horses – wounded.

'*European officers*, 13; native officers, 2; non-commissioned officers, drummers, rank and file, 192; syces., &c. 8; killed. – Grand total, 215.

'*European officers*, 39; native officers, 9; non-commissioned officers, drummers, rank and file, 192; syces, &c. 21; wounded. – Grand total, 657.

'Grand total of all ranks, killed and wounded, 872.

'*Return of Ordnance captured from the Sikh Army, at the Battle of Moodkee, on the 18th of December, 1845, by the Army of the Sutlej, under the Command of His Excellency Sir Hugh Gough, G.C.B., Commander-in-Chief.*

			in.	*tenths*	
6	Guns	Brass	4	6	12-pounder.
1	Howizter	do.	6	5	6½
4	Guns	do.	4	2	9
3	do.	do.	3	6	6
1	do.	do.	2	9	3

'*Remarks.* – The number of guns captured, 15. It was impossible to compute the quantity of metal in these guns, but it was evident that they were much heavier than those of a similar calibre in the Bengal Artillery.

'The carriages were all in good repair, with the exception of one or two struck by your shot. The whole were destroyed, and the guns left in the fort of Moodkee.

'Four more guns reported to have been dismounted by the men of the horse artillery, and left on the field from want of means to bring them away.

GEO. BROOKE, *Brigadier,*
Commanding Artillery, Army of the Sutlej.'

Hardinge always maintained that sepoys resembled the Portuguese in that they had their fighting days. In reaching this conclusion he obviously drew upon his experiences in the Peninsula some 40 years previously. At the close of the campaign, when their dread of the Khalsa had more or less disappeared, they fought at Sobraon with a determination sharply contrasting to their former unsteadiness, and vied with the European troops in their attack upon the breastworks.

Part of the loss must be ascribed not only to the courage, but to the fanaticism, of the Sikhs. Their gallantry and discipline in the fighting evoked admiration from all, but, brave as they were, they expected no mercy and gave none. They killed and mutilated the wounded in the same way as did the Zulus and Dervishes of later colonial wars. Even when their own lives had been spared by the orders of British officers, the Sikhs were known, on several occasions, to have fired upon their deliverers as soon as their backs were turned. So strong was the indignation excited among the 3rd Light Dragoons, who were horrified to find their comrades, wounded in the splendid charge, cruelly murdered, that 'Remember Mudki' became a battle-cry and many Sikhs were ruthlessly slain who would otherwise have been spared.

The Sikh losses were severe, the ground being covered with their dead and wounded, although one account claims that it is possible that their casualties did not exceed those of the British. Seventeen of their guns were captured, five being carried away. The British cavalry were masters of the field, and it is difficult to understand how they permitted a fleeing foe to take with him nearly 25 per cent of his artillery strength. The Sikhs had also lost the field of battle, but they had not lost their honour, having been less decisively beaten than were most Indian armies.

THE BATTLE OF FEROZESHAH – 21–22 DECEMBER 1845

The most terrible battle of British Indian history, Ferozeshah was fought on the shortest day of the year, three days after the unexpected 'battle in the dust' at Mudki. It began at 2.00 am on 21 December when, in perfect silence, Gough's force was called to arms at Mudki; by 3.00 am the camp had been struck and packed on camels, and by 4.00 am the army was formed up in line of columns ready to match. Each man carried 60 rounds of ball ammunition and a leather-covered water-bottle over the shoulder. Two days' cooked rations were prepared, each man taking as much as he could in his haversack; greatcoats were not carried. Two native infantry regiments were left at Mudki to protect the wounded, for whom there was no transport, and the baggage. They marched light and unencumbered over the sandy plain, advancing in line of columns for about four miles, ready to deploy into line should the Sikhs be encountered. Then it was discovered that the enemy was concentrated around Ferozeshah, and the force moved in column of route.

First in pitch darkness and cold, then under an increasingly hot sun, they made very slow progress on what was a mere track through the jungle. On the broad front of the army, they took nearly six hours to traverse a few miles until arriving about two miles from the enemy position at 10.00 am. Here they rested briefly and made a scratch breakfast from the food in their haversacks. The welcome dawn had revealed a broad expanse of level plain, dotted here and there with low jungle, and the enemy occupying a position in the shape of a large horseshoe, entrenched around the village of Ferozeshah. It was the usual Punjab mud village, with a high house or two in the centre, lying across the road to

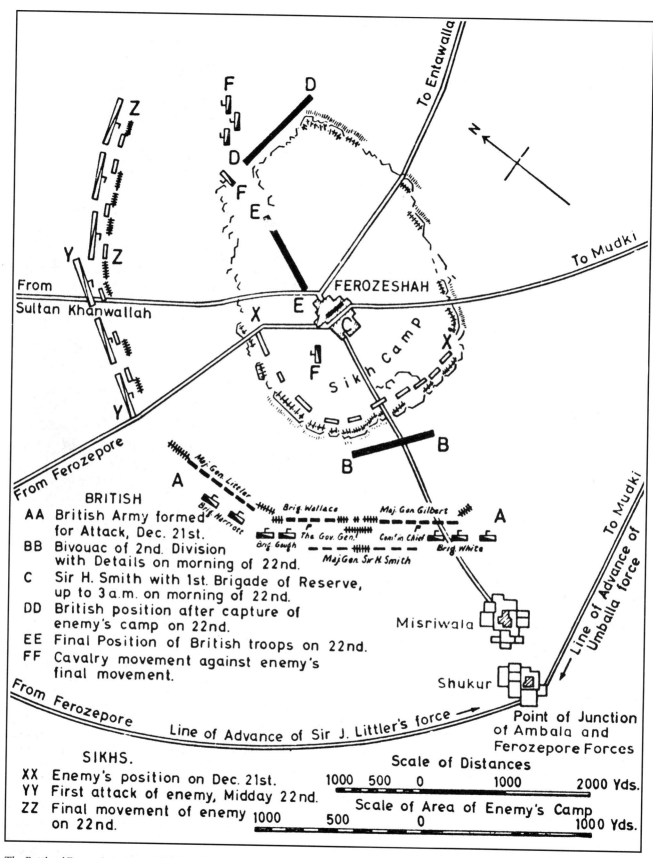

The Battle of Ferozeshah, 21 and 22 December 1845.

risk as little as I possibly can. At this extremity of the Empire a defeat is almost the loss of India.

'I have told Gough I have a right to interfere, and control him in all and every matter. We are on good terms. I have praised him as he deserves in my general orders, and political expediency requires that I do him full justice. But the public safety also requires that you should be informed of the truth, and I should be deficient in fortitude and moral courage if I did not reveal to you opinions, and facts, which render it most important that the invading army should be placed in other hands; and in my opinion the most proper arrangement will be to make Napier C.-in-C. of the Punjab army.

'In our present state I shall not write to Napier; and in case of accident to myself, Mr. Currie, my chief secretary, and my son Charles are the only persons who are aware of the contents of this letter.'

Sir Robert Peel's answer was brief and guarded:

'My Dear Hardinge,

'Your loss has been very severe. It demonstrates the extent of the danger and the necessity for unparalleled exertion. We are astonished at the numbers, the power of concentration and the skill and courage of the enemy. On all matters of reinforcement, I hope Lord Ripon will write you as fully as the short time will allow. We shall lay some of your letter on the table of the House, tending to show the policy which you had resolved to pursue, and the unprovoked and wicked aggression which you have repelled. Your escape and that of your sons, amid all the perils that surrounded you, has filled us with delight.

'God bless you, my dear Hardinge. Excuse my hurried letter. I am fighting a desperate battle here. Shall probably drive my opponents across the Sutlej, but what is to come afterward, I know not.

Ever affectionately yours,
R. Peel.'

THE BATTLE OF ALIWAL – 28 JANUARY 1846

Said by Sir John Fortescue, historian of the British Army, to be 'the battle without a mistake', this action belongs to Sir Harry Smith, a gallant and very dashing soldier, at that time probably the longest serving British soldier, having joined the army in 1805 and still to perform some very active service in South Africa against the Boers and Kaffirs. He was 57 years of age when dashing forward with the 50th's colour at Mudki and commanding with dash and vigour at Ferozeshah, Budowal and Aliwal. In the First Sikh War, a campaign not exactly noted for its tactical standards, a remark of Sir Harry's after Aliwal puts him in true historical perspective: 'I steered the course invariably pursued by my great master the Duke, never needlessly to risk your troops or fight a battle without an objective.'

He qualified that, and his admiration for the Duke of Wellington, in a letter written on 24 February 1846 to an old comrade, Sir James Kempt: 'my fight at Aliwal was a little sweeping second edition of Salamanca – a standup gentlemanlike battle, a mixing of all arms and laying-on,

Sir Harry Smith.

carrying everything before us by weight of attack and combination, all hands at work from one end of the field to the other.'

Early in January 1846, the Sikhs, in force, crossed the River Sutlej at Phillaur, about six miles north of Ludhiana, and established a bridge there under the cover of an old fortress. Their force of 8,000 men and 70 guns was under the command of Ranjur Singh, who apparently intended to garrison the forts of Dhurmkote, which was midway between Ludhiana and Ferozeshah, and Fatehgarh, which was 12 miles to the east of Gough's position.

On 16 January the Commander-in-Chief sent for Sir Harry Smith and told him that the Governor-General wanted to reduce the two fortresses. Gough said: 'A brigade will be sufficient to send, with the 3rd Light Cavalry and some Irregular Horse; but who will you send?' Sir Harry characteristically replied that he would rather go himself. Gough was very pleased with this ready assent, because Hardinge had already indicated that he wanted Smith to do the job. On being told that there was no hurry, Smith replied: 'Soon after this time tomorrow I shall be writing my report that I have reduced them both.'

Gough laughed. 'Why, the distance to Dhurmkote is twenty-six miles from your right.'

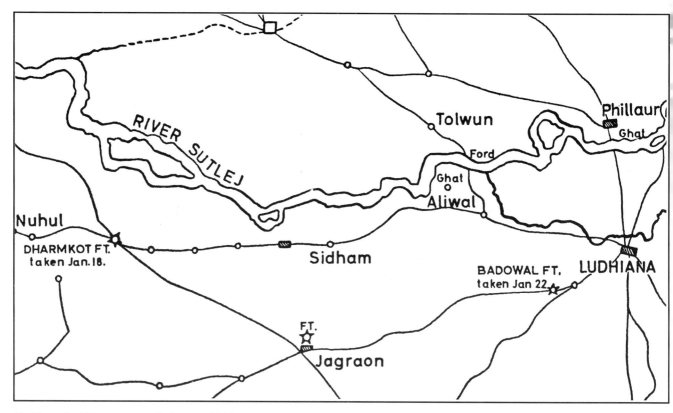

Sir Harry Smith's movements in January 1846.

'I know that, still what I say shall be, provided that the officer and the Engineers supply me in time with the powder I want to blow in the gates in case of necessity.'

Quite evidently Sir Harry was determined to follow Wellington's maxim to waste not a minute. Collecting everything he wanted from what was left in the camp, he marched two hours before daylight. Fatehgahr was abandoned, so he pushed on to Dhurmkote, which he found occupied by the enemy but without guns. He parleyed with the garrison commander and gave him 20 minutes to surrender, with the promise, 'I will endeavour to secure all hands six weeks pay'. A few shots had to be fired from the 9-pounders and the howitzer, then the Sikh flag came down and the white flag was hoisted. Sir Harry made his report to the Commander-in-Chief as promised.

He rested on 22 January while preparing to attack Ranjur at Budowal. Quietly, during the night, the Sikh leader, with sound judgement, evacuated the place and marched northwards towards the river, where he picked up a reinforcement of 12 guns, 4,000 regular infantry of Avitabile's corps, and some cavalry at the Tulwun Ghaut eight miles lower down the Sutlej. Sir Harry immediately moved forward and occupied Budowal, where he halted for a few days, leaving Godby at Ludhiana.

'While he was engaged with the enemy on this march, which he made in order to perform a part of his instructions – namely, to maintain the communication with Loodiana, they came out from the entrenched camp and carried off his baggage. I desire to explain that, because it was the only check which the gallant officer met with throughout the whole of this operation, and in fact it is the only misfortune, trifling as it is, which has happened during the whole operations that have taken place in that part of the country. The loss of the baggage, such as it is, has been written up as a great misfortune; but, in point of fact, it could not be otherwise. He was obliged to march within sight of the entrenched camp, from which the enemy had an opportunity of attacking him on his march.' (From a speech by the Duke of Wellington in the House of Lords, on 2 April 1846, when moving a motion of thanks to Sir Harry Smith.)

Hardinge was very anxious that Ludhiana should be relieved and, before hearing of Smith's arrival there, had ridden down to Gough's camp in the middle of the night to request him to reinforce Sir Harry at once. Wheeler's brigade, with two regiments of native cavalry and four guns, was ordered to march for that purpose during the night, the Brigadier having recovered from the wound he had sustained at Mudki. On the evening of 22 January they reached Dhurmkote. Not having heard of the action at Budowal on the previous day, Wheeler continued his march on the 23rd direct to Ludhiana, but on arriving at Sidham he heard that a large Sikh force was on the road between him and the rest of the British soldiers. With the same lack of resolution that was to cost him his life at Cawnpore 11 years later, he decided to return to Dhurmkote and follow a circuitous route to Jagraon. This meant a hard day's

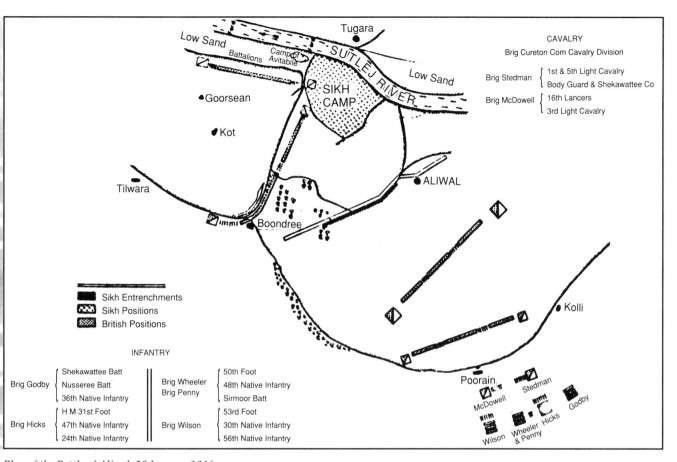

CAVALRY

Brig Cureton Com Cavalry Division

Brig Stedman { 1st & 5th Light Cavalry
{ Body Guard & Shekawattee Co

Brig McDowell { 16th Lancers
{ 3rd Light Cavalry

- Sikh Entrenchments
- Sikh Positions
- British Positions

INFANTRY

Brig Godby	{ Shekawattee Batt		Brig Wheeler	{ 50th Foot
	{ Nusseree Batt		Brig Penny	{ 48th Native Infantry
	{ 36th Native Infantry			{ Sirmoor Batt
Brig Hicks	{ H M 31st Foot		Brig Wilson	{ 53rd Foot
	{ 47th Native Infantry			{ 30th Native Infantry
	{ 24th Native Infantry			{ 56th Native Infantry

Plan of the Battle of Aliwal, 28 January 1846.

march of 30 miles through heavy sand and under a hot sun. Finally, on 26 January, he joined Sir Harry Smith, but Ranjur Singh, hearing of Wheeler's advance and fearing that he might be attacked from both Dhurmkote and Ludhiana, had moved from Budowal on the 22nd.

The loss of Smith's baggage and his casualties at Budowal had been greatly magnified, and cries of disaster caused Hardinge and Gough to tremble for the safety of the siege-train and convoy of ammunition. In addition to moving Wheeler's force as a reinforcement, Hardinge rode down to Gough's camp again on the morning of the 27th and, after some consultation, they ordered Brigadier Taylor to move to Dhurmkote and the Shekawati brigade to move from Basian to Jagraon.

Subsequent events followed the course described in the Duke of Wellington's speech to the House. These movements culminated in Sir Harry Smith's force coming up to the Sikh position at Aliwal on the morning of 28 January 1846. There can be no better way of describing the momentuous happenings of that day than to let Sir Harry's official despatch tell the story, but before he penned it on 30 January, with characteristic exuberance and on the field of battle, he scribbled a pencil note to Gough:

Copy of a Pencil Express, written on the Field of Battle, by Sir Harry Smith, to the Commander-in-Chief.

BANK OF THE SUTLEJ, *28th January*

'Hearing the enemy had received a reinforcement yesterday of twelve guns, and 4,000 men last night, I moved my troops at daylight this morning to attack. I think I have taken every gun he had, and driven him over the river. My guns are now battering him from the opposite bank. He came out to fight me. I expect fifty guns are on the field at least. My loss I hope not great. The cavalry charged several times, both black and white, like soldiers, – and infantry, vied with each other in bravery. To the God of Victory we are all indebted. God bless you, dear Sir Hugh. My Staff all right – Mackeson and Cunningham, of the Political Department, bore heavily on some villages. The enemy required all I could do with such brave fellows to teach him to swim.

(Signed) H. G. SMITH, Major-General.'

Major-General Sir Harry Smith, K.C.B., to the Adjutant-General of the Army.

CAMP, FIELD OF THE BATTLE OF ALIWAL, *Jan. 30, 1846.*

'SIR,

'My despatches to his Excellency the Commander-in-Chief of the 23rd instant, will have put his Excellency in possession of the position of the force under my command, after having formed a junction with the troops at Loodiana, hemmed in by a formidable body of the Sikh army under Runjoor Singh and the Rajah of

Ladwa. The enemy strongly entrenched himself around the little fort of Budhowal by breast-works and "abbatis," which he precipitately abandoned on the night of the 22nd instant (retiring, as it were, upon the ford of Tulwun), having ordered all the boats which were opposite Philour to that Ghat. This movement he effected during the night, and, by making a considerable detour, placed himself at a distance of ten miles, and consequently out of my reach. I could, therefore, only push forward my cavalry so soon as I had ascertained he had marched during the night, and I occupied immediately his vacated position. It appeared subsequently he had no intention of recrossing the Sutlej, but moved down to the Ghat of Tulwun (being cut off from that of Philour, by the position my force occupied after its relief of Loodiana), for the purpose of protecting the passage of a very considerable reinforcement of twelve guns and 4,000 of the regular, or "Aieen" troops, called Avitabile's battalion, entrenching himself strongly in a semicircle, his flanks resting on a river, his position covered with from forty to fifty guns (generally of large calibre), howitzers, and mortars. The reinforcement crossed during the night of the 27th instant, and encamped to the right of the main army.

'Meanwhile, his Excellency the Commander-in-Chief, with that foresight and judgment which mark the able general, had reinforced me by a considerable addition to my cavalry, some guns, and the 2nd brigade of my own division, under Brigadier Wheeler, C.B. This reinforcement reached me on the 26th, and I had intended the next morning to move upon the enemy in his entrenchments, but the troops required one day's rest after the long marches Brigadier Wheeler had made.

'I have now the honour to lay before you the operations of my united forces on the morning of the eventful 28th January, for his Excellency's information. The body of troops under my command having been increased, it became necessary so to organize and brigade them as to render them manageable in action. The cavalry under the command of Brigadier Cureton, and horse artillery under Major Lawrenson, were put into two brigades; the one under Brigadier MacDowell, D.B., and the other under Brigadier Stedman. The 1st division as it stood, two brigades: – Her Majesty's 53rd and 30th Native Infantry, under Brigadier Wilson, of the latter corps; – the 36th Native Infantry, and Nusseree battalion, under Brigadier Godby; – and the Shekawattee brigade under Major Forster. The Sirmoor battalion I attached to Brigadier Wheeler's brigade of the 1st division; the 42nd Native Infantry having been left at head quarters.

'At daylight on the 28th, my order of advance was – the Cavalry in front, in contiguous columns of squadrons of regiments, two troops of horse artillery in the interval of brigades; – the infantry in contiguous columns of brigades at intervals of deploying distance; – artillery in the intervals, followed by two 8-inch howitzers on travelling carriages, brought into the field from the fort of Loodiana, by the indefatigable exertions of Lieutenant-Colonel Lane, Horse Artillery; – Brigadier

Godby's brigade, which I had marched out from Loodiana the previous evening, on the right; – the Shekawattee infantry on the left; – the 4th Irregular Cavalry considerably to the right, for the purpose of sweeping the banks of the wet nullah on my right, and preventing any of the enemy's horse attempting an inroad towards Loodiana, or any attempt upon the baggage assembled round the fort of Budhowal.

'In this order the troops moved forward towards the enemy, a distance of six miles, the advance conducted by Captain Waugh, 16th Lancers, the Deputy Assistant Quarter-Master of Cavalry, Major Bradford, of the 1st Cavalry, and Lieutenant Strachey of the Engineers, who had been jointly employed in the conduct of patrols up to the enemy's position, and for the purpose of reporting upon the facility and point of approach. Previously to the march of the troops it had been intimated to me, by Major Mackeson, that the information by spies, led to the belief the enemy would move somewhere at daylight, either on Jugraon, my position of Budhowal, or Loodiana. On a near approach to his outposts, this rumour was confirmed by a spy, who had just left the camp, saying the Sikh army was actually in march towards Jugraon. My advance was steady; my troops well in hand; and if he had anticipated me on the Jugraon road, I could have fallen upon his centre with advantage.

'From the tops of the houses of the village of Poorein, I had a distant view of the enemy. He was in motion, and appeared directly opposite my front on a ridge, of which the village of Aliwal may be regarded as the centre. His left appeared still to occupy its ground in the circular entrenchment; his right was brought forward and occupied the ridge. I immediately deployed the cavalry into line, and moved on. As I neared the enemy, the ground became most favourable for the troops to manœuvre, being open and hard grass land. I ordered the cavalry to take ground to the right and left by brigades; thus displaying the heads of the infantry columns; and, as they reached the hard ground, I directed them to deploy into line. Brigadier Godby's brigade was in direct échellon to the rear of the right; the Shekawattee infantry in like manner to the rear of my left; – the cavalry in direct échellon on, and well to the rear of, both flanks of the infantry; – the artillery massed on the right, and centre and left. After deployment, I observed the enemy's left to outflank me, I therefore broke into open column and took ground to my right. When I had gained sufficient ground, the troops wheeled into line. There was no dust, the sun shone brightly. These manœuvres were performed with the celerity and precision of the most correct field day. The glistening of the bayonets and swords of this order of battle was most imposing; and the line advanced. Scarcely had it moved 150 yards, when, at ten o'clock, the enemy opened a fierce cannonade from his whole line. At first his balls fell short, but quickly reached us. Thus upon him, and capable of better ascertaining his position, I was compelled to halt the line, though under

A trooper in one of the company's Indian cavalry regiments.

the most gallant manner dashed in among them, and drove them back upon their infantry. Meanwhile a second gallant charge to my right was made by the light cavalry and the body guard. The Shekawattee brigade was moved well to the right, in support of Brigadier Cureton, when I observed the enemy's encampment, and saw it was full of infantry: I immediately brought upon it Brigadier Godby's brigade, by changing front, and taking the enemy's infantry "en-reverse." They drove them before them, and took some guns without a check.

'While these operations were going on upon the right; and the enemy's left flank was thus driven back, I occasionally observed the brigade under Brigadier Wheeler, an officer in whom I have the greatest confidence, charging and carrying guns and everything before it, again connecting his line, and moving on, in a manner which ably displayed the coolness of the Brigadier and the gallantry of his irresistible brigade, – Her Majesty's 50th Foot, the 48th Native Infantry, and the Sirmoor Battalion, although the loss was, I regret to say, severe in the 50th. Upon the left, Brigadier Wilson, with Her Majesty's 53rd and the 30th Native Infantry equalled in celerity and regularity their comrades on the right; and this brigade was opposed to the "Aieen" troops, called Avitabile's, when the fight was fiercely raging.

'The enemy, well driven back on his left and centre, endeavoured to hold his right to cover the passage of the river, and he strongly occupied the village of Bhoondree – I directed a squadron of the 16th Lancers, under Major Smyth and Captain Pearson, to charge a body to the right of a village, which they did in the most gallant and determined style, bearing everything before them, as a squadron under Captain Bere had previously done, going right through a square in the most intrepid manner with the deadly lance. – This charge was accompanied by the 3rd Light Cavalry under Major Angelo, and as gallantly sustained. The largest gun upon the field, and seven others, were then captured, while the 53rd Regiment carried the village by the bayonet, and the 30th Native Infantry wheeled round to the rear in a most spirited manner. Lieut.-Col. Alexander's and Capt. Turton's troops of horse artillery, under Major Lawrenson, dashed among the flying infantry, committing great havoc, until about 800 or 1,000 men rallied under the high bank of a nullah, and opened a heavy but ineffectual fire from below the bank. I immediately directed the 30th Native Infantry to charge them, which they were able to do upon their left flank, while in a line in rear of the village. This native corps nobly obeyed my orders, and rushed among the Avitabile troops, driving them from under the bank, and exposing them once more to a deadly fire of twelve guns within 300 yards. The destruction was very great, as may be supposed, from guns served as these were. Her Majesty's 53rd Regiment moved forward in support of the 30th Native Infantry by the right of the village. The battle was won; our troops advancing with the most perfect order to the common focus – the passage of the river. The enemy,

fire, for a few moments, until I ascertained that, by bringing up my right, and carrying the village of Aliwal, I could with great effect precipitate myself upon his left and centre. I therefore quickly brought up Brigadier Godby's brigade; and, with it, and the 1st brigade under Brigadier Hicks, made a rapid and noble charge, carried the village, and two guns of large calibre. The line I ordered to advance – Her Majesty's 31st Foot and the native regiments contending for the front; and the battle became general. The enemy had a numerous body of cavalry on the heights to his left, and I ordered Brigadier Cureton to bring up the right brigade of cavalry, who, in completely hemmed in, were flying from our fire, and precipitating themselves in disordered masses into the ford and boats, in the utmost confusion and consternation; our 8-inch howitzers soon began to play upon their boats, when the "débris" of the Sikh army appeared upon the opposite and high bank of the river, flying in every direction, although a sort of line was attempted to countenance their retreat, until *all* our guns commenced a furious cannonade, when they quickly receded. Nine guns were on the river by the ford. It appears as if they had been unlimbered to cover the ford. These being loaded, were fired once upon our advance; two others were sticking in the river, one of them we got out; two were seen to sink in the quicksands; two were dragged to the opposite bank and abandoned. These, and the one in the middle of the river, were gallantly spiked by Lieutenant Holmes, of the 11th Irregular Cavalry, and Gunner Scott, of the 1st troop 2nd brigade horse artillery, who rode into the stream, and crossed for the purpose, covered by our guns and light infantry.

'Thus ended the battle of Aliwal, one of the most glorious victories ever achieved in India, by the united efforts of Her Majesty's and the Honourable Company's troops. *Every gun* the enemy had fell into our hands, as I infer from his never opening one upon us from the opposite bank of the river, which is high and favourable for the purpose – fifty-two guns are now in the Ordnance Park; two sank in the bed of the Sutlej; and two were spiked on the opposite bank; making a total of fifty-six pieces of cannon captured or destroyed. Many jingalls which were attached to Avitabile's corps, and which aided in the defence of the village of Bhoondree, have also been taken. The whole army of the enemy has been driven headlong over the difficult ford of a broad river; his camp, baggage, stores of ammunition and of grain, – his all, in fact, wrested from him, by the repeated charges of cavalry and infantry, aided by the guns of Alexander, Turton, Lane, Mill, Boileau, and of the Shekawattee brigade, and by the 8-inch howitzers; – our guns literally being constantly ahead of everything. The determined bravery of all was as conspicuous as noble. I am unwont to praise when praise is not merited; and I here most unavowedly express my firm opinion and conviction, that no troops in any battle on record ever behaved more nobly; – British and native, no distinction; cavalry, all vying with H.M.'s 16th Lancers, and striving to head in the repeated charges. Our guns and gunners, officers and men, may be equalled, but cannot be excelled, by any artillery in the world. Throughout the day no hesitation – a bold and intrepid advance; – and thus it is that our loss is comparatively small, though I deeply regret to say, severe. The enemy fought with much resolution; they maintained frequent rencontres with our cavalry hand to hand. In one charge, upon infantry, of H.M.'s 16th Lancers, they threw away their muskets and came on with their swords and targets against the lance.

'The fort of Goongrana has, subsequently to the battle, been evacuated, and I yesterday evening blew up the fort of Budhowal. I shall now blow up that of Noorpoor. A portion of the peasantry, *viz.*, the Sikhs, appear less friendly to us, while the Mussulmans rejoice in being under our Government. I have, &c.

(True copy). H. G. SMITH, *Major-General Commanding.*
(Signed) P. GRANT, Major, *Deputy-Adjutant-General of the Army.'*

'*Casualty Return of the Force under the Command of Major-General Sir H. G. Smith, K.C.B.*

CAMP, ALIWAL, *January 29, 1846.*

'*Artillery.* – 3 men, 30 horses – killed; 15 men, 9 horses – wounded; 5 men, 12 horses – missing.

'*Cavalry.*

'*1st brigade.* – 3 European officers, 2 native officers, 83 men, 120 horses, – killed; 6 European officers, 1 native officer, 100 men, 32 horses – wounded; 1 man, 73 horses – missing.

'*2nd brigade.* – 11 men, 25 horses – killed; 2 European officers, 3 native officers, 34 men, 38 horses wounded; 12 horses – missing.

'*Infantry.*

'*1st brigade.* – 2 men killed; 2 European officers, 28 men – wounded; 7 men missing.

'*2nd brigade.* – 1 European officer, 1 native officer, 27 men, 2 horses – killed; 14 European officers, 2 native officers, 134 men – wounded; 4 men missing.

'*3rd brigade.* – 7 men killed; 32 men wounded; 3 men missing.

'*4th brigade.* – 9 men killed; 1 European officer, 26 men – wounded; 1 man missing.

'*Shekawattee Infantry.* – 2 men killed; 13 men wounded; 4 men missing.

'*Sappers and Miners.* – None killed or wounded.

'*Total killed* – 151 men, 177 horses; *total wounded* – 413 men, 79 horses; *total missing* – 25 men, 97 horses.

'*Grand total of killed, wounded, and missing* – 589 men; 353 horses.

H. G. SMITH, *Major-General.'*

'*Return of Ordnance captured from the Enemy, in action at Aliwal, by the 1st Division of the Army of the Sutlej, under the personal Command of Major-General Sir Harry Smith, K.C.B., on the 29th January, 1846.*

CAMP, ALIWAL, *January 30, 1846.*

'*Serviceable* – 12 howitzers, 4 mortars, 33 guns; total – 49; unserviceable – 1 howitzer, 2 guns; total – 3; sunk in the Sutlej, and spiked on the opposite shore – 13 guns; since brought in – 2 guns. Grand total, 67.

'*Forty swivel camel guns also captured, which have been destroyed.*

G. LAWRENCE, *Major, 2nd Brigade Horse Artillery, Commanding Artillery, 1st Division Army of the Sutlej.'*

Perhaps the most memorable feature of this stirring battle was the manner in which the 16th Lancers repeatedly broke through formed squares of courageous, trained Sikh infantry, a feat rare in warfare of the period

The charge of the 16th (Queen's Own) Lancers at Aliwal on 28 January 1846

or in the Napoleonic Wars which preceded it by 50 or so years. There are many first-hand accounts, and following are from Henry Graham's *The History of the 16th, The Queen's Light Dragoons (Lancers)* (1912). Sergeant Gould of C Troop wrote:

'At a trumpet note to trot, off we went. "Now," said Major Smyth, "I am going to give the word to charge. Three cheers for the Queen!" There was a terrific burst of cheering in reply, and we swept down on the guns. Bullets were flying around like a hailstorm. A big Sergeant, Harry Newsome, mounted on a grey charger, shouted, "Hullo, boys, here goes for death or a commission!" and forced his horse over the front rank of the kneeling Sikhs, bristling with bayonets. He leant over to grasp one of their standards, but fell from his horse, pierced by 19 bayonet wounds.

'When we got out on the other side of the square our troop had lost both lieutenants, the cornet, troop sergeant-major and two sergeants. I was the only sergeant left. Some of the men shouted: "Bill, you've got command! They're all down!" Back we went through the disorganised square, the Sikhs peppering us in all directions. One of the men had both arms frightfully slashed by a Sikh, who was down under his horse's hooves and made upward cuts at him.'

Corporal F. B. Cowtan wrote afterwards:

'As for myself, I went through cavalry and infantry squares repeatedly, at the first charge I dismounted two cavalrymen and on retiring we passed through a square of their infantry, and I left three on the ground killed or wounded. One fellow was taking deliberate aim at me when I put my horse at him, and just in time, for his priming blackened my face. Sergeant Brown was riding next to me and cleaving everyone down before him with his sword when his horse was shot under him, and before he reached the ground he received no less than a dozen sabre-cuts, which of course killed him. My comrade on my left, just as we cheered before charging, had his heart torn from his side by a cannon-ball, but my heart sickens at the recollection of what I witnessed that day. The killed and wounded alone in my squadron was forty-two.'

Writing afterwards about Captain Bere's charge, a man of his squadron said:

'They gave us a volley at forty yards, a ball from which struck the chain of my lance-cap just over the left cheekbone. I was into them by then, and delivered a point at one fellow but could not quite reach him, and was about to settle a second when a blow from a sabre from behind severed my arm just above the wrist, and my hand, grasping the lance, fell to the ground. Not being able to make my horse break the ranks, I slipped my feet out of the stirrups and endeavoured to throw myself off. In doing this my sword belt caught the cantle of the saddle, but fortunately, the belt broke, and I found myself on the ground. I lay for a few moments reflecting on what I should do, when a ball came within a few feet of my head, which at once convinced me that this was no place of safety, On getting up to make my way to the rear I was met by a Sikh who, seeing my helpless condition, placed his musket within a yard of my head. Just at that moment I lifted my arm as though to strike him, and fell forward to the ground. He fired, and his charge burnt a portion of the hair off the back of my head, the ball entering my left shoulder. I lay for a few moments expecting the cowardly rascal to finish me with his bayonet, but while he was reloading, an artilleryman came up and gave him the contents of his pistol, but as this only wounded him, he dismounted and ran him through with his sword. After this I got up and grasping the stump of my right arm, again made for the rear. I had not gone far before I found myself in front of a troop of our artillery, who were only waiting for our squadron to get out of the way before opening fire on the retreating enemy. I managed to get be-

tween two of the guns and then bolted as fast as I could, walking on for about a mile when I met with a doctor, who applied a tourniquet to my arm and gave me a glass of brandy-and-water. He directed me to a field hospital where, on arriving in a very exhausted condition, it was found necessary to amputate my arm just below the elbow.' (The writer of that letter recovered and returned to England, he was invalided out of the army and granted the munificent pension of £13.00 per annum!)

Writing in February 1846, Trooper Eaton of the 16th Lancers, gives a very characteristic picture of Sir Harry Smith:

'The General told us that when our regiment was in Lahore in 1837, the King thought us all gentlemen, but had he seen us on that day (at Aliwal) he would have proclaimed us all devils, "for you charged their ranks more like them than anything else". As he left us we saw tears in the poor old man's eyes, and he said, "God bless you, my brave boys; I love you".'

While Sir Harry was fighting at Aliwal, the Commander-

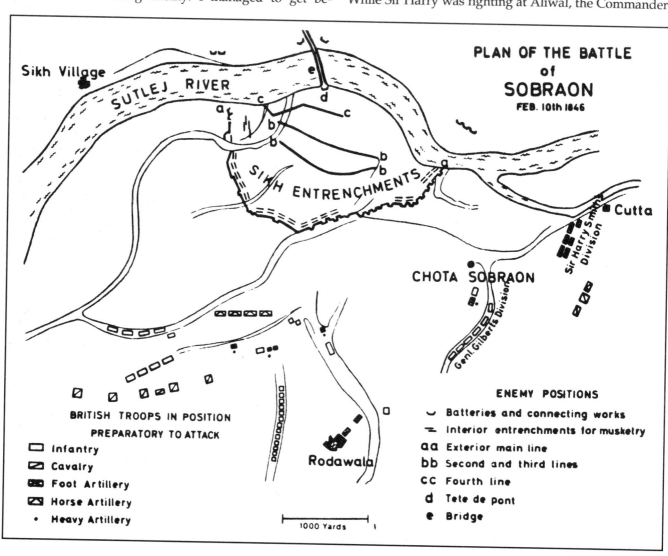

64

in-Chief and the Governor-General were watching the Sikh camp at Sobraon. From Bootawallah, where they were conversing on the morning of 28 January, they could hear the sound of artillery, and an officer who was with Sir Hugh wrote of the scene:

'From not having heard of Sir Harry Smith and various native rumours in the camp, Sir Hugh was really very miserably anxious about him, and the fine force he had given him; and I must now tell you of that gallant, glorious, good old Chief. We heard the cannonading which was, while it lasted, fearful. I asked him what he thought of it. "Think of it! Why, 'tis the most glorious thing I ever heard. I know by the sound of the guns that Smith has carried the position and silenced their artillery." "I hope, Sir," I said, "he has not found it too strong, and retired to wait for our reinforcements." "Retire," he cried, "No! No British force would ever retire before such a cannonade as we have just heard!" He spoke with such likely confidence that, although I had gone to him fully impressed with the conviction that Smith had failed, I left him perfectly assured that I was wrong, and that victory had been ours. He sent Bagot and Becher to bring an express. When he heard the news he was nearly frantic with joy; but Bagot told me that ere the lapse of two minutes he saw the dear old man on his knees by his couch, offering up his thanks to that Power which alone gave the victory.'

THE BATTLE OF SOBRAON – 10 FEBRUARY 1846

'General Sir Hugh Gough, Bart., G.C.B., Commander-in-Chief in India, to the Governor-General.
CAMP, NIHALKEE, *February 1, 1846*.

'After its final repulse, on the 22nd of December, the Sikh army retired, in great confusion, across the ferries and fords of the Sutlej.

'On the 12th of January, I determined to bring my whole force into a position, from which it might more closely observe the movements of the enemy, now posted near the greater Sobraon, on the right bank.

'The enemy, on his side, reinforced his army on the right bank, completed and strengthened his bridge, and increased the force of his posts and picquets on the left bank. These parties having, on the 14th, evinced more than usual audacity, I caused that body of his infantry which held the head of the bridge, to be driven in by the fire of artillery and rockets, supported by the presence of our light troops. On the following day, a partial cannonade, which was again opened, on our side, upon the boats of the Sikhs, on their outposts on the left bank, and their encampment on the right, enabled me to ascertain, from the direction of their corresponding fire, the nature of all their defensive dispositions.'

In the British camp there was a natural disappointment at the slow progress of the siege-train. Herbert Edwards, at that time ADC to Sir Hugh Gough, wrote in the *Calcutta Review*: 'The Army is sickening for want of a battle; a malignant fever or epidemic of horrors must have broken out at Sobraon had it been delayed another week.'

'General Sir Hugh Gough, Bart., G.C.B., Commander-in-Chief of the Forces in India, to the Governor-General of India.
HEAD QUARTERS, ARMY OF THE SUTLEJ, CAMP KUSSOOR, *February 13, 1846*.

'RIGHT HONOURABLE SIR,

'This is the fourth despatch which I have the honour of addressing to you since the opening of the campaign. Thanks to Almighty God, whose hand I desire to acknowledge in all our successes, the occasion of my writing now is to announce a fourth and most glorious and decisive victory.

'My last communication detailed the movements of the Sikhs and our counter-manœuvres since the great day of Ferozeshah. Defeated on the Upper Sutlej, the enemy continued to occupy his position on the right bank, and his formidable *tête du pont* and entrenchments on the left bank of the river, in front of the main body of our army. But, on the 10th instant, all that he held of British territory, which was comprised in the ground on which one of his camps stood, was stormed from his grasp, and his audacity was again signally punished by a blow, sudden, heavy, and overwhelming. It is my gratifying duty to detail the measures which had led to this glorious result.

'The enemy's works had been repeatedly reconnoitered during the time of my head quarters being fixed at Nihalkee, by myself, my departmental staff, and my engineer and artillery officers. Our observations, coupled with the reports of spies, convinced us that there had devolved on us the arduous task of attacking a position covered with formidable entrenchments, not fewer than 30,000 men, the best of the Khalsa troops, with seventy pieces of cannon, united by a good bridge to a reserve on the opposite bank, on which the enemy had a considerable camp and some artillery, commanding and flanking his field-works on our side. . . . Major General Sir Harry Smith's division having rejoined me on the evening of the 8th, and part of my siege train having come up with me, I resolved, on the morning of the 10th, to dispose our mortars and battering guns on the alluvial land within good range of the enemy's picquets at the post of observation in front of Kodeewalla, and at the Little Sobraon. It was directed that this should be done during the night of the 9th, but the execution of this part of the plan was deferred owing to misconceptions and casual circumstances until near daybreak. The delay was of little importance, as the event showed that the Sikhs had followed our example, in occupying the two posts in force by day only. Of both, therefore, possession was taken without opposition. The battering and disposable field artillery was then put in position on an extended semi-circle, embracing within its fire the works of the Sikhs. It had been intended that the cannonade should have commenced at daybreak; but so heavy a mist hung over the plain and river that it became necessary to wait until the rays of the sun had penetrated it and cleared the atmosphere.'

The historical record of the 1st Bengal European Light Infantry describes the scene:

'The rising sun rapidly dispelled the fog, when a magnificent picture presented itself. The batteries of artillery were seen in position ready to open fire and the plain was covered with our troops, the fortified village Rhoadawallah on our left being strongly held by our infantry. Immediately the guns opened a heavy fire. The enemy appeared suddenly to realise their danger, their drums beat the alarm, their bugles sounded to "arms!" and in a few minutes their batteries were manned, and pouring shot and shell upon our troops.'

Even in old Gough, man of action rather than of letters, this artillery barrage aroused an emotional feeling, causing him later to write:

'Nothing could be conceived grander than the effect of the batteries when they opened, as the cannonade passed along from the Sutlej to Little Sobraon, in one continued roar of guns and mortars; while, ever and anon, the rocket, like a spirit of fire, winged its rapid flight high over the batteries in its progress toward the Sikh entrenchments. . . .

'Meanwhile on the margin of the Sutlej, on our left, two brigades of Major-General Robert Dick's division, under his personal command, stood ready to commence the assault against the enemy's extreme right. His 7th brigade, in which was the 10th Foot, reinforced by the 53rd Foot, and led by Brigadier Stacy, was to head the attack, supported, at 200 yards distance, by the 6th brigade, under Brigadier Wilkinson. In reserve was the 5th brigade, under Brigadier the Honourable T. Ashburnham, which was to move foward from the entrenched village of Kodeewalla, leaving, if necessary, a regiment for its defence. In the centre, Major-General Gilbert's division was deployed for support or attack, its right resting on and in the village of the Little Sobraon. Major-General Sir Harry Smith's division was formed near the village of Guttah, with its right thrown up towards the Sutlej. Brigadier Cureton's cavalry threatened, by feigned attacks, the ford at Hurrekee and the enemy's horse, under Rajah Lal Singh Misr, on the opposite bank. Brigadier Campbell, taking an intermediate position in the rear between Major-General Gilbert's right and Major-General Sir Harry Smith's left, protected both. Major-General Sir Thomas Thackwell, under whom was Brigadier Scott, held in reserve on our left, ready to act as circumstances might demand, the rest of the cavalry.

'Our battery of nine-pounders, enlarged into twelves, opened near the Little Sobraon with a brigade of howitzers formed from the light field batteries and troops of horse artillery, shortly after daybreak. But it was half-past six before the whole of our artillery fire was developed. It was most spirited and well directed. I cannot speak in terms too high of the judicious disposition of the guns, their admirable practice, or the activity with which the cannonade was sustained. But, notwithstanding the formidable calibre of our iron guns, mortars, and howitzers, and the admirable way in which they were served, and aided by a rocket battery, it would have been visionary to expect that they could, within any limited time, silence the fire of seventy pieces behind well-constructed batteries of earth, plank, and fascines, or dislodge troops, covered either by redoubts or epaulments, or within a treble line of trenches. The effect of the cannonade was, as has been since proved by an inspection of the camp, most severely felt by the enemy; but it soon became evident that the issue of this struggle must be brought to the arbitrement of musketry and the bayonet.'

Despite delaying his assault until the heavy guns had arrived from Delhi, it was never far from Gough's mind that this was a battle to be settled by cold steel. Thus, when the ammunition of the heavy guns began to run out and their fire slackened, his heart possibly lightened, so that, to the surprise of those around him, he showed no signs of alarm or hesitation, crying to the officer who brought the news: 'Thank God! Then I'll be at them with the bayonet!'

Colonel Benson, a member of Hardinge's staff, arrived with a message. He had been instructed by the Governor-General to tell the Commander-in-Chief that if he doubted the issue, he was at liberty to call off the assault, but that if he only anticipated heavy loss he might go on. Unfortunately, Colonel Benson transposed this relatively harmless message into these words: 'If Gough did not feel confident of success without great loss he had better withdraw the troops and work up to the enemy's entrenchments by regular approaches.' The effect of this peremptory, thrice-repeated message upon the choleric Sir Hugh was galvanic: 'What? Withdraw the troops after the action has commenced! Indeed I will not!' And, turning to his nephew, Colonel J. B. Gough, and Quartermaster-General, he cried: 'Tell Sir Robert Dick to move on, in the name of God!'

Gough's despatch again:

'At nine o'clock, Brigadier Stacy's brigade, supported on either flank by Captains Horsford's and Fordyce's batteries, and Lieutenant-Colonel Lane's troop of horse artillery, moved to the attack in admirable order. The infantry and guns aided each other correlatively. The former marched steadily on in line, which they halted only to correct when necessary. The latter took up successive positions at the gallop, until at length they were within three hundred yards of the heavy batteries of the Sikhs; but, notwithstanding the regularity and coolness, and scientific character of this assault, which Brigadier Wilkinson well supported, so hot was the fire of cannon, musketry, and zumboorucks, kept up by the Khalsa troops, that it seemed for some moments impossible that the entrenchments could be won under it; but soon, persevering gallantry triumphed, and the whole army had the satisfaction to see the gallant Brigadier Stacy's soldiers driving the Sikhs in confusion before them within the area of their encampment. The 10th Foot, under Lieutenant-Colonel Franks, now for the first time brought into serious contact with the enemy, greatly distinguished themselves. This regiment never fired a shot until it had got within the works of the enemy.'

One reads of the steady British infantry but rarely realises the effect they had on those on whom they were advancing. Hookhum Singh, a Sikh gunner in battery upon the right wing of the enemy army, directly opposed to the advance of the 10th Foot, wrote:

'Nearer and nearer they came, as steadily as if they were on their own parade ground, in perfect silence. A creeping feeling came over me; this silence seemed so unnatural. We Sikhs are, as you know, brave, but when we attack we begin firing our muskets and shouting our famous war-cry; but these men, saying never a word, advanced in perfect silence. They appeared to me as demons, evil spirits, bent on our destruction, and I could hardly refrain from firing.

'At last the order came, "Fire", and our whole battery as if from one gun fired into the advancing mass. The smoke was so great that for a few minutes I could not see the effect of our fire, but fully expected that we had destroyed the demons, so, what was my astonishment, when the smoke cleared away, to see them still advancing in perfect silence, but their numbers reduced to about one half. Loading my cannon, I fired again and again into them, making a gap or lane in their ranks each time; but on they came, in that awful silence, till they were within a short distance of our guns, when their colonel ordered them to halt and take breath, which they did under heavy fire.

'Then with a shout, such as only angry demons could give and which is still ringing in my ears, they made a rush for our guns, led by their colonel. In ten minutes it was all over; they leapt into the deep ditch or moat in our front, soon filling it, and then swarming up the opposite side on the shoulders of their comrades, dashed for the guns, which were still defended by a strong body of our infantry, who fought bravely. But who could withstand such fierce demons, with those awful bayonets, which they preferred to their guns – for not a shot did they fire the whole time – and then, with a ringing cheer, which was heard for miles, they announced their victory.'

In his despatch, Gough states:

'The onset of Her Majesty's 53rd Foot was as gallant and effective. The 43rd and 59th Native Infantry, brigaded with them, emulated both in cool determination.

'At the moment of this first success, I directed Brigadier the Hon. T. Ashburnham's brigade to move on in support; and Major-General Gilbert's and Sir Harry Smith's divisions to throw out their light troops to threaten the works, aided by artillery. As these attacks of the centre and right commenced, the fire of our heavy guns had first to be directed to the right, and then gradually to cease; but, at one time, the thunder of full 120 pieces of ordnance reverberated in this mighty combat through the valley of the Sutlej; and as it was soon seen that the weight of the whole force within the Sikh camp was likely to be thrown upon the two brigades that had passed its trenches, it became necessary to convert into

Officer and other ranks of the 29th Foot (Worcestershire Regiment) at Ferozeshah and Sobraon.

close and serious attacks the demonstrations with skirmishers and artillery of the centre and right; and the battle raged with inconceivable fury from right to left. The Sikhs, even when at particular points their entrenchments were mastered with the bayonet, strove to regain them by the fiercest conflict, sword in hand.'

At the same time as Gough had ordered Smith forward, the Governor-General, feeling that the situation was becoming critical, had directed Gilbert's division in the centre to attack. Rushing forward, the troops crossed a dry nullah, to be exposed to a murderous fire of musketry from Sikhs concealed behind walls too high for them to climb. Three times did the 29th Foot of Taylor's brigade go forward to charge the works, and three times were they obliged to retire, Sikh cavalry following them and butchering the wounded. They were ably supported by Maclaren's brigade, whose brigadier was killed, Gilbert being wounded at the same time. Gough, watching the assault, was moved to cry out: 'Good God, they'll be annihilated!'

Meanwhile, Smith's division, on the British right attacking the left of the Sikh position, was heavily engaged, so much so that even Sir Harry himself, veteran of so many bloody encounters, thought it a hard battle. In a letter to his sister, Mrs Sargant, dated 'Camp Lahore, 25th February 1846', he says:

'Our last fight was an awful one. My reduced in numbers Division – only 2,400 bayonets – was, as in other fights, placed in reserve, but pretty soon brought into action, and as at Ferozeshuhur again I had the good luck to turn the fortune of the day. In so doing I lost out of my 2,400 men, 635 killed and wounded (100 more than out of 12,000 men at Aliwal). My first attack on the entrenchments was repulsed. I attacked when I did not wish, and had to take ground close to the river on the enemy's left, consequently our right. (Never catch a butting animal by the horns, though, as a good soldier, obey your superior's orders). By dint of the hardest fighting I ever saw (except Badajoz, New Orleans, and Waterloo) I carried the entrenchments. By Jupiter! the enemy were within a hairsbreadth of driving me back. Their numbers exceeded mine. And such a hand-to-hand conflict ensued, for 25 minutes I could barely hold my own. Mixed together, swords and targets against bayonets, and a fire on both sides. I never was in such a

Charge of cavalry through the breaches at Sobraon.

personal fight for half the time, but my bulldogs of the 31st and the old 50th stood up like men, were well supported by the native regiments, and my position closed the fight which staggered everywhere. Then such a scene of shooting men fording a deep river, as no-one I believe ever saw before. The bodies *made a bridge*, but the fire of our musketry and cannon killed everyone who rushed. The hand of Almighty God has been upon me, for I may say to you what all the army knows, I was foremost in the fight, and on a noble horse the whole time, which sprang over the enemy's works like a deer, neither he nor I nor my clothes being scratched. It was a miracle for which I am, I trust, even more grateful to God than humble towards my comrades.'

In another letter, to Sir James Kempt, Smith added some extra details:

'Behind such formidable entrenchments, I could not get in where I was ordered to attack, but had to turn my right close to the river, where, if left alone, I should have commenced. I carried the works by dint of English pluck, although the native corps stuck close to me, and when I got in, such hand-to-hand work I have never witnessed. For 25 minutes we were at it against four times my numbers, sometimes receding (never turning round, though) sometimes advancing. The old 31st and 50th laid on like devils . . . This last was a brutal bulldog fight, although of vast political and definite results; but my fight at Aliwal was a little sweeping second edition of Salamanca – a stand-up gentlemanlike battle, a mixing of all arms and laying on, carrying everything before us by weight of attack and combination, all hands at work from one end of the field to the other.'

Gough's despatch takes up the account:

'Nor was it until the cavalry of the left, under Major-General Sir Joseph Thackwell, had moved forward and ridden through the openings in the entrenchments made by our sappers, in single file, and reformed as they passed them; and the 3rd Dragoons, whom no obstacle usually held formidable by horse appears to check, had on this day, as at Ferozeshah, galloped over and cut down the obstinate defenders of batteries and field-works, and until the full weight of three divisions of infantry, with every field artillery gun which could be sent to their aid, had been cast into the scale, that victory finally declared for the British. . . .

'The fire of the Sikhs first slackened, and then nearly ceased; and the victors then pressing them on every side, precipitated them in masses over their bridge, and into the Sutlej, which a sudden rise of seven inches had rendered hardly fordable. In their efforts to reach the right bank through the deepened water, they suffered from our horse artillery a terrible carnage. Hundreds fell under this cannonade; hundreds upon hundreds were drowned in attempting the perilous passage.

'The loss of the enemy has been immense; an estimate must be formed with a due allowance for the spirit of exaggeration which pervades all statements of Asiatics where their interest leads them to magnify numbers; but our own observation on the river banks and in the

The Sikh trophy guns 'forming up', in the Fort of Monghyr.
Illustrated London News, *March 1847.*

enemy's camp, combined with the reports brought to our intelligence department, convince me that the Khalsa casualties were between 8,000 and 10,000 men killed and wounded in action and drowned in the passage of the river.

'Sixty-seven pieces of cannon, upwards of 200 camel-swivels (zumboorucks), numerous standards, and vast munitions of war, captured by our troops, are the pledges and trophies of our victory. The battle was over by eleven in the morning; and, in the forenoon, I caused our engineers to burn a part and to sink a part of the vaunted bridge of the Khalsa army, across which they had boastfully come once more to defy us, and to threaten India with ruin and devastation.

'Their awful slaughter, confusion, and dismay were such as would have excited compassion in the hearts of their generous conquerors, if the Khalsa troops had not, in the earlier part of the action, sullied their gallantry by slaughtering and barbarously mangling every wounded soldier whom, in the vicissitudes of attack, the fortune of war left at their mercy.'

Hodson, a well-known soldier of the period, wrote: 'The river is literally choked with corpses and their camp is full of dead and dying. An intercepted letter of theirs shows that they have lost 20,000 killed and wounded; all their guns remain in our hands. I had the pleasure myself of spiking two guns that were turned on us.'

Few escaped and none surrendered: by 10.30 there was not a live Sikh remaining on the left bank of the Sutlej. The British 'defiled with dust, smoke and carnage, stood mute indeed for a moment until, the glory of their success rushing upon their minds, they gave expression to their feelings and hailed their victorious commanders with reiterated shouts of triumph and congratulation.'

Gough's despatch concludes:

'I must pause in this narrative especially to notice the determined hardihood and bravery with which our two battalions of Ghoorkhas, the Sirmoor and Nusseree, met the Sikhs, wherever they were opposed to them. Soldiers, of small stature but indomitable spirit, they vied in ardent courage in the charge with the grenadiers of our own nation, and, armed with the short weapon of their mountains, were a terror to the Sikhs throughout this great combat.

'The consequences of this great action have yet to be fully developed. It has at least, in God's providence, once more expelled the Sikhs from our territory, and planted our standards on the soil of the Punjaub. After occupying their entrenched position for nearly a month, the Khalsa army had perhaps mistaken the caution which had induced us to wait for the necessary material, for timidity. But they must now deeply feel that the blow which has fallen on them from the British arm has only been the heavier for being long delayed.'

Gurkha soldier.

'Return of the Killed, Wounded, and Missing of the Army of the Sutlej, under the Command of His Excellency General Sir Hugh Gough, Bart., G.C.B., Commander-in-Chief, in the Action at Sobraon, on 10th February, 1846.

'ABSTRACT.

'*Staff.* – 2 European officers wounded.

'*Artillery Division.* – 1 European officer, 3 rank and file, 3 syce drivers, 17 horses – killed; 1 European officer, 1 sergeant, 33 rank and file, 5 lascars, 5 syces, 23 horses – wounded; 5 horses missing.

'*Engineers and Sappers and Miners.* – 2 rank and file – killed; 3 European officers, 1 native ditto, 16 rank and file – wounded.

'*Cavalry Division.* – 6 rank and file, 13 horses – killed; 4 European officers, 2 trumpeters, 36 rank and file, 53 horses – wounded; 24 horses missing.

'*1st Infantry Division.* – 2 European officers, 1 native officer, 97 rank and file – killed; 28 European officers, 13 native officers, 489 rank and file – wounded.

'*2nd Infantry Division.* – 5 European officers, 1 native officer, 5 sergeants, 109 rank and file, 1 horse – killed; 38 European officers, 12 native officers, 46 sergeants, 2 drummers, 685 rank and file, 1 horse – wounded.

'*3rd Infantry Division.* – 5 European officers, 1 native officer, 3 sergeants, 1 drummer, 75 rank and file, 5 horses – killed; 25 European officers, 13 native officers, 27 sergeants, 3 drummers, 573 rank and file, 6 horses – wounded.

'*Total* – 13 European officers, 3 native officers, 8 sergeants, 1 drummer, 292 rank and file, 3 syces, and 36 horses – killed; 101 European officers, 39 native officers, 74 sergeants and havildars, 7 trumpeters and drummers, 832 rank and file, 5 lascars, 5 syces, 83 horses – wounded; 29 horses missing.

'*European officers.* – 13 killed, 101 wounded.

'*Native officers.* – 3 killed, 39 wounded.

'*Warrant and non-commissioned officers, rank and file.* – 301 killed, 1,913 wounded.

'*Lascars, syce drivers, syce, &c.* – 3 killed, 10 wounded.

'*Total* – 320 killed, 2,063 wounded.

'*Grand Total of killed, wounded, and missing, 2,383.*'

The losses were more evenly distributed among the British and Indian troops than in any previous action of the war, for the sepoys had learned their lesson at Aliwal and fought in a determined manner, doing their duty well, and the two battalions of Gurkhas greatly distinguished themselves.

The Sikh losses had been fearful. Five days after the action and when the walls of the entrenchment had been levelled to the ground, the sandbank in the middle of the river was completely covered with their dead bodies, and the ground within their encampment thickly strewn with the carcasses of men and horses. With the permission of the Commander-in-Chief they returned to carry off their dead, but the task was found too irksome, and many not swept away by the river were left as food for the jackal, the wild dog and the vulture. The heirs of

Landing of the 31st Regiment, Ordnance Wharf, Gravesend.

3,125 Sikh soldiers killed claimed arrears of pay, from which it can be estimated that they had between 8,000 and 12,000 casualties.

As is probably the invariable case with all major battles, there were 'inquests' on the handling of Sobraon, some from the principal characters involved. Sir Harry Smith wrote:

'In my own mind I very much disagreed with my gallant Commander-in-Chief as to the place of his attack being the most eligible one. I saw at once that the fundamental principle of "being superior to your enemy at the point of attack" was lost sight of, and the whole of our army, with the exception of my division, which was reduced to 2,400 bayonets, was held in reserve just out of reach of the enemy's guns.'

There was certainly mismanagement of the heavy artillery, and particularly of the 18-pounders, which, if properly handled, might have dismounted at least part of the Sikh artillery. Gough's biographer does not agree with this; he claims that, as Sir Hugh stated in his despatch, it would have been 'visionary to expect that our guns could, within any limited time, silence the fire of 70 pieces behind well constructed batteries of earth, planks and fascines, or dislodge troops, covered by either redoubts or epaulments or within a treble line of trenches'. Gough wished to use his artillery so as to

THE MEDAL ordered by her Majesty for distribution amongst the officers and soldiers of her Majesty's and the Company's Service, who took part in the late campaign in the Punjaub, have at length been completed. The design, which is by Mr. W. Wyon, R.A., of the Mint, is one of great beauty. It is appropriate, and marked by classical feeling. The obverse gives an excellent profile of the Queen, with the name; while the reverse represents a figure of Victory, holding out a wreath to the army of the Sutlej in one hand, and in the other she bears a palm branch; at her feet are military weapons, tastefully grouped. In the exergue, are the names of the battles in which the particular wearer took part. Medals have been sent to the several regiments at present in England; and 20,000 have been forwarded to India. It is expected that about 4',000 will be struck. The tie is a blue ribbon, with a red border. As in the case of the Waterloo Medal, there will be no distinction made in the value of the decoration; all will be of silver.

The original announcement in the Illustrated London News *of 8 April 1848, of the issue of medals for the 1st Sikh War, 1845–1846.*

weaken the Sikhs sufficiently to allow the issue to be brought to 'the arbitrament of the musket and the bayonet'. The Duke of Wellington, referring to Sobraon and exploring what *he* would have done with his guns, exclaimed: 'The fire of that battery would have gone right in among them, so that, by Heavens, I would not have left a cat there with room to stand . . . Ah, the truth is, they are not masters of their game!'

BATTLE HONOURS FOR THE FIRST SIKH WAR 1845/6

MUDKI

3rd (King's Own) Regt. of Light Dragoons
9th (East Norfolk) Regt. of Foot
31st (Huntingdonshire) Regt. of Foot
80th (Staffordshire Volunteers) Regt. of Foot
50th (The Queen's Own) Regt. of Foot

Indian Army

Governor General's Body Guard
4th Regt. Bengal Irregular Cavalry
8th Regt. Bengal Irregular Cavalry
42nd Regt. Bengal Native (Light) Infantry
47th Regt. Bengal Native Infantry

FEROZESHAH

3rd (King's Own) Regt. of Light Dragoons
9th (East Norfolk) Regt. of Foot
29th (Worcestershire) Regt. of Foot
31st (Huntingdonshire) Regt. of Foot
80th (Staffordshire Volunteers) Regt. of Foot
50th (The Queen's Own) Regt. of Foot
62nd (Wiltshire) Regt. of Foot
H.E.I.C. 1st Bengal European Regt. (Light Infantry)

Indian Army

Governor General's Body Guard
4th Regt. Bengal Irregular Cavalry
8th Regt. Bengal Irregular Cavalry
Corps of Bengal Sappers & Miners
33rd Regt. Bengal Native Infantry
42nd Regt. Bengal Native (Light) Infantry
47th Regt. Bengal Native Infantry

ALIWAL

16th (The Queen's) Light Dragoons (Lancers)
31st (Huntingdonshire) Regt. of Foot
50th (The Queen's Own) Regt. of Foot
53rd (Shropshire) Regt. of Foot

Indian Army

Governor General's Body Guard
4th Regt. Bengal Irregular Cavalry
47th Regt. Bengal Native Infantry
The Shekhawati Brigade
4th or Nasiri Local Battalion
6th or Sirmoor Local Battalion

SOBRAON

3rd (King's Own) Regt. of Light Dragoons
9th (Queen's Royal) Regt. of Light Dragoons (Lancers)
16th (The Queen's) Light Dragoons (Lancers)
9th (East Norfolk) Regt. of Foot
10th (North Lincolnshire) Regt. of Foot
29th (Worcestershire) Regt. of Foot
31st (Huntingdonshire) Regt. of Foot
80th (Staffordshire Volunteers) Regt. of Foot
50th (The Queen's Own) Regt. of Foot
53rd (Shropshire) Regt. of Foot
62nd (Wiltshire) Regt. of Foot
H.E.I.C. 1st Bengal European Regt. (Light Infantry)

Indian Army

Governor General's Body Guard
2nd Regt. Bengal Irregular Cavalry
8th Regt. Bengal Irregular Cavalry
Corps of Bengal Sappers & Miners
33rd Regt. Bengal Native Infantry
42nd Regt. Bengal Native (Light) Infantry
43rd Regt. Bengal Native (Light) Infantry
47th Regt. Bengal Native Infantry
59th Regt. Bengal Native Infantry
4th or Nasiri Local Battalion
6th or Sirmoor Local Battalion
63rd Regt. Bengal Native Infantry

Return of H.M. Regiments with the Army of the Sutlej, showing the effective strength before entering into Action, and the Casualties after each subsequent Engagement.

HEAD QUARTERS, CAMP LAHORE, 2nd March, 1846.

Regiment	Eff. Off	Eff. Men	Moodkee K-Off	Moodkee K-Men	Moodkee W-Off	Moodkee W-Men	Moodkee M-Off	Moodkee M-Men	Ferozeshah K-Off	Ferozeshah K-Men	Ferozeshah W-Off	Ferozeshah W-Men	Ferozeshah M-Off	Ferozeshah M-Men	Budeewal K-Off	Budeewal K-Men	Budeewal W-Off	Budeewal W-Men	Budeewal M-Off	Budeewal M-Men	Aliwal K-Off	Aliwal K-Men	Aliwal W-Off	Aliwal W-Men	Aliwal M-Off	Aliwal M-Men	Sobraon K-Off	Sobraon K-Men	Sobraon W-Off	Sobraon W-Men	Sobraon M-Off	Sobraon M-Men	Total K-Off	Total K-Men	Total W-Off	Total W-Men	Total M-Off	Total M-Men
3rd LIGHT DRAGOONS, Before the Action at Moodkee, on the 18th December, 1845	27	518	3	58	3	32	..	..	3	53	7	67	..	..	..	..	..	..	..	..	..	9	..	..	..	..	..	4	5	22	..	..	6	124	15	121	..	..
9th LANCERS, Before the Action at Sobraon, on the 10th February, 1846	33	599	..	..	..	..	..	..	..	..	..	..	..	..	..	..	..	..	..	..	..	..	..	..	..	..	..	1	..	1	..	..	..	1	..	1	..	..
16th LANCERS, Before the Skirmish at Budeewal, on the 21st January, 1846	23	539	..	..	..	..	..	..	..	..	..	..	..	..	..	2	..	1	..	..	2	57	6	77	..	..	..	..	..	..	..	..	2	59	6	78	..	..
9th FOOT, Before the Action at Moodkee, on the 18th December, 1845	30	874	1	2	1	49	..	..	3	67	6	197	..	18	..	..	..	..	..	..	..	..	..	..	..	..	..	5	1	28	..	..	4	74	8	274	..	18
10th FOOT, Before the Action at Sobraon, on the 10th February, 1846	36	742	..	..	..	..	..	..	..	..	..	..	..	..	..	..	..	..	..	..	..	..	..	..	..	..	1	29	2	101	..	..	1	29	2	101	..	..
29th FOOT, Before the Action at Ferozeshah, on the 21st December, 1856	28	765	..	..	..	..	..	..	3	52	3	185	..	..	..	..	..	..	..	..	..	..	..	..	..	..	1	35	13	159	..	..	4	87	16	344	..	..
31st FOOT, Before the Action at Moodkee, on the 18th December, 1845	31	844	1	24	8	126	..	6	2	59	5	97	..	19	..	12	..	9	..	19	..	1	1	14	..	..	..	33	8	112	..	2	3	129	22	358	..	46
50th FOOT, Before the Action at Moodkee, on the 18th December, 1845	31	675	1	21	6	94	..	4	..	24	3	89	..	2	..	4	..	13	..	8	..	8	8	59	..	..	2	37	12	184	..	..	3	94	29	439	..	14
53rd FOOT, Before the Skirmish at Budeewal, on the 21st January, 1846	47	861	..	..	..	..	..	..	..	..	..	..	..	..	..	26	2	15	..	20	1	3	1	7	..	1	..	4	7	105	..	3	1	33	10	127	..	24
62nd FOOT, Before the Action at Ferozeshah, on the 21st December, 1845	24	768	..	..	..	..	..	..	7	88	10	161	..	..	..	..	..	..	..	..	..	..	..	..	..	..	1	3	1	43	..	..	8	91	11	204	..	..
80th FOOT, Before the Action at Moodkee, on the 18th December, 1845	26	795	..	5	1	20	..	..	5	35	1	73	..	..	..	..	..	..	..	..	..	..	..	..	..	..	..	13	5	74	..	..	5	53	7	167	..	..
TOTAL	336	7980	6	110	19	321	..	10	23	378	35	869	..	39	..	44	2	38	..	47	3	78	16	157	..	1	5	164	54	829	..	5	37	774	126	2214	..	102

EDWARD LUGARD, Captain,
Acting-Assistant-Adjutant-General of H.M. Forces in India.

4 · The Second Sikh War
1848–1849

The arrival of Calcutta news to the 8th of May puts the public in possession of the particulars of the threatened renewal of the war in the Punjaub. It was expected, after the summary chastisement inflicted upon the Sikhs by the victories of Moodkee, Aliwal, and Sobraon, that during the present generation, at least, we should hear no more of any great difficulties in that quarter; but it appears that the Sikhs are not yet sufficiently convinced of the invincibility of our arms, and of our determination to keep India quiet. They are still intriguing against British supremacy; and still, as it would appear, indulge in the belief that we may be driven from India. The district of Moultan has been the scene of a new intrigue and outbreak. The Viceroy, Dewan Moolraj, was confirmed, or rather left in power by Lord Hardinge, after the campaign of the Sutlej; but as the administrative reforms carried on by Col. Lawrence in the other portions of the Sikh territory rendered it necessary to establish uniformity in this district as well as the rest, a negotiation was entered into, and amicably concluded with this ruler, for the peaceable absorption of Moultan into the general system of the Punjaub. Mr. Vans Agnew and Lieut. Anderson were deputed, on the part of the Indian Government, to proceed to Moultan to carry the treaty into effect, and left Lahore for that purpose with an escort of three hundred Sikh troops. The day after their arrival they were attacked by the Moultanese; their escort proved faithless, and turned against them, and both were murdered. Sir Frederick Currie, the resident at Lahore, at first imagined that the murder was the result of individual fanaticism; but, on receiving fuller information, he came to the conclusion that it was the preconcerted signal for a general rising of the Sikhs in Moultan, under their Viceroy, Dewan Moolraj, against the British. He has since taken his measures accordingly; and we may expect by the next arrival, or as soon as the hot season in India shall have allowed the troops to advance with impunity, to hear of a renewal of hostilities with one portion of the Sikhs of the Punjaub occupying a fortress hitherto deemed to be impregnable. There can be no doubt that our arms will be once more successful; but it is fearful to contemplate at what a cost of life to them, and to us the victory may have to be purchased.

ILLUSTRATED LONDON NEWS, *Saturday, 24 June 1848*

Subsequent events are related in the Victorian part-work *England's Battles by Sea and Land* by William Cooke Stafford:

'At the time when Moolraj committed his outrage – for that it was his there is no doubt – upon the British officials, a young English officer (Lieutenant Edwardes) was engaged in settling the country ceded to the company by the second article of the treaty of Lahore. Mr. Vans Agnew, after he was wounded and taken to the Eedgah, found means to dispatch a messenger to this officer, who instantly concerted measures with the rajah of Bhawulpore, to array a force at once, to assist him [Edwardes] in his attempt to rescue his countrymen, and to protect Colonel Cortlandt, who at that time was at the head of a small garrison in the town of Dera Ismael Khan. Without waiting for the rajah's troops, Lieutenant Edwardes, collecting the little force which had been sent to the Indus under his orders, crossed that river, and proceeded at once to Moultan. [Edwarde's small force consisted of 12 company's of infantry, 350 horse, two guns, and 20 zamburucks (camel-guns).] Moolraj did not long remain quiet. He sent a force, in May, to attack a party of 300 horse, left by Lieutenant Edwardes to collect the revenue at Leia, an important commercial town, situate on a small branch of the Indus, about eleven miles to the eastward of the main stream. The attack took place on the 18th of May; but Moolraj's troops were completely defeated, and compelled to retreat, leaving ten light guns in the hands of the victors. About the same time, Colonel Cortlandt left Dera Ismael Khan, with 4,000 troops; and having captured Sunghur (a fortress on the west of the Indus) on the way, effected a junction with Lieutenant Edwardes. The united force – chiefly Sikhs, and a corps of Mohammedans raised by Edwardes – defeated a large detachment of Moolraj's army on the 20th of May; the slaughter amongst the enemy, and their loss of guns, being considerable.

'On the 10th and 11th of June, the two commanders recrossed the Indus, for the purpose of effecting a junction with the troops of the rajah of Bhawulpore. Moolraj, apprised by some of his emissaries of their route, and its purpose, crossed the Chenaub on the 14th; and on the 16th, the two forces were opposite to each other, on different sides of that river. The troops of the rajah were then marching to join Edwardes, who, on the 18th of June, crossed the Chenaub to meet them, with 3,000 irregular infantry; Cortlandt being left to follow with the cavalry and the guns. Before the latter, however, could effect the passage, Edwardes and his force were attacked by Moolraj's army, the number of which has been variously estimated at from 7,000 to 10,000 men, with ten guns. Gallantly the inferior force resisted the attack; they beat back the repeated assaults of the enemy, which were made with all the desperate bravery of the Sikhs; till at length Cortlandt – who had got over gun after gun, with some small bodies of troops – joined; and then the men under Lieutenant Edwardes became the assailants, and defeated Moolraj's army, with great loss to the latter in men, baggage, and stores; six guns were also taken. This action, which lasted nine hours, is called the battle of Kineyree. – The fugitives retreated on Moultan, and were followed by Lieutenant Edwardes and Colonel Cortlandt; who, on the 1st of July, were within a short distance of the city. Moolraj resolved to arrest their further progress; and he left Moultan for that purpose at the head of 11,000 men, taking up his position behind a strong breastwork at the village of Suddoosam. There they were attacked by Lieutenant Edwardes' army, and another fierce fight of six hours' duration ensued, ending in the defeat of Moolraj, who with difficulty got back into the fortress; before which Lieutenant Edwardes now encamped his force, augmented by the arrival of a large body of men, under Sheikh Imaum-ood-deen, to 18,000. But though strong in men, he was deficient in siege *matériel*. Sir Frederick Currie, who had succeeded Sir Henry Lawrence as political resident at Lahore, on learning the position of this force, dispatched, a siege-train, under a competent escort, to the camp; but it was a long while before it arrived.

'The British resident at Lahore, on first hearing of the murder of the officials at Moultan, and of the movements of Moolraj, had urged upon the government at Calcutta, the propriety of sending a British force to capture that city; but both the governor-general and the commander-in-chief were of opinion, that the time was very unfit for a European force to commence operations,

Sir Herbert Edwardes.

it being the hottest season of the year, and the district around Moultan the hottest in India. The British government also thought, that it was a case for the Sikhs to act in; and they [according to Lord Dalhousie, the Governor-General] "were called upon to punish Moolraj as a rebel against their own sovereign, and to exact reparation for the British government, whose protection they had previously invoked". As time progressed, however, and the Sikh government did nothing to restore tranquillity, Sir F. Currie sent General Whish from Lahore to Moultan, with her majesty's 8th regiment, a troop of horse artillery, a regiment of irregular cavalry, and two native regiments, the 8th and 52nd. He reached his destination on the 18th of August; and on the next day a still larger body arrived from Ferozepore, comprising her majesty's 32nd foot, the 11th regular and the 11th irregular cavalry the 49th, 51st and 72nd native infantry, a troop of horse artillery, and a battering train of 30 heavy guns. These reinforcements increased the besieging army to near 28,000 men, of which General Whish took the command.'

James Grant's *Illustrated History of India*, which was published during the second half of the nineteenth century, describes Multan and the opposing forces:

'The native force' which had assembled before this, consisted of 8,415 cavalry, and 14,327 infantry, with forty-five horse artillery guns, four mortars, and 158 zumboorucks. Of this column, including that of General Cortlandt, 7,718 infantry and 4,033 cavalry were commanded by Lieutenant Edwardes; 5,700 infantry and 1,900 calvary formed the Bhawulpore army, commanded by Lieutenant Lake; and 909 infantry and 3,382 cavalry, formed the Sikh army, commanded by Rajah Shere Sing. To this besieging force of nearly 32,000 men Moolraj was not able to oppose more than a garrison of 12,000 men, with an artillery of fifty-four guns and five mortars. This great disparity of numbers was compensated by the strength of the works.

'Moultan is built on a mound of considerable height, formed of the accumulated debris of many cities that have occupied the same site, on the left bank of the Chenab.

'The citadel, on which the banner of Moolraj was waving, is an irregular hexagon, constructed on an eminence, and girt by a ditch twenty-five feet deep by forty wide. The city surrounds the hill which this citadel crowns. Prior to the late defeat of Moolraj, an old brick wall was its only defence, but now, by unremitting exertions, he had surrounded it by an enormous rampart of mud, having six gates. The citadel was undoubtedly one of the strongest and most regular of Indian fortresses constructed by native engineers. Beyond its deep wide ditch, which was faced with masonry, rose a wall, strengthened by thirty great towers. Within, everything had been done for its security, and its magazines were stored for a protracted siege. Around the city are populous suburbs, groves of date-trees, and beautiful gardens.

'On the 4th of September, 1848, General Whish issued a proclamation to the people and garrison of the city, demanding an unconditional surrender within twenty-

Citizen of Multan and Sikh soldiers.

four hours after the firing of a royal salute at sunrise tomorrow, in honour of her most gracious Majesty the Queen of Great Britain and her ally his Highness Maharajah Dhuleep Sing. In the event of non-compliance, death and destruction was threatened to the rebel traitor and all his adherents, who, having begun their resistance to lawful authority with a most cowardly act of treachery and murder, seek to uphold their unrighteous cause by an appeal to religion, which every one must know to be sheer hypocrisy.

'The only reply to this was a cannon-shot from the citadel, which buried itself in the earth, close by General Whish and his staff.'

Grant then tells of an event that completely changed the situation:

'The speedy capture of Moultan was confidently anticipated, when an unlooked-for event took place.

'On the 14th of September Shere Sing threw off all disguise, and, at the head of all his contingent, marched to join the enemy in Moultan, ordering the *dhurum kha dosa*, or religious drum to be beaten, and proclaiming a sacred war, "under the auspices of the holy *Gooroo* [against] the cruel *Feringhees*," surrounded all who had eaten the salt of the Maharajah to come forth and destroy them. The arrival of Shere Sing was a source of high satisfaction to Moolraj, though the latter was far from having confidence in his new allies; thus, instead of admitting them into the citadel, he cautiously kept them under its guns in the city, while he took all the officers to a temple and made them swear that they had no designs of treachery.

'Even this oath proved insufficient to allay the suspicions of Moolraj, who was anxious for the withdrawal of Shere. . . . Hence Shere Sing, on the 9th of October, marched to join his father, and became the leader in a new Sikh war. . . .

'General Whish held a council of war, which was unanimously of opinion that the siege was no longer practicable. Our troops were in consequences withdrawn from their advanced positions to new ground, to await the arrival of such reinforcements as Lord Gough might send.'

This manœuvre was not carried out without interference, as Stafford explains:

'During their march, Shere Sing detached 1,000 of his cavalry to harass and annoy his late friends. Colonel Cortlandt, however, halted the troop he commanded, and opening his guns upon the pursuers, they speedily turned their horses' heads and fled. – Shortly after this movement, intelligence was received, that Lieutenant Edwardes had been raised to the local rank of major, and created a knight-commander of the Bath. . . .

'Meanwhile, many suspicious events were occurring elsewhere. Among them was a formidable revolt led by Chuttur Sing in the Hazareh country in the north-west of the Punjaub, where the people are of Tartar origin, and, like our Highland clans of old, are almost constantly at variance with each other. They are, moreover, an irritable, fierce, and capricious race, good matchlock-men, and excellent archers. Their outbreak derived significant importance from the fact that Chuttur was the father of Shere Sing, who though now encamped with his troops before Moultan, affecting to be part of the besieging force, must have been acquainted with his father's designs, and no doubt sanctioned them.'

INDIA
'RETREAT OF THE BRITISH FORCES FROM MOULTAN

'Advices in anticipation of the Overland Mail have been received this week; they are dated Calcutta, September 22; Madras, 25th; and Bombay, October 3. The intelligence thus received is not very satisfactory either as regards the operations of the siege of Moultan or the general state of the Punjaub. At Moultan our forces have suffered a check, in consequence of the defection of the auxiliary Sikh troops. Just as the operations of General Whish's brigade had commenced in the most brilliant manner, Shere Singh, with a force of nearly 5,000 men under his command, on the 14th of September, went over to the Dewan, evidently upon a pre-arranged plot – an event which compelled General Whish instantly to change his tactics, to raise the siege, and, having made a retrograde movement to unite his forces in an entrenched camp at some fifteen miles from the citadel, there to await in a more favourable position the junction of the reinforcements from Ferozepore and Scinde. Two engineer officers had since fallen into the hands of the enemy.

'The operations before Moultan (previous to this disaster) are thus described in the *Bombay Times*: – "On the 5th (of Sept.) it was intimated that twenty-four hours would be allowed for those to retire who wished to quit the town. On the 6th the mortar batteries began to fire. It was at first proposed to attempt the town by assault. The guns were first to clear the suburbs, then to advance within 600 yards of the walls. It was expected that in twenty-four hours a practicable breach would be effected. After the storming party had been told off, it was discovered that the suburbs were very strong and well defended; and regular approaches were next determined on. The trenches were begun to be opened on the 7th, and from this till the 9th a succession of severe skirmishes ensued, in which we were successful. On the morning of this day we were compelled to retire with severe loss from a strong post we had endeavoured to capture. Further skirmishing ensued, and on the morning of the 12th a strong party was directed to capture the stronghold before which we had formerly been foiled, and which ever since had been annoying us. We succeeded, but not without heavy loss. Up to this time five officers had been killed and 21 wounded, and nearly 200 men had been killed and wounded. A furious attack was made on Edwardes' camp on the 13th; and on the 14th we carried a strong outwork, which enabled us to bring our guns within easy breaching distance. At this time all our plans were thrown into confusion by the desertion of the Durbar leader, Shere Singh, with 4,000 Singhs, and it then became plain that the attack could no longer be maintained with any hope of success."

'Expresses were immediately sent off requesting reinforcements. An army of above 20,000 was ordered to be immediately formed at Ferozepore, to proceed either in whole or in part to Moultan. Moolraj, by Shere Singh's defection, had augmented his adherents to about 20,000 men, with the probability of a further accession of nearly as many more. Chutter Singh, the rebel leader in the Hazareh, was marching with about 10,000 men to join the Dewan; and, although Gholab Singh had not more positively than heretofore gone over to the conspiracy, two of his regiments, with stores and baggage, had left to join the Hazareh Sikhs.

'Troops were being poured into Scinde by sea from Bombay, to occupy the line of the middle Indus, and to march, should their services be required upon the Punjaub. The Bombay force, when united, would amount to about 10,000 men. Some of the Madras regiments would reinforce the Bombay stations, at the same time that a general advance was preparing from the Bengal frontier. From the latter direction, a well-apportioned force, amounting to about 20,000 men, were to march upon Moultan, under General Gilbert. No troops could be spared from Lahore; but it was considered the cavalry regiments still left in Ferozepore would be quite sufficient to keep open the line of communication with the camp of General Whish; in other words, to frustrate any rising between him and the capital. Under these circumstances, the position of the British force in the field, strongly entrenched, with a park of artillery of seventy guns, and their flank on the river, at some fifteen miles from Moultan, may be regarded as secure under any contingency.'

Illustrated London News, 4 November 1848

Once Lord Gough felt ready to move, he advanced rapidly and was in Lahore on 16 November, where he stayed three days, before joining the force near Ramnuggur on 21 November.

Almost complete except for the heavy artillery and the besieging force outside Multan, the army consisted of:

'Cavalry Division, under Brigadier Cureton:

'1st Brigade – 3rd and 14th Light Dragoons, and 5th and 8th Light Native Cavalry, under Brigadier White.

'2nd Brigade – 9th Lancers, and 1st and 6th Native Light Cavalry, under Brigadier Pope.

'Infantry. Gilbert's Division:

'1st Brigade – H.M.'s 29th Foot, 30th and 56th Native Infantry, under Brigadier Mountain.

'2nd Brigade – 2nd European Light Infantry, and 31st and 70th Native Infantry, under Brigadier Godby.

'Thackwell's Division:

'1st Brigade – H.M.'s 24th Foot, 25th and 45th Native Infantry, under Brigadier Pennycuick.

'2nd Brigade – H.M.'s 61st Foot, 36th and 6th Native Infantry, under Brigadier Hoggan.

'3rd Brigade – 15th, 20th, and 69th Native Infantry, under Brigadier Penny.

'Artillery. Horse Artillery, under Lieut.-Colonel Huthwaite:

'Six troops, commanded by Lieut.-Colonel Lane, and Majors Christie, Huish, Warner, Duncan, and Fordyce.

'Field Batteries – Three, under Major Dawes, and Captains Kinleside and Austin.

'Heavy Batteries – Two, under Major Horsford.'

THE ACTION AT RAMNUGGUR – 22 NOVEMBER 1848

Gough was anxious lest Shere Singh should attempt to carry the war into the difficult country across the Indus, and he made immediate arrangements to enter the Punjab. In a letter to his son, written on 16 November, he revealed the force he had at his disposal:

'I deemed it right at once to order on the Force, which I had taken on myself to collect there [at Ferozepore], but which the Government have since entirely approved, consisting of six Regiments of Infantry (including the 24th and 25th Foot), one Light Field Battery, and six siege guns (drawn by elephants, with bullocks to take them into action), with a reserve Company of Artillery and a Pontoon Train. I have in advance, eight regiments of cavalry (including the 3rd and 14th Light Dragoons and the 9th Lancers), and six regiments of Infantry (including the 2nd European infantry), with five troops of Horse Artillery, and two Light Field Batteries – exclusive of Brigadier Wheeler, who is acting on my right flank, with one troop of Horse Artillery, and one Light Field Battery, three regiments of Cavalry and two of Infantry (including the 61st Foot). Coming on in my support are a brigade of Infantry, two regiments Irregular Cavalry, and a siege train, whilst I have, to protect the N.W. frontier, a Brigade of Infantry (one regiment of which is European, the 98th) and a Brigade of Irregular Cavalry, exclusive of the corps doing station duty at Ferozepore, Ludhiana, and Umballa. At Lahore, I have six regiments of Infantry (including the 53rd Foot), a troop of Horse Artillery, and a Light Field Battery, with a regiment of Irregular Cavalry coming from the rear, from the lower provinces, I have six regiments of Infantry, including the 18th Royal Irish. So you perceive I am now moving as an Army with Advance, Centre Column, Flank Corps, with support and Reserve.'

Gough had scarcely arrived at the camp when he decided to put the army into motion, attacking the Sikh outposts and guns on the left bank of the Chenab. He described the action in a letter to Lord Fitzroy Somerset on 26 November 1848:

'Deeming it necessary to attack this force, if possible, before it could get across the Chenab, which is a difficult river, I directed Brigadier-General Campbell, commanding the troops in advance, with an Infantry Brigade, and the whole of the Cavalry Division, with three troops of Horse Artillery and one Light Field Battery, under Brigadier-General Cureton, to proceed during the night of the 21st to effect this; the Troops under my personal command coming up, in support, the following morning, should the enemy be in too great force. I joined the advance at three in the morning, to witness the opera-

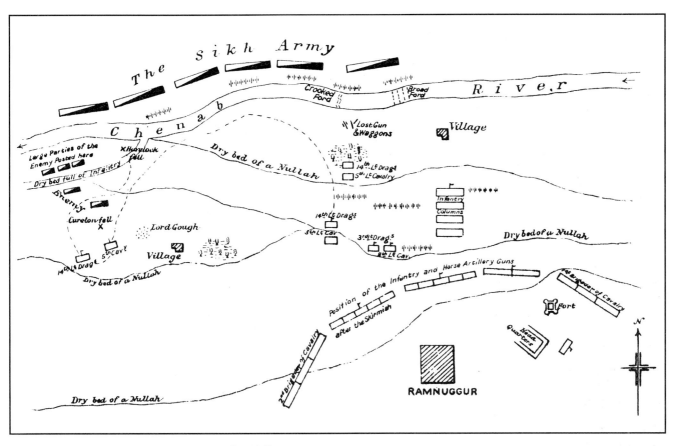

The cavalry skirmish at Ramnuggur, 22 November 1848.

tion. Just as the day dawned, the Troops were brought up in beautiful order to the town of Ramnuggur, situated on rather a high bank, having a commanding view of the low ground between it and the river, distant about two miles. The enemy appeared to have crossed with the main body of his force, but there were several large bodies of Horse upon the flat, to drive away which, with as much punishment as possible, two troops of Horse Artillery, with five Regiments of Cavalry, were ordered to advance as rapidly as the nature of the ground would admit, and to punish the enemy in crossing the river. I regret to say the Artillery, in their eagerness to overtake the enemy, pushed to the very banks of the river, and the leading gun was precipitated down a bank of several feet into a deep sand, and this, under the guns of the Enemy, which opened from the opposite bank, placed in battery. Every exertion was made to get it free, so much so, that Brigadier Campbell dismounted personally to assist; but in vain, and it was spiked and abandoned.'

Gough's biographer, Rait, enlarges upon the situation:

'Lord Gough's object had been accomplished; the casualties were slight, and the loss of the gun and two ammunition-waggons would have been borne with equanimity had no further blunder occurred.

'To the left of the scene of conflict there was another ford, and some Sikh light cavalry ("Gorchurras") crossed and threatened our flank. Lord Gough ordered the commanding officer of the 14th Light Dragoons,

Lieut.-Colonel William Havelock, to deliver a charge and clear the ground. Havelock was a brave man, and he possessed the gift of inspiring courage in others. "Now we'll win our spurs," he said, and, in his brother's words, "happy as a lover, he placed himself in front of his cherished dragoons." Cureton sat watching the result. Havelock pushed on, but apparently "losing the direction of the body of Gorchurras which General Cureton had sanctioned his attacking, he charged across an arm of the river, under the bank of which numbers both of Infantry and Cavalry were concealed." "My God!" exclaimed Cureton, "this isn't the way to use cavalry!" and he immediately started off, with a few of the escort of the 5th Light Cavalry, to warn Havelock not to charge into the sand of the river-bed. He had ridden only a short distance when he was shot through the heart. The escort returned to say that the General was dead. Lord Gough, unaware of Cureton's intention, sent Major Tucker to Havelock with a similar warning; "but he went at such a pace that Major Tucker could not overtake him . . . leaving the body of cavalry he was supposed to be about to attack about half way between us and where he was. These men, finding themselves free, moved to attack the reserve, a squadron of the 5th Light Cavalry. . . . Seeing the 5th hesitate, I naturally was anxious that the 14th reserve should charge." They did so, and effectually. But meanwhile Havelock had charged into the sandy river-bed, lined with the enemy and commanded by their guns. He paid for his mistake with his life; the regiment (though it suffered sadly) made its way back, but without its Colonel. . . .

'The loss, though not large in numbers, was severe in proportion to the troops engaged. Twenty-six were killed or missing, and fifty-nine were wounded. Among the killed the most important were Cureton and Havelock. Cureton was a general of great ability, in whom Lord Gough placed special confidence. He had risen from the ranks to the grade of Brigadier-General, and the skill with which he handled cavalry in the Sutlej Campaign had induced the Commander-in-Chief to place him in command of the cavalry division of the army of the Punjab. "A better or a braver soldier," said Lord Gough's report, "never fell in his country's service." Of Havelock, too, the Commander-in-Chief spoke most warmly, suggesting explanations for his misinterpretation of his orders, and emphasizing the courage which had marked his whole career.'

The subsequent course of operations is reported in Gough's official despatch:

'HEADQUARTERS, FLYING CAMP, HILLAH, *December 5th, 1848.*

'MY LORD,

'It has pleased Almighty God to vouchsafe to the British arms the most successful issue to the extensive combinations rendered necessary for the purpose of effecting the passage of the Chenab, the defeat and dispersion of the Sikh force under the insurgent Rajah Shere Sing, and the numerous Sikh sirdars, who had the temerity to set at defiance the British power. This force, from all my information, amounted to from 30,000 to 40,000 men, with 28 guns, and was strongly entrenched on the right bank of the Chenab, at the principal ford, about two miles from the town of Ramnuggar.

'My despatch of November 23rd will have made your Lordship acquainted with the motives which induced me to penetrate thus far into the Punjaub, and the occurrences of the previous day, when the enemy were ejected from the left bank of the Chenab. My daily private communications will have placed your Lordship in possession of the difficulties I had to encounter in a country so little known, and in the passage of a river, the fords of which were most strictly watched by a numerous and vigilant enemy, and presenting more difficulties than most rivers, whilst I was surrounded by a hostile peasantry.

'Finding that to force the passage at the ford in my front must have been attended with considerable loss, from the very strong entrenchments and well-selected batteries which protected the passage, I instructed the field-engineer, Major Tremenhere, in co-operation with the Quartermaster-General's department, to ascertain (under the difficulties before noticed) the practicability of the several fords reported to exist on both by flanks, while I had batteries erected and made demonstrations so as to draw the attention of the enemy to the main ford in my front, and with the view, if my batteries could silence their guns, to act simultaneously with the

force I proposed to detach under an officer of much experience in India, Major-General Sir Joseph Thackwell.

'On the night of November 30th, this officer, in command of the following force, and more particularly detailed in the accompanying memorandum:

	European.	Native.	Total.
3 Troops Horse Artillery	3	0	3
2 Light Field Batteries	2	0	2
1 Brigade of Cavalry	1	4	5
3 Brigades of Infantry	2	6	8

' . . . two eighteen-pounders with elephant draft and detail artillery, pontoon train, with two companies, moved up the river in light marching order, without tents and with three days' provisions, upon a ford which I had every reason to consider very practicable (and which I have since ascertained was so), but which the Major-General deemed so dangerous and difficult that he proceeded (as he was instructed should such turn out to be the case) to Wuzeerabad, a town 22 miles up the river, where Lieutenant Nicholson, a most energetic assistant to the Resident at Lahore, had secured 16 boats, with the aid of which this force effected the passage on the evening of the 1st and morning of the 2nd instant.'

Brigadier Colin Campbell, commanding the infantry in this outflanking force, was not happy about the operation: 'the movement was, in my view, and in that of the General [Thackwell] a hazardous one – the placing of a force under 7,000 in a position in which they could not be supported, and where they might be opposed by 30,000.'

Campbell's diary of the day contains the following statement:

'After a march of fourteen or fifteen miles, we arrived at a part of the river which was guarded on the opposite bank by the enemy. It was the ford of Ranni-ki-Patten; *and above this, about a mile higher up, was the ford at which it was intended the force should pass.* Lieutenant Paton, Assistant Quartermaster-General, was sent to examine it and the approaches to it. His report was that it was of this shape and breast-high in some places; that the sand through which the guns must pass was very deep and heavy, and that the bullocks with the pontoon train would certainly not be able to drag the pontoons through it . . . *The enemy, moreover, were on the opposite side, ready to oppose our passage, and in such cover as to make it difficult for our guns to drive them from it.'*

Lord Gough's despatch continues:

'Upon learning from an aide-de-camp sent for the purpose that the Major-General's force had crossed and was in movement, I directed a heavy cannonade to commence upon the enemy's batteries and encampment at Ramnuggar, which was returned by only a few guns, which guarded effectually the ford, but so buried that,

Sir Colin Campbell.

although the practice of our artillery was admirable under Major Mowatt and Captain Sir Richmond Shakespear, we could not, from the width of the river, silence them. This cannonade, however, inflicted very severe loss to the enemy in their camp and batteries, and forced him to fall back with his camp about two miles, which enabled me, without loss of a man, to push my batteries and breastworks, on the night of the 2nd, to the bank of the river, the principal ford of which I then commanded. By this I was enabled to detach another brigade of infantry, under Brigadier Godby, at daylight on the 3rd, which effected the passage, with the aid of pontoon train, six miles up the river, and got into communication with Major-General Sir Joseph Thackwell.

'The cannonade and demonstration to cross at Ramnuggar were kept up on the 2nd and 3rd, so as to fix a large portion of the enemy there to defend that point. Having communicated to Sir Joseph my views and intentions, and although giving discretionary power to attack any portion of the Sikh force sent to oppose him, I expressed a wish that when he covered the crossing of Brigadier Godby's brigade he should await their junction, except the enemy attempt to retreat; this induced him to halt within about two or three miles of the left of their position. About 2 o'clock on the 3rd, the principal part of the enemy's force, encouraged by the halt, moved to attack the detached column, when a smart cannonade on the part of the enemy took place, and an attempt to turn both Major-General Sir Joseph

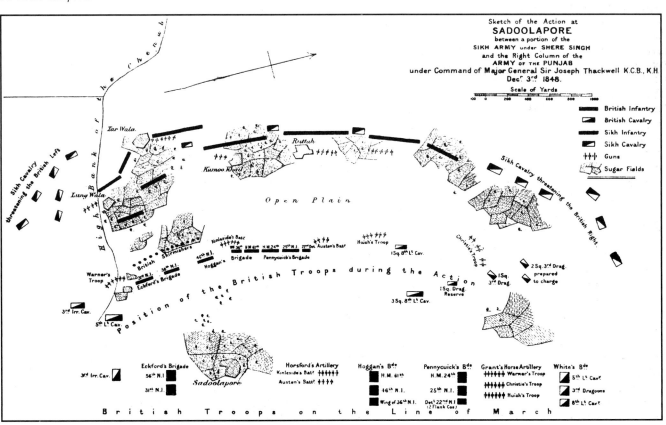

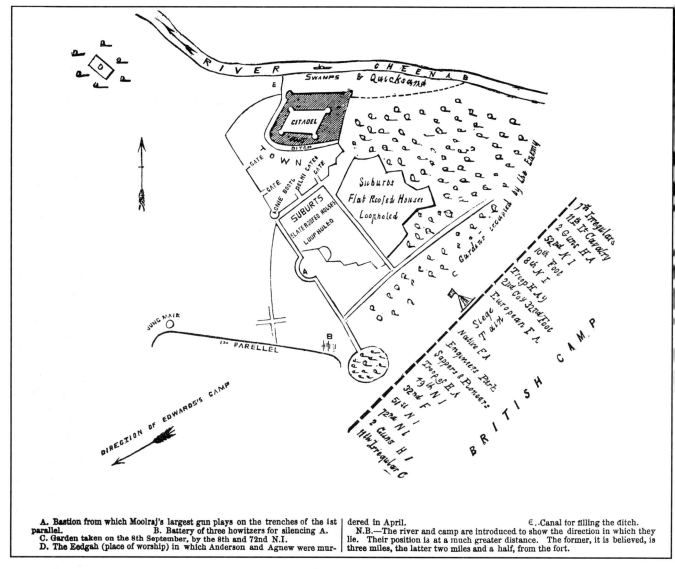

A. **Bastion** from which Moolraj's largest gun plays on the trenches of the 1st parallel.   B. **Battery** of three howitzers for silencing A.
C. **Garden** taken on the 8th September, by the 8th and 72nd N.I.
D. **The Eedgah** (place of worship) in which Anderson and Agnew were murdered in April.   E..Canal for filling the ditch.

N.B.—The river and camp are introduced to show the direction in which they lie. Their position is at a much greater distance. The former, it is believed, is three miles, the latter two miles and a half, from the fort.

Plan of the operations before Multan, from the Illustrated London News, *4 November 1848.*

Thackwell's flanks by numerous bodies of cavalry was made. After about one hour's distant cannonade on the part of the Sikhs, the British artillery never returning a shot, the enemy took courage and advanced, when our artillery, commanded by that excellent officer Lieutenant-Colonel C. Grant, poured in upon them a most destructive fire, which soon silenced all their guns and frustrated all their operations, with very severe loss upon their side; but the exhausted state of both man and horse induced the Major-General to postpone the attack upon their flanks and rear, as he was directed, until the following morning, the day having nearly closed when the cannonade ceased.

'I regret to say that during the night of the 3rd the whole of the Sikh force, precipitately fled, concealing or carrying with them their artillery, and exploding their magazines. I immediately pushed across the river the 9th Lancers and 14th Light Dragoons in pursuit, under

that most energetic officer, Major-General Sir Walter Gilbert. The Sikhs, it appears, retreated in the greatest disorder, leaving in the villages numerous wounded men. They have subdivided into three divisions, which have become more a flight than a retreat; and I understand a great portion of those not belonging to the revolted Khalsa army have dispersed and returned to their homes, thus, I trust, effectually frustrating the views of the rebel Shere Sing and his rebel associates.

'I have not received Major-General Sir Joseph Thackwell's report, nor the returns of his loss, but I am most thankful to say that our whole loss, subsequent to November 22nd, does not much exceed 40 men; no officers have been killed, and but three wounded. Captain Austin, of the artillery, only appears severely so.

'I have to congratulate your Lordship upon events so fraught with importance, and which will, I have no doubt, with God's blessing, tend to most momentous results. It is, as I anticipate, most gratifying to me to assure your Lordship that the noble army under my command has, in these operations, upheld the well-established fame of the arms of India, both European and native, each vying who should best perform his duty. Every officer, from the general of division to the youngest subaltern, well supported their Commander-in-Chief, and cheerfully carried out his views, which at a future period, and when we shall have effected the views of the Government, I shall feel proud in bringing to your Lordship's notice.'

THE END OF THE SIEGE OF MULTAN – 22 JANUARY 1849

At Multan, General Whish and his army remained quiet in their entrenchments during the months of October, November and December; but it was not a period of idleness, as 15,000 gabions and 12,000 fascines were prepared during that time. Similiarly, Mulraj was equally active in improving his defences, already among the strongest in that part of India by the employment for more than two years of every artisan and labourer in the place.

On 21 December the Bombay Division marched in, increasing Whish's force to 32,000 men and 150 guns; nearly half of the soldiers were British. On 25 December the Bengal Division arrived, and on the 27th the siege was resumed, the enemy being driven out of the suburbs and the place invested. The course of the siege is described by Stafford:

'Several very brilliant affairs occurred during the day. The suburbs are extensive; and the enemy had posted themselves in some brick-kilns, in a cemetery, and in Moolraj's garden. They were driven from every one of their positions; and the besiegers were enabled to advance within 400 yards of the city walls. The garrison made a sally on the 29th, but were beaten back. On the 30th, a shell from one of the mortars, laid by Lieutenant Newall, of the Bengal artillery, fell into the principal magazine of the citadel, said to contain 400,000 lbs. of powder. The explosion was one of the most terrible ever witnessed. The great mosque, several other temples, and a number of houses, were destroyed, and 800 men killed. The fortifications were not injured, and Moolraj still refused to surrender, saying he had yet powder enough to last for twelve months.'

Stafford mentions the presence of a naval brigade at this siege:

'The sailors were landed from Captain Powell's steamers, a part of the Indus flotilla, which had ascended the river to Moultan; and they worked the guns of an 18-pounder battery with as much good will and bravery as were displayed by the "blue-jackets" under Captains Lushington and Peel, at the siege of Sebastopol. The battery attracted the particular notice of the garrison, who sent so many shells in that direction, that it was completely destroyed: the tars, however, carried off both powder and guns.'

The events leading up to Multan's capitulation are graphically described by Grant in his *Illustrated History of India*:

'By the 2nd of January, 1849, one breach in the city wall was declared practicable, and another sufficient to allow of its being assailed by a column. The latter proved very imperfect, for the stormers who approached it were subjected to a heavy cross-fire, and after passing through a deep intervening hollow, found to their bewilderment the old city wall in their front – about thirty feet high — unbreached and impracticable. They were thus compelled to retire. The other breach was carried with brilliant success, though the Sikhs are said to have fought with "the tenacity of men and the ferocity of wild beasts"; but the town was stormed by two columns, one of the Bombay, and the other of the Bengal army: the first British colours planted on Moultan being by the hands of a brave sergeant-major of the Company's Fusiliers. The city presented a melancholy spectacle after 120 hours' cannonade; every house was roofless; but the citadel, however, held out, and there was every prospect that it would be desperately defended by Moolraj, who had retired into it, at the head of 3,000 picked men; for as soon as he saw the city was lost, he closed the gates of the former, and left the rest of his troops to shift for themselves. By the 4th of January, a brigade of the Bombay division encamped on the north communicating with a Bengal brigade on the east; the irregulars were on the west, and thus the investment was complete. Even the desperate courage of Moolraj now began to give way, and he made overtures to Herbert Edwardes – now deservedly major – in the hope of obtaining terms. He was referred to General Whish, who refused to receive any messenger but one who would announce when Moolraj would yield himself a prisoner.

'The latter had not made up his mind to this humiliation, but continued his defence, and, on the night of the 12th, made a furious sortie on our trenches. By this time parallels of approach had been made, mines sunk, and the walls were incessantly battered by iron showers of shot and shell, direct and vertical. On the 14th our sappers crowned the crest of the glacis at the north-east angle of the citadel, with a cavalier only fifteen feet from the edge of the ditch; on the 18th and counterscarp was blown into the latter. By the 21st two practicable breaches were made, and the troops were ordered to hold themselves in readiness for a general assault.

'But when the day of the intended storm dawned, Moolraj came forth, mounted on a beautiful Arab charger, magnificently caparisoned, and, while his chiefs and soldiers prostrated themselves in passionate devotion as he did so, he gave up his sword, which was returned to him. He was at once placed under guard, and the citadel was taken possession of. As his partisans in the country were numerous, it was deemed unsafe to leave him near the city; thus, when our army marched along the bank of the Chenab, to wheel off to the camp of the Governor-General by the road leading to Lahore, he was conveyed with it.

'During the siege, which had lasted twenty-seven days, our losses were 210 killed, and 910 wounded. Moolraj was afterwards tried at Lahore, and sentenced

The British troops entering Multan.

o be hanged; but the court recommended him to mercy, o the award was commuted to banishment beyond the eas.'

THE BATTLE OF CHILLIANWALLAH – 13 JANUARY 1849

After abandoning Ramnuggur and being defeated by Thackwell at Sadoolapore, Shere Singh, his troops unbroken in spirit and his artillery intact, continued to retire until taking up a position of some strength on the Jhelum. The Sikh strength had increased to 40,000 men and 62 guns, and their main body was posted in ravines, strengthened by fieldworks. The Jhelum covered their rear and to their front was a broad and dense jungle.

Gough remained inactive for some six weeks in an area between the Chenab and the Jhelum, awaiting the fall of Multan so as to effect a junction of troops.

Gough's army was formed as follows:
'Cavalry Division, under Sir Joseph Thackwell:
'1st Brigade – 3rd (and 14th) Light Dragoons, and 5th and 8th Native Light Cavalry under Brigadier White.
'2nd Brigade – 9th Lancers, and 1st and 6th Native Light Cavalry under Brigadier Pope. The 14th Light Dragoons were attached to this brigade at Chillianwalla.
'Infantry: Gilbert's Division:
'1st Brigade (Mountain's) – H.M.'s 29th Foot, and the 30th and 56th Regiments Native Infantry.
'2nd Brigade (Godby's) – 2nd European Light Infantry, 31st and 70th Native Infantry.
'Campbell's Division:
'1st Brigade (Pennycuick's) – H.M.'s 24th Foot, and 25th and 45th Native Infantry.
'2nd Brigade (Hoggan's) – H.M.'s 61st Foot, and 36th and 46th Native Infantry.
'3rd Brigade (Penny's) – 15th, 20th, and 69th Native Infantry.
'Artillery, under Brigadier Tennant.
'The six troops of Horse Artillery (Lane, Christie, Huish, Warner, Duncan, and Fordyce) were commanded by Brigadier Brooke, with Colonels Brind and C. Grant.
'Foot Artillery under Brigadier Hathwaite:
'Two heavy Batteries (Shakespear and Ludlow) under Major Horsford.
'Three Field Batteries (Walker, Robertson, Dawes; Kinleside being ill, and Austin wounded).'

Without waiting for the Multan troops, on 12 January 1849 the army moved to Dingee, to find Shere Singh posted in the vicinity. Lord Gough's official despatch relates the events that transpired:

From his Excellency The Commander-In-Chief, to The Right Honourable The Governor-General of India.
HEADQUARTERS CAMP, CHILLIANWALLAH, *January 16th, 1849.*

MY LORD,
'Major Mackeson, your Lordship's political agent with my camp, officially communicated to me, on the 10th instant, the fall of Attock and the advance of Sirdar Chutter Sing in order to concentrate his force with the

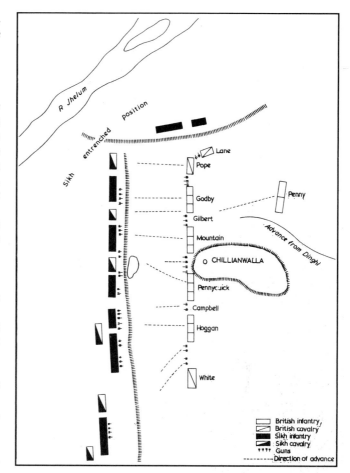

Battle of Chillianwallah, 13 January 1849.

army in my front, under Shere Sing, already amounting to from 30,000 to 40,000 men, with 62 guns, concluding his letter thus: "I would urge, in the event of your Lordship's finding yourself strong enough with the army under your command to strike an effectual blow at the enemy in our front, that the blow should be struck with the least possible delay."

'Concurring entirely with Major Mackeson, and feeling that I was perfectly competent effectually to overthrow Shere Sing's army, I moved from Loah Tibba, at daylight on the 12th, to Dingee, about 12 miles. Having learnt from my spies, and from other sources of information, that Shere Sing still held with his right the village of Lukhneewalla and Futtehshaw-ke-Chuck, having the great body of his force at the village of Woolianwalla, with his left at Russool, on the Jhelum, strongly occupying the southern extremity of a low range of hills, intersected by ravines, which extend nearly to that village, I made my arrangements accordingly that evening, and communicated them to the commanders of the several divisions; but to insure correct information as to the nature of the country, which I believed to be excessively difficult and ill-adapted to the advance of a regular army, I determined upon moving on this village with a view to reconnoitre.

'On the morning of the 13th the force advanced. I

made a considerable detour to my right, partly in order to distract the enemy's attention, but principally to get as clear as I could of the jungle, on which it would appear that the enemy mainly relied.

'We approached this village about 12 o'clock, and I found, on a mound close to it, a strong picquet of the enemy's cavalry and infantry, which we at once dispersed, obtaining from the mound a very extended view of the country before us, and the enemy drawn out in battle array, he having, either during the night or that morning, moved out of his several positions, and occupied the ground in our front, which, though not dense, was still a difficult jungle, his right in advance of Futtehshaw-ke-Chuck, and his left on the furrowed hills before described.

'The day being so far advanced, I decided upon taking up a position in rear of the village, in order to reconnoitre my front, finding that I could not turn the enemy's flanks, which rested upon a dense jungle, extending nearly to Hillah, which I had previously occupied for some time, and the neighbourhood of which I knew, and upon the raviney hills near Russool, without detaching a force to a distance; this I considered both inexpedient and dangerous.

'The engineer department had been ordered to examine the country before us and the Quartermaster-General was in the act of taking up ground for the encampment, when the enemy advanced some horse artillery, and opened fire on the skirmishers in front of the village.

'I immediately ordered them to be silenced by a few rounds from our heavy guns, which advanced to an open space in front of the village. Their fire was instantly returned by that of nearly the whole of the enemy's field artillery; thus exposing the position of his guns, which the jungle had hitherto concealed.

'It was now evident that the enemy intended to fight, and would probably advance his guns so as to reach the encampment during the night.

'I therefore drew up in order of battle. . . .'

In a letter to his father, written two days after the battle, an officer describes the opening events:

'The whole force approached the ground where the battle was fought about 12 noon and having driven in one of the enemy's outposts in an entrenched mound, with a few shells, the Quarter Masters were sent for to take up ground for encamping, as thus far the original intention of waiting quietly until the enemy's position had been reconnoitred was intended to have been carried out. The enemy however posted in the jungle about a mile or more off fired three round shots from six pounders at some part of our force – this was enough for our Chief – like a hunter at the sound of horns he was determined to dash on at all risks – contrary to his own original plans and to the advice of all connected with him.'

Thus began one of the most controversial battles in the history of the British Raj, when Gough, apparently incensed by the Sikh artillery fire, decided that it was imperative to give battle at once, at two o'clock on a short winter's day. Grant explains it thus: 'From the tenor of his own words, there can be little doubt that Lord Gough intended to delay giving battle till he had made a careful reconnaissance, when the shots from the advanced guns of the Sikhs roused that spirit of defiance and antagonism which were so natural to him, overcame his sober judgement, and made him issue orders for the uncasing of the colours, and immediate action.'

The resulting 'soldier's battle' caused such heavy casualties that, back home in Britain, the ageing Duke of Wellington said to Sir Charles Napier: 'If you don't go [to India, as the Commander-in-Chief] then I must.'

As given in his official despatch, Gough's order of battle was:

'Sir Walter Gilbert's division on the right, flanked by Brigadier Pope's brigade of cavalry, which I strengthened by the 14th Light Dragoons, well aware that the enemy was strong in cavalry upon his left. To this were attached three troops of horse artillery under Lieutenant-Colonel Grant.

'The heavy guns were in the centre.

'Brigadier-General Campbell's division formed the left, flanked by Brigadier White's brigade of cavalry and three troops of horse artillery under Lieutenant Colonel Brind.

'The field batteries were with the infantry divisions.

'Thus formed, the troops were ordered to lie down whilst the heavy guns, under Major Horsford, ably seconded by Brevet-Majors Ludlow and Sir Richmond Shakespear, opened a well-directed and powerful fire upon the enemy's centre, where his guns appeared principally to be placed; and this fire was ably supported on the flanks by the field batteries of the infantry divisions.

'After about an hour's fire the enemy appeared to be if not silenced, sufficiently disabled to justify an advance upon his position and guns.

'I then ordered my left division to advance, which had to move over a great extent of ground, and in front of which the enemy seemed not to have many guns.'

In his book *The Narrative of the Second Seikh War*, E. J. Thackwell states that the staff officer who brought to Campbell the order to advance directed him to 'carry the guns in his front without delay at the point of the bayonet'. Campbell himself makes no mention of this in his journal, but the officer who succeeded to the command of the 24th, when the Colonel was killed, has left it on record that Campbell particularly enjoined the regiment to advance without firing and Lawrence Archer, who was attached to the 24th Regiment, recounts that the Brigadier-General Campbell addressed the men saying: 'there must be no firing, the bayonet must do the work.' In his report of the action, too, Campbell states that 'the batteries were carried without a shot being fired by the regiment or a musket taken from the shoulder', which Gough describes as 'an act of madness', adding, according to Rait, that if proper precautions had been taken 'the 24th would not have been cut up, as they were, without firing a shot'.

Colonel Smith, who succeeded to the command of the 24th after Chillianwallah, said in a letter to Colonel Mountain (quoted by Rait):

'The 24th advanced with loaded firelocks, but the greatest pains were taken by Campbell (previous to going into action) to inculcate upon them the merit of taking the Enemy Guns [sic] without firing a shot. He told me so himself, and blamed himself for it – and for a long time previous to Gujerat, I drilled the Regiment by his order, in firing by files while advancing. There seems to be a confusion of Principle in this. To stop to fire after the Charge is commenced – supposing it is not begun till within reasonable distance, is of course a grievous error, but the 24th were told to march up, under a storm of fire, in front of the muzzles of Guns, for several hundred yards, without attempting to stagger or dismay the Enemy by making use of the arms.'

Gough takes up the story in his despatch:

'Soon after, I directed Sir Walter Gilbert to advance, and sent orders to Brigadier Pope to protect the flank and support the movement. Brigadier Penny's brigade was held in reserve, while the irregular cavalry under Brigadier Hearsey, with the 20th Native Infantry, was ordered to protect the enormous amount of provision and baggage that so hampers the movement of an Indian army.

'Some time after the advance, I found that Brigadier Pennycuick's brigade had failed in maintaining the position it had carried, and immediately ordered Brigadier Penny's reserve to its support; but Brigadier-General Campbell, with that steady coolness and military decision for which he is so remarkable, having pushed on his left brigade and formed line to his right, carried everything before him, and soon overthrew that portion of the enemy which had obtained a temporary advantage over his right brigade.'

In a letter written immediately after the battle, an officer, who was present, describes the scene:

'The line was ordered to advance, the Artillery was brought into play & after firing for half an hour the Brigade were ordered to charge the enemys' guns. To give any connected detail of the battle is out of anyones power. No one knew where the next Brigade was, hidden as they were by jungle, the enemy firing on their flanks & rear in more than one instance had some Brigades to face about their rear ranks & fire for the position of their own rear. The Brigade in which were the H.M. 61st, 29th & 2nd Europeans [this brigading of units does not coincide with the accepted order of battle] being lucky enough to have the support of guns carried all before them, & turned the right of the enemys' position, but such was the confusion, so totally without plan or foresight were operations carried on that several Artillery Officers were on the point of firing into our troops under the impression that they were Sikhs, who are dressed in red. James will have told you that when his Brigade advanced they were left alone to themselves neither seeing nor being seen by any other part of the force, surrounded by the enemy closing in on them on all sides, when luckily two guns which they met acci-

dentally rescued them with grape shot from inevitable destruction.'

The initial movements of Hoggan's brigade, which Campbell accompanied, are described in his report:

'Although the jungle through which the Brigade passed was glose and thick, causing frequent breaks to be made in the line, yet, by regulating the pace so as to make allowance for these obstructions, the Left Brigade, after an advance of half a mile, reached a comparatively open tract of country in a tolerably connected Line. On this open tract we found, formed in our front, a large body of Cavalry and regular Seik infantry, with four guns, which had played upon us during our advance. H.M.'s 61st Regiment charged this Cavalry, and put it to an immediate and disorderly flight, while the 36th Native Infantry on the right made an attack upon the Infantry, which, however, was not successful, and, in consequence, they (the Sikhs) came down upon the 36th Regt., obliging it to retreat in rear of H.M.'s 61st. The two right companies of the 61st were instantly made to change front to the right, and, while the 'remainder of the Regiment was ordered to form rapidly in the same direction, the two right companies charged the two guns, and captured them. The fire of those two companies upon the Enemy who were in pursuit of the 36th compelled them to desist and retreat.'

The despatches now tell of one of the most controversial features of the battle, which culminated in the death of Campbell's 1st Brigade commander, Brigadier Pennycuick:

'This last brigade, I am informed, mistook for the signal to move in double time the action of their brave leaders, Brigadier Pennycuick and Lieutenant-Colonel Brooks (two officers not surpassed for sound judgment and military daring in this or any other army), who waved their swords over their heads as they cheered on their gallant comrades. This unhappy mistake led to the Europeans outstripping the native corps, which could not keep pace, and arriving, completely blown, at a belt of thick jungle, where they got into some confusion, and Lieutenant-Colonel Brooks, leading the 24th, was killed between the enemy's guns. At this moment a large body of infantry, which supported their guns, opened upon them so destructive a fire that the brigade was forced to retire, having lost their gallant and lamented leader, Brigadier Pennycuick, and the three other field-officers of the 24th, and nearly half the regiment before it gave way, the native regiment, when it came up, also suffering severely. In justice to this brigade, I must be allowed to state that they behaved, heroically, and, but for their too hasty, and consequently disorderly advance, would have emulated the conduct of their left brigade, which, left unsupported for a time, had to charge to their front and right wherever an enemy appeared. The brigade of horse artillery on their left, under Lieutenant-Colonel Brind, judiciously and gallantly aiding, maintained an effective fire.'

Gough's despatch records:

'Major-General Sir J. Thackwell, on the extreme left

and rear, charged the enemy's cavalry wherever they showed themselves.

'The right attack of infantry, under that able officer Major-General Sir Walter Gilbert, was most praiseworthy and successful. The left brigade, under Brigadier Mountain, advanced under a heavy fire upon the enemy's guns, in a manner that did credit to the brigadier and his gallant brigade, which came first into action and suffered severely; the right brigade, under Brigadier Godby, ably supported the advance.

Finding the colours of the 24th Regiment after the Battle of Chillianwallah, January 1849.

'This division nobly maintained the character of the Indian army, taking and spiking the whole of the enemy's guns, in their front, and dispersing the Sikhs wherever they were seen.

'The Major-General reports most favourably of the fire of his field battery.'

Extracts from General Sir Walter Gilbert's report give colour to the words of the despatch:

'Both of my brigades were deployed on reaching the height about a mile in front of the village of Chillianwallah, and advanced steadily in line on the

Enemy's position of Lullian, where the Brigade led by Brigadier A. S. Mountain CB charged a large battery in its front, driving out the Enemy at the point of the bayonet, and almost immediately afterwards, the Brigade led by Brigadier G. Godby CB., carried the guns on the extreme left of the Seikh position.

'The flank and rear of both my Brigades were, at different times, endeavoured to be turned by the Seikhs and each time was obliged to change its front, by which movement the Enemy were not only out-manoeuvred but their very severe attacks were successfully repulsed.

'It is with extreme regret I lay before H.E. a very heavy list of casualties, but it could hardly be otherwise, considering the obstinate and vigorous resistance of the Enemy, with all the advantages, which they as Irregular Troops, possessed over ours, fighting in a jungle.'

Even more colourful is the account of the action by an officer of the 2nd Bengal European Regiment of Godby's Brigade:

'The word came for the infantry to advance. "Fix bayonets! Load! Deploy into line! Quick March!" And just then came a roll of musketry that drove us almost to madness. "Quick March!" And into the jungle we plunged in line, with a deafening cheer, the roll of musketry increasing every moment. On we went at a rapid double, dashing through the bushes and bounding over every impediment; faster rolled the musketry – crash upon the cannon poured forth its deadly contents. On swept our brigade and, gaining an open space in the jungle, the whole of the enemy's line burst on our view. "Charge!" ran the word through our ranks, and the men bounded forward like angry bulldogs, pouring in a murderous fire. The enemy's bullets whizzed above our heads; the very air seemed teeming with them; man after man was struck down and rolled in the dust. But a passing glance was all we could give them. And onward we went, bearing on their line with a steadiness which nothing could resist. They fired a last volley, wavered, and then turned and fled, leaving the ground covered with dead and wounded.'

It was remarked in several narratives that the Sikhs fought ferociously, drunk and maddened by hemp-seed or bhang, that they exhibited 'frightful ferocity' and, with their sharp tulwars, hewed off heads and hands and arms by a single blow. An officer who fought in the battle later said: 'They fought like devils, singly, sword in hand, and strove to break our lines.' James Grant wrote: 'On this day, the deficiency of our cavalry in proper weapons and accoutrements was rendered painfully apparent. The weight, badness of balance, and the wretched steel of which their swords were made, gave the enemy a vast superiority over them at close quarters. Like most Asiatics, the Sikhs kept their short handy swords as keen as razors – swords that sliced at every stroke; and we are told that "our poor fellows laboured in vain with their long, awkward, and blunt sabres to draw blood".'

These aspects are also mentioned by Thackwell:

'It may be here observed that that flimsy, diminutive piece of steel called the infantry regulation sword, proved useless to the gallant officer. The powerful tulwar of the Seikh shivered it to atoms with a blow. It may answer the purpose of saluting, but it is insufficient as a means of protection. The cook's spit is far preferable to this infantry spit.'

Gough's despatch continues:

'The right brigade of cavalry, under Brigadier Pope, was not I regret to say, so successful. Either by some order, or misapprehension of an order, they got into much confusion, hampered the fine brigade of horse artillery, which, while getting into action, against a body of the enemy's cavalry that was coming down upon them, had their horses separated from their guns by the false movements of our cavalry, and notwithstanding the heroic conduct of the gunners, four of whose guns were disabled to an extent which rendered their withdrawal, at the moment, impossible. The moment the artillery was extricated and the cavalry re-formed, a few rounds put to flight the enemy that had occasioned this confusion.'

That is a very low profile account of a notoriously ignominious affair, of which Grant wrote what he termed 'the actual details':

'When our line of cavalry advanced, it was broken up by clumps of trees and jungle bushes into small sections that were forced to cover each other in succession to the rear; and while in this useless order, a body of Sikh horsemen, maddened with intoxicating drugs, rushed on their centre in one wild galloping mass, inspiring utter terror among the native cavalry; and at this crisis, it is said, that one of our 14th Light Dragoons cried: "Three's about!" on which the whole regiment wheeled in obedience and made rearward in confusion and, while the exulting Sikh horsemen pressed on, galloped in helpless panic through the cannon and waggons posted in their rear. Entering the line of artillery with our own dragoons, the Sikhs captured four guns.'

In his diary, quoted by Rait, Sir Frederick Haines (one of Gough's staff) wrote:

'We were watching the Infantry attacks, when news came that the Ghoorchurras were on our right flank, and were overpowering our cavalry and the Horse Artillery (the three troops which had been rendered useless by Pope's advance) They had, in effect, come down . . . turned, and rode over the guns of the Troop (Christie's), upsetting some in their headlong course, and causing infinite confusion. The consequence was the Artillery were entirely paralysed, carried off the field in fact, and the Ghoorchurras captured the guns that had been upset. Some of these men continued their flight until they rode over our Field Hospital, and were rallied by our Chaplain (the Rev. W. Whiting). Eventually, two guns were opened, which sent the Ghoorchurras to the right-about immediately.'

Lord Gough's despatch concludes:

'With this exception, the conduct of the troops generally was most exemplary, some corps, both European and native, acting under most trying circumstances (from the temporary failure on our left centre and right, and the cover which the jungle afforded to the enemy's movements), and with a gallantry worthy of the highest admiration.

'Although the enemy, who defended not only his guns but his position, with desperation, was driven in much confusion, and with heavy loss, from every part of it and the greater part of his field artillery was actually captured, the march of brigades to their flanks to repel parties that had rallied, and the want of numbers and consequent support to our right flank, aided by the cover of the jungle and the close of the day, enabled him, upon our further advance in pursuit, to return and carry off unobserved the greater position of the guns we had thus gallantly carried at the point of the bayonet.

'I remained with Brigadier-General Campbell's division, which had been reinforced by Brigadier Mountain's brigade, until near 8 o'clock, in order to effect the bringing in of the captured ordnance and of the wounded, and I hoped to bring in the rest of the guns next morning. But I did not feel justified in remaining longer out. The night was very dark. I knew not how far I had advanced. There were no wells nearer than the line of this village. The troops had been arduously employed all day, and there was every appearance of a wet night; rain did fall before morning.

'I should have felt greater satisfaction if I were enabled to state that my expectations in regard to the guns had been realised; but although a brigade of cavalry, under Brigadier White, with a troop of horse artillery, were on the ground soon after daylight, we found that the enemy, assisted by the neighbouring villagers, had carried off their guns, excepting twelve, which we had brought in the night before. Most of the captured waggons I had caused to be blown up before leaving the ground.

'The victory was complete, as to the total overthrow of the enemy; and his sense of utter discomfiture and defeat will, I trust, soon be made apparent, unless, indeed, the rumours prevalent this day, of his having been joined by Chutter Sing, proved correct.

'I am informed that the loss the Sikhs has been very great, and chiefly amongst their old and tried soldiers. In no action do I remember seeing so many of an enemy's slain upon the same space – Sobraon perhaps only excepted.'

The confused nature of the fighting and the conclusion of the battle is indicated when General Sir Walter Gilbert with other senior officers decided upon a 'retrograde movement' because they were 'quite unsupported' as night began to fall. The movement was seemingly going on quite satisfactorily until Major Galloway 'consulting his pocket compass . . . managed . . . to make out by the light of his cigar' that they were marching due north towards the enemy lines instead of due south, as intended. The campfires glittering to their front were those of the Sikhs and not of Gough's army. (R. E. Scouller, *The Journal of the Society for Army Historical Research, Vol. LXII, no. 252.*)

Out of a total strength of just over 13,000, Gough's force lost 2,338 killed and wounded — approximately 18 per cent — formed of 22 British officers and 16 native officers killed and 659 men dead; 67 British officers, 27 native officers and 1,547 rank-and-file wounded. John Curtis Binkley, who fought in the battle with the 61st Regiment, wrote to his sister on 9 February 1849: 'many of those which are returned as wounded died as soon as they reached hospital, and many of them even before that time, and those that are returned as missing were killed on the field, but darkness comes so soon that we could not collect our dead and wounded and in the morning these were missing and most likely were carried away by wolves, jackals or some other beasts of prey which are always prowling about this country.' (P. Beattie, *The Journal of the Society for Army Historical Research, vol. LXI, no. 245.*)

In Britain the news of Chillianwallah was received by an incredulous and impassioned outcry against Lord Gough, as the British public learned with emotion and consternation the number of casualties and that four British guns had been taken and the colours of three regiments lost. The wild and hysterical accusations hurled against the Commander-in-Chief took no account of the fact that the Sikhs had been driven out of their position, suffering heavy casualties and losing 13 guns. Strong pressure was put upon the Government, and in Parliament Lord John Russell's demand that Sir Charles Napier be sent to India as Commander-in-Chief was received with cheers, even though it was recognised that the war would be over before he arrived to conduct it. However, it did succeed in forcing the Directors of the East India Company to supersede Lord Gough and to appoint Sir Charles Napier to succeed him. Napier's biographer (his brother Sir William Napier) reflects Sir Charles' calm appreciation of the situation and reveals how little he was affected by the unintelligent abuse showered upon Sir Hugh, by saying:

'If he was proud of such testimony in his favour, he was still more indignant that the call for himself should be coupled with an unjust and ignoble outcry against Lord Gough . . . who was a noble soldier of fifty years service, and had always been victorious, whether obeying or commanding; no man heard, because no man dared to say, that personal comfort or idleness, or fear, had induced him to shrink from danger, responsibility or labour. What then was his crime? He had fought a drawn battle – the enemy was not crushed.'

Gough's biographer, Rait, commented: 'To those of the general public who sympathised with Lord Gough, it seemed as if the Duke of Wellington had taken advantage of a moment of popular excitement in order to force Sir Charles Napier upon the Directors of the East India Company.' If confidence in the generalship of Lord Gough had waned in Britain, in India his Army of the Punjab continued to reveal their emotional ties with their commander, as Rait describes:

'So great was the impression made by the British infantry charges at Chillianwallah that the Sikhs, when next they met the British in field, did not attempt to withstand an attack of the infantry – the lesson taught them there rendered the task easier at Gujerat. If this view of Chillianwallah has not found its way into the history books, the Army of the Punjab, at all events, felt secure under the guidance of the Commander-in-Chief. Officers and men alike have borne frequent testimony to the love borne by the Indian Army for Lord Gough; and never was this affection more touchingly manifested than on the morrow of Chillianwallah, when he rode down the line after the battle.

'The lull between the storms in India is described in the contemporary publication *England's Battles by Sea and Land*:

'The Sikhs do not appear to have been driven from their position in the battle of the 13th. They occupied it for nearly a month after; the British camp being pitched on their left flank, with their own left thrown back. The weather, probably, prevented either army from moving. The night of the 13th set in cold, with a bleak northerly wind, and a drizzling rain. On the morning of the 14th it came down in torrents, and continued till the 16th. The encamping-ground, especially on the right flank, was completely covered with water. "My tent [said an officer of the 6th light cavalry] was surrounded with a pool knee-deep; and what was worse, our chief dared not move either one way or the other – not to the rear, for fear of giving the enemy a word to say against us; nor to the front, for the fear of bringing down their fire and another engagement," which he was not just then prepared to encounter. Thus the two antagonists lay till the 12th of February, "in a vile country, but with a magnificent view of the Cashmere hills, distant about a hundred miles, resplendent with snow". – On the 12th of February, the Sikhs drew up their cavalry in a body outside their camp, to cover the striking of their tents; and, that task performed, they retreated in the direction of Goojerat – a considerable walled town of the Punjab, about eight miles from the right bank of the Chenaub, and on the great route from Attock to Lahore. As they moved towards Vizierabad, their intention was, probably, to cross the Chenaub, and make for Lahore; but General Whish, with the cavalry and part of the infantry, had reached Ramnuggur from Moultan, and he forwarded a strong detachment to Vizierabad, which prevented their crossing; and they took up a position near Goojerat. Here Shere Sing was joined by his father, Chuttur Sing, and also by a body of 1,500 Affghan horse, under Akram Khan, a son of Dost Mahomed. Thus [wrote the Governor-General], "for the first time, Sikhs and Affghans were banded together against the British power; and it thus became an occasion which demanded the putting forth of all the means at our disposal, and of making such a conspicuous manifestation of the superiority of our armies as should appal each enemy, and dissolve at once their compact by fatal proof of its fatality."

'The British left their encampment on the 15th of February, and on the 16th, arrived at Sudalpore, a

Sikh soldier.

village five miles from the Chenaub, and not far from Goojerat. On the 17th, General Whish crossed the Chenaub, and put his army in communication with Lord Gough; and on the 21st, the latter resolved again to attack the enemy, who were concentrated in a camp encircling the town of Goojerat, having an effective force of 60,000 men, and 59 pieces of cannon.'

THE BATTLE OF GUJERAT – 21 FEBRUARY 1949

Writing in *The Punjab in Peace and War*, Thorburn relates that: 'Throughout the 20th the two armies lay opposite to each other, the Sikhs round the town of Gujerat, the British about three miles to the south, their left resting on the small town of Kunjah, their centre on the large village of Shadiwal, and their right extending to the low alluvial lands on the Gujerat side of the ford at Wazirabad. The whole country was perfectly flat, open, and cultivated, dotted by populous villages, and covered with young spring crops, chiefly wheat and barley, at that time of the year standing a few inches high. Had Lord Gough searched all India for a battlefield better adapted for the overthrow of the Sikhs, he could have found none more suitable.'

In his camp Gough had an army of about 24,000 men, not counting baggage guards and so forth. He could put about 20,000 men into the field, formed of those regiments that were at Chillianwallah, plus the infantry division from Multan under General Whish, now known as the 1st Division of the Army of the Punjab (Gilbert's being the 2nd, and Campbell's the 3rd). Whish's division was formed of two brigades, as follows:

'Markham's Brigade: H.M.'s 32nd Foot, and 49th and 51st Native Infantry. Hervey's Brigade: H.M's 10th Foot, and 8th and 72nd Native Infantry.

'Dundas's Bombay Column: 60th Rifles, 3rd Bombay, Native Infantry, Bombay Fusiliers, and 19th Native Infantry.'

Wylly, in *The Military Memoirs of Lieutenant-General Sir Joseph Thackwell*, elaborated on Gough's position:

'Although his numbers were thus less than half those of the enemy, he was now very strong in artillery, having, besides heavy guns, thirteen other batteries, of which all but one – which remained with the baggage escort in rear of the army – were brought into action. The Commander-in-Chief could now dispose of 18 heavy guns, viz. ten 18-pounders and eight 8-inch howitzers, while he had a large number of 9-pounders. In all, and allowing for the guns lost at Chillianwala, Lord Gough was able to bring 94 guns of varying calibre into action, *including* the Bombay Light Field Battery with the baggage guard.

'There has been considerable difference of opinion among various writers as to the number of British guns actually present at the battle of Gujerat, the total being given as 106, 96, and 88, while Sir Joseph gives the number as 90, viz. 18 heavy guns, 42 9-pounders, and 30 6-pounders. Taking the reports of the officers commanding respectively the Bengal and Bombay Artillery, there would appear to have been in all 18 heavy guns, 9 troops of horse artillery, and 4 light field batteries – making a total of 96 guns which should have been present. Stubbs, however, in his "History of the Bengal Artillery", writes of "the fire of the 88 guns", from which it is apparent that, as the Bengal Artillery could only number at most 84 guns, he must be *including* the Bombay horse battery which was engaged, and *excluding* the Bombay light field battery, which, being with the baggage guard, did not fire. It is evident also from Stubb's figures that two at least of the guns lost at Chillianwala had not been replaced; but as all accounts seem in agreement that Duncan and Huish on the left had 12 guns between them, it would appear that while Huish's troops had been again made up to six guns, that of Christie – now Kinleside – had not. If these figures and deductions are correct, there must have been altogether 94 guns present in the field.

'The 18 heavy guns seem to have been divided into four batteries, or among four artillery companies, viz. six in one, and four in each of the other three.'

James Grant tells how these guns were employed:

'Lord Gough began the action by employing his superior force of artillery, and certainly used it with success, causing great havoc in the ranks of the enemy, while dashing to pieces the gun-carriages and tumbrils along their line. Our oldest officers had never witnessed a cannonade like this for magnificence and effect. He was resolved on this occasion, by no precipitancy as elsewhere, to give advantage to the foe; but to meet him on the strictest principles of military science, so that no more unfavourable critiques and comparisons might be made of his generalship at home.'

That evening, Lord Gough was able to dash off a hurried despatch to the Governor-General, briefly outlining details of his triumph.

'*From His Excellency the Commander-in-Chief in India, to the Right Honourable the Governor-General.*
CAMP IN FRONT OF GOOJERAT, *February 21st, 1849.*

'MY LORD,
'I have the honour to report to your Lordship that I have this day obtained a victory of no common order, either in its character, or, I trust, in its effects.
'I was joined yesterday by Brigadier Markham's brigade, Brigadier-General Dundas having joined late the preceding night. I moved on in the afternoon of yesterday, as soon as these troops were refreshed, from Trikur, to the village of Shadiwal, and at 7 this morning I moved to the attack, which commenced at half-past 8 o'clock, and by 1 o'clock I was in possession of the whole of the Sikh position, with all his camp equipage, baggage, magazines, and, I hope, a large proportion of his guns; the exact number I cannot at present state, from the great extent of his position and length of pursuit, as I followed up the enemy from four to five miles on the Bimber road, and pushed on Sir Joseph Thackwell with the cavalry. The rout has been most complete; the whole road for twelve miles is strewed with guns, ammunition, waggons, arms, and baggage.
'My loss was comparatively small (I hope within 300 killed and wounded) when it is considered I had to attack 60,000 Sikhs, in a very strong position, armed with upwards of 60 guns. The loss of the enemy must have been very severe.
'The conduct of the whole army, in every arm, was conspicuous for steadiness in movement and gallantry in action. The details I shall furnish hereafter.
'I have, etc.,
(*Signed*) GOUGH, *General, Commander-in-Chief in India.*
By order of the Right Honourable the Governor-General of India.
(*Signed*) "H. M. ELLIOT.
Secretary to the Government of India, with the Governor-General.
(*Signed*) "J. STUART, *Colonel,
Secretary to the Government of India, Military Department, with the Governor-General.*'

This was followed, a week later, by an official despatch giving full details of the battle that ended the Second Sikh War:

From the right Honourable the Commander-In-Chief in India, to the Right Honourable the Governor-General of India.
HEADQUARTERS CAMP, GOOJERAT *February 26th, 1849.*

MY LORD,

'By my letter of the 21st instant, written on the field of battle immediately after the action, your Lordship will have been made acquainted with the glorious result of my operations on that day against the Sikh army, calculated from all credible reports at 60,000 men of all arms and 59 pieces of artillery, under the command of Sirdar Chutter Sing and Rajah Shere Sing, with a body of 1,500 Afghan Horse led by Akram Khan, son of the Ameer Dost Mahomed Khan; a result, my Lord, glorious indeed for the ever-victorious army of India! the ranks of the enemy broken, their position carried, their guns, ammunition, camp equipage, and baggage captured, their flying masses driven before the victorious pursuers from mid-day to dusk, receiving a most severe punishment in their flight; and, my Lord with gratitude to a merciful Providence, I have the satisfaction of adding that, notwithstanding the obstinate resistance of the enemy, this triumphant success, this brilliant victory has been achieved with comparatively little loss on our side.

'The number of guns taken into action and captured in the line of pursuit, I now find to be 53.

'On the same day a reconnaissance was made of the enemy's position, and it was ascertained that their camp nearly encircled the town of Goojerat, their regular troops being placed immediately fronting us between the town and a deep watercourse, the dry bed of the River Dwara – this nullah, which is very tortuous, passing round nearly two sides of the town of Goojerat, diverging to a considerable distance on the north and west faces, and then taking a southerly direction, running through the centre of the ground I occupied at Shadiwal. Thus the enemy's position on the right was generally strengthened, the nullah giving cover to his infantry in front of his guns, whilst another deep, though narrow wet nullah running from the east of the town and falling into the Chenab, in the direction of Wuzeerabad, covered his left.

'The ground between these nullahs, for a space of nearly three miles, being well calculated for the operations of all arms, and presenting no obstacle to the movement of my heavy guns, I determined to make my principal attack in that direction and dispose my force accordingly.

'On the extreme left I placed the Bombay column, commanded by Brigadier the Honourable H. Dundas, supported by Brigadier White's brigade of cavalry and the Scinde Horse, under Sir Joseph Thackwell, to protect the left and to prevent large bodies of Sikh and Afghan cavalry from turning that flank; with this cavalry I placed Captains Duncan and Huish's troops of horse artillery, whilst the infantry was covered by the Bombay troop of horse artillery under Major Blood.

'On the right of the Bombay column, and with its right resting on the nullah, I placed Brigadier-General Campbell's division of infantry, covered by No. 5 and No. 10 Light Field Batteries, under Major Ludlow and Lieutenant Robertson, having Brigadier Hoggan's brigade of infantry in reserve.

'Upon the right of the nullah I placed the Infantry division of Major-General Sir Walter Gilbert, the heavy guns, 18 in number under Majors Day and Horsford, with Captain Shakspear and Brevet-Majors Day and Horsford, with Captain Shakspear and Brevet-Major Sir Richmond Shakspear, commanding batteries, being disposed in two divisions upon the flanks of his left brigade.

'This line was prolonged by Major-General Whish's division of infantry, under Brigadier Markham, in support of second line, and the whole covered by three troops of horse artillery, Major Fordyce's Captains Mackenzie's, and Anderson's; No. 17 Light Field Battery, under Captain Dawes, with Lieutenant-Colonel Lane's and Captain Kinleside's troops of horse artillery, in a second line in reserve, under Lieutenant-Colonel Brind.

'My right flank was protected by Brigadiers Hearsey's and Lockwood's brigades of cavalry, with Captain Warner's troop of horse artillery.

'The 5th and 6th Light Cavalry, with the Bombay Light Field Battery, and the 45th and 69th Regiments, under the command of Lieutenant-Colonel Mercer, most effectually protected my rear and baggage.

'With my right wing I proposed penetrating the centre of the enemy's line, so as to turn the position of their force in rear of the nullah, and thus enable my left wing to cross it with little loss, and in co-operation with the right to double upon the centre of the wing of the enemy's force to them.'

Both Durand, writing in the *Calcutta Review* (quoted by Rait), and Grant paint a similar picture of a British/Indian army going into battle, in much the same way as their fathers and grandfathers had done in the Peninsula. First Durand:

'The morning dawned calm and fair, and the natural beauty of the scene could not fail to impress even those who had much else to think of.

'As the enemy's masses had very early taken up their positions, there was no dust of moving columns to cloud the purity of the air and sky. The snowy ranges of the Himalayah, forming a truly magnificent background to Guzerat and the village-dotted plain, seemed on that beautiful morning, to have drawn nearer, as if like a calm spectator, to gaze on the military spectacle.'

'The army, invigorated by rest and food, was in full motion by half past seven. The morning was clear and cloudless, and the brilliant sun shone on the long lines of fixed bayonets and drawn swords, advancing in two parallel lines, with cavalry on the flanks, and eighty-four pieces of cannon in front.' (Grant).

Gough's despatch notes:

'At half-past 7 o'clock the army advanced in the order described, with the precision of a parade movement. The enemy opened their fire at a very long distance, which exposed to my artillery both the position and

The Battle of Gujerat.

range of their guns. I halted the infantry just out of fire, and advanced the whole of my artillery, covered by skirmishers.'

Rait takes up the story:

'The Sikhs, with less than their usual wisdom, at once opened fire and exposed to Lord Gough the situation of their guns. The advance was therefore continued until the infantry were just beyond the Sikh range, when (about nine o'clock) the line halted and the British artillery proceeded to the front. "The cannonade now opened upon the enemy [Gough's dispatch recorded] was the most terrible I ever witnessed, and as terrible in its effect. The Sikh guns were served with their accustomed rapidity, and the enemy well and resolutely maintained his position; but the terrific force of our fire obliged them, after an obstinate resistance, to fall back." The result of this artillery duel somewhat surprised the Sikhs, who thought that the British did not sufficiently understand the use of their guns. They had formed this opinion partly in ignorance of the weakness of the British ordnance, but it was partly the natural effect of the wild rush of Pennycuick's Brigade at Chillianwalla. Our weakness in artillery had long been deplored by Lord Gough, and when, for the only time throughout

the Sikh wars, he excelled in that important arm, he made full use of the opportunity. "We stood two hours in hell," was a Sikh's description of the battle; "and, after that, we saw six miles of infantry."

'For two and a half hours the merciless fire of the British artillery was continued. The Sikh reply had not been without effect, but the result was overwhelmingly in favour of the British.'

The account given in *Battles of the 19th Century* reveals that Gough did not have things all his own way:

'The infantry line began its advance, but had more than once to lie down to avoid the hail of grape and round slot which fell thick among the batteries in front. The gunners suffered heavily; Fordyce's troop had to fall back twice for men, horses, and ammunition. The inevitable end drew nearer and nearer as the men and horses of the enemy went down amid shattered tumbrils and disabled guns under the crushing fire of Gough's siege-guns.

'But the Sikhs fought on with the high courage of their race. The gunners were mostly expended, but the grand old Khalsa infantry and the staunch Bunnoo regiments showed still a gallant front. The Sikh cavalry hovered on either flank, eager to pass round into the British rear; but their efforts were thwarted by the fire of Warner's guns and the counterstrokes of Hearsey's and Lockwood's Horse. One band of desperadoes did accomplish the turning movement, and made a bold and desperate dash on the spot where stood Gough alongside of the heavy guns; but a charge by the chief's escort cut the daring band to pieces.

'During the cannonade the infantry, excepting the skirmishers, had not fired a shot.'

It was now nearly noon, and Gough ordered a general advance, still covered by the artillery. Gough's despatch tells of this:

'The village of Burra-Kalra, the left one of those of that name, in which the enemy had concealed a large body of infantry, and which was apparently the key of their position, lay immediately in the line of Major-General Sir Walter Gilbert's advance, and was carried in the most brilliant style, by a spirited attack of the Third Brigade, under Brigadier Penny, consisting of the 2nd Europeans, 31st and 70th Regiments of Native Infantry, which drove the enemy from their cover with great slaughter.'

Pushing forward his light troops to force the enemy to reveal their position, Gilbert describes the advance:

'I immediately advanced the troop of Horse Artillery and Dawes' light field-battery, which instantly drew a very heavy and well-directed fire from two large batteries which the enemy had established on either side of the village of Kalerah [Burra Kalra], by which they were nearly screened from the fire of our guns, which, with the light companies, were then still further pushed forward, followed by the division, which had deployed into line; the heavy guns in our centre at this time opening, a very destructive cannonade. Up to this time the village above named seemed to be unoccupied, and I directed a party of infantry to take possession of it. Upon the approach of this party a tremendous fire of musketry was opened from the walls, which were loopholed in every direction; the 2nd European Regiment was then ordered up in support, under the command of Major Steele, and soon carried it, after a most obstinate resistance, in which that most gallant regiment suffered rather severely, as well as upon its emerging from the village, soon after which the enemy left many of their guns, and fled in the greatest confusion.'

'Gough's despatch continues:

'A very spirited and successful movement was also made about the same time against a heavy body of the enemy's troops, in and about Chota-Kalra, by part of Brigadier Hervey's brigade, most gallantly led by Lieutenant-Colonel Franks of H.M.'s 10th Foot.

'The heavy artillery continued to advance with extraordinary celerity, taking up successive forward positions, driving the enemy from those they had retired to, whilst the rapid advance and beautiful fire of the horse artillery and light field batteries, which I strengthened by bringing to the front the two reserved troops of horse artillery under Lieutenant-Colonel Brind – Brigadier Brooke having the general superintendence of the whole of the horse artillery – broke the ranks of the enemy at all points. The whole infantry line now rapidly advanced and drove the enemy before it; the nullah was cleared, several villages stormed, the guns that were in position carried, the camp captured, and the enemy routed in every direction! – the right wing and Brigadier-General Campbell's division passing in pursuit to the eastward, the Bombay column to the westward of the town.'

Gough's despatch now tells of the cavalry actions and the Sikh retreat:

'The retreat of the Sikh army, thus hotly pressed, soon became a perfect flight, all arms dispersing over the country, rapidly pursued by our troops for a distance of twelve miles, their track strewed with their wounded, their arms, and military equipments, which they threw away to conceal that they were soldiers.

'Throughout the operations thus detailed, the cavalry brigades on the flanks were threatened, and occasionally attacked by vast masses of the enemy's cavalry, which were, in every instance, put to flight by the steady movements and spirited manœuvres of our cavalry, most zealously and judiciously supported by the troops of horse artillery attached to them, from whom the enemy received the severest punishment.

'On the left, a most successful and gallant charge was made upon the Afghan cavalry and a large body of Goorchurras, by the Scinde Horse and a party of the 9th Lancers, when some standards were captured.' (General Thackwell's own report on these operations should also be studied.)

Sir Charles Gough, in his account of the *Battles of Chillianwala and Gujerat*, says:

'It was a glorious sight to see the Scinde Horse and the 9th Lancers sweeping forward over the open plain, and in a few minutes the whole force of Afghan Cavalry turned and fled, and Thackwell . . . found that his advance had completely turned the right of the Sikh line.'

Thackwell now threw in the rest of his cavalry, who rushed on with great dash, dispersing, riding over and trampling down the Sikh infantry, capturing guns and waggons and converting the discomforted enemy into a shapeless mass of fugitives. The pursuing troopers did not draw rein until they had ridden 10 miles beyond Gujerat, by which time the army of Shere Singh was an utter wreck, deprived of its camp, its standards and 53 of its cherished guns. This is praised in both Thackwell's report and Gough's official despatch as follows:

'The determined front shown by the 14th Light Dragoons and the other cavalry regiments on the right, both regular and irregular, completely overawed the enemy, and contributed much to the success of the day; the conduct of all in following up the fugitive enemy was beyond all praise.'

The son and aide-de-camp of Sir Joseph Thackwell, E. Thackwell, wrote in his book *Narrative of the Second Seikh War* of the pursuit, in which he took a personal part:

'The slaughter, perpetrated by the British Dragoons in

Sikh guns at Windsor Castle, from the Illustrated London News, *14 October 1848.*

the pursuit, was fearful. No quarter was given, and every Sikh, armed or unarmed, fell under the sword or the pistol.'

Hope Grant, who was with the 9th Lancers, says: 'It was horrible work slaughtering these wretched fugitives, who had taken refuge in trees and in the standing corn hoping to evade discovery. . . . Our men were enraged with the Sikhs, owing to the brutal manner in which they had slaughtered our wounded at Chillianwala.'

Gough's despatch continues: 'A competent force, under the command of Major-General Sir Walter Gilbert, resumed the pursuit towards the Jhelum on the following morning, with a view of cutting off the enemy from the only practicable gun road to the Jhelum.'

At the same time, another division under Brigadier-General Campbell, consisting of his infantry division, the 9th Lancers, 8th Light Cavalry, and some Horse Artillery, advanced on the road to Bimber, scouring, as we learn from the conclusion of Gough's despatch: 'the country in that direction, to prevent their carrying off the guns by that route, and a body of cavalry, under Lieutenant-Colonel Bradford, successfully pushed on several miles into the hills, and twenty-four from Goojerat, accompanied by that most energetic political officer, Captain Nicholson, for the same purpose, whilst I remained in possession of the field for the purpose of supporting these operations, covering the fords of the Chenab, and destroying the vast magazine of ammunition left scattered about in all directions. I am happy to add that these combinations have been entirely successful, the detached parties coming at every step on the wreck of the dispersed and flying foe.

'Having thus endeavoured to convey to your Lordship the particulars of the operations of the battle of Goojerat, I beg now to offer my heartfelt congratulations to your Lordship, and to the Government of India, upon this signal victory achieved under the blessing of Divine providence by the united efforts and indomitable gallantry of the noble army under my command.'

At home in Britain, the news of Gough's final victory caused the tone of the press to change rapidly, substituting praise for abuse. The situation was summed up with considerable candour by *Punch*, whose pages had hitherto carried much from the skilful pen of Thackeray in praise of Napier at the expense of Gough:

'*Punch* hereby begs to present his thanks to Lord Gough, and the officers and soldiers of the British Army in India for the brilliant victory which they had the good fortune to gain the other day at Goojerat; and *Punch* by these presents, extols his Lordship and his troops to the skies. A few weeks ago *Punch* sent Lord Gough his dismissal, which *Mr. Punch* is now glad did not arrive in time to prevent the triumph for which he is thus thankful. Having violently abused Lord Gough for losing the day at Chillianwallah, *Punch* outrageously glorifies him for winning the fight at Goojerat. When Lord Gough met with a reverse, *Punch* set him down for an incompetent octogenarian; now that he has been fortunate, *Punch* believes him to be a gallant veteran; for *Mr. Punch*, like many other people, of course looks merely to results; and takes as his only criterion of merit, success.'

That noble old warrior General Sir Colin Campbell (who still had a lot of fighting to do in India during the Mutiny nine years later) knew brave men when he saw them, and was much moved by the fine attitude of the Sikh soldiers of the Khalsa. Later, he wrote in his journal:

'There was nothing cringing in the manner of these men in laying down their arms. They acknowledged themselves beaten, and they were starving – destitute

A cannon with an ornate carriage and a solid mortar were two of the prizes taken by the British when the Punjab Revolt was crushed in 1849.

alike of food and money. Each man as he laid down his arms received a rupee to enable him to support himself on his way to his home. The greater number of the old men especially, when laying down their arms, made a deep reverence as they placed their swords on the heap, with the muttered words "Runjeet Singh is dead to-day!" This was said with deep feeling: they were undoubtedly a fine and brave people.'

His opinions were to be borne out a thousand-fold in subsequent years when Sikh soldiers faithfully served the British Crown in many wars.

When Sir Charles Napier landed at Calcutta, bearing the Queen's commission to take command of the army 'without loss of time', he found that the war was over. *In The Life of Sir Charles Napier* W. N. Bruce tells of his reactions:

'You will have heard . . . that the war is over in India, and Lord Gough has come off with flying colours. Both these things rejoice me much . . . I like that noble old fellow Gough more than ever. I told him that my wish was that he would order me home; it would be a kindness, and so saying I told him the truth . . . Again let me express my delight with old Gough; he is so good, so honest, so noble-minded.'

Needless to say, Gough did not order him home. He

at once laid down his office, deriving, as Rait explains, no small comfort in his sadness 'from the gentle and considerate kindness which he received from his successor and from the Governor General [Lord Dalhousie] . . . who ordered that during Lord Gough's stay in India he should receive all the honour that had been his due as Commander-in-Chief, and he was unremitting in his efforts to show him all possible deference.'

It is fitting that the epilogue to the Sikh Wars should be in the form of the following prophetic words, which were written by E. Thackwell, who served in the conflict:

'India, from the mouth of the Ganges to the hill-girt Peshawur, inhabited by millions of warlike people, is now tributary to England. What an awful responsibility! The more extensive the tract, the more slippery becomes the British ascendancy. There is a greater need than ever of energetic, enlightened rulers, like Dalhousie, Ellenborough, and Hardinge. The question now occurs, are there sufficient British Regiments in India? No. Fifty Queen's infantry regiments would not do more than maintain our supremacy in the event of well-organised insurrection. If railways were established fewer men might suffice. We hold India by the bayonet; but, rest assured, it is a very dangerous weapon in the hands of the native soldiery.'

BATTLE HONOURS FOR THE SECOND SIKH WAR 1848–9

MOOLTAN

10th (North Lincolnshire) Regt. of Foot
32nd (Cornwall) Regt. of Foot
1st Bn. 60th (The King's Royal Rifle Corps)
H.E.I.C. 1st Bombay (European) Fusiliers

Indian Army

7th Regt. Bengal Irregular Cavalry
1st Regt. Bombay Light Cavalry (Lancers)
1st Regt. Scinde Irregular Horse
2nd Regt. Scinde Irregular Horse
Corps of Guides
1st Co. 4th Battalion, Bombay Foot Artillery
Corps of Bengal Sappers & Miners
Corps of Bombay Sappers & Miners
3rd Regt. Bombay Native Infantry
4th Regt. Bombay Native Infantry (or Rifle Corps)
9th Regt. Bombay Native Infantry
19th Regt. Bombay Native Infantry

CHILLIANWALLAH

3rd (King's Own) Regt. of Light Dragoons
9th (Queen's Royal) Regt. of Light Dragoons (Lancers)
14th (The King's) Regt. of Light Dragoons
24th (2nd Warwickshire) Regt. of Foot
61st (South Gloucestershire) Regt. of Foot
29th (Worcestershire) Regt. of Foot
H.E.I.C. 2nd Bengal (European) Regt.

Indian Army

31st Regt. Bengal Native Infantry
70th Regt. Bengal Native Infantry

GUJERAT

3rd (King's Own) Regt. of Light Dragoons
9th (Queen's Royal) Regt. of Light Dragoons (Lancers)
14th (The King's) Regt. of Light Dragoons
10th (North Lincolnshire) Regt. of Foot
24th (2nd Warwickshire) Regt. of Foot
61st (South Gloucestershire) Regt. of Foot
29th (Worcestershire) Regt. of Foot
32nd (Cornwall) Regt. of Foot
53rd (Shropshire) Regt. of Foot
1st Bn. 60th (The King's Royal Rifle Corps)
H.E.I.C. 2nd Bengal (European) Fusiliers
H.E.I.C. 1st Bombay (European) Fusiliers

Indian Army

1st Regt. Scinde Irregular Horse
2nd Regt. Scinde Irregular Horse
Corps of Guides
Corps of Bengal Sappers & Miners
Corps of Bombay Sappers & Miners
31st Regt. Bengal Native Infantry
70th Regt. Bengal Native Infantry
3rd Regt. Bombay Native Infantry
19th Regt. Bombay Native Infantry

PUNJAUB

3rd (King's Own) Regt. of Light Dragoons
9th (Queen's Royal) Regt. of Light Dragoons (Lancers)
14th (The King's) Regt. of Light Dragoons
10th (North Lincolnshire) Regt. of Foot
24th (2nd Warwickshire) Regt. of Foot
61st (South Gloucestershire) Regt. of Foot
29th (Worcestershire) Regt. of Foot
32nd (Cornwall) Regt. of Foot
53rd (Shropshire) Regt. of Foot
1st Bn. 60th (The King's Royal Rifle Corps)
98th (The Prince of Wales's) Regt. of Foot
H.E.I.C. 2nd Bengal (European) Fusiliers
H.E.I.C. 1st Bombay (European) Fusiliers

Indian Army

2nd Regt. Bengal Irregular Cavalry
7th Regt. Bengal Irregular Cavalry
17th Regt. Bengal Irregular Cavalry
1st Regt. Bombay Light Cavalry (Lancers)
1st Regt. Scinde Irregular Horse
2nd Regt. Scinde Irregular Horse
Corps of Guides
1st Co. 4th Battalion, Bombay Foot Artillery
Corps of Bengal Sappers & Miners
Corps of Bombay Sappers & Miners
31st Regt. Bengal Native Infantry
70th Regt. Bengal Native Infantry
1st Regt. Sikh Local Infantry
2nd (or Hill) Regt. Sikh Local Infantry
3rd Regt. Bombay Native Infantry
4th Regt. Bombay Native Infantry
9th Regt. Bombay Native Infantry
19th Regt. Bombay Native Infantry
The Marine Battalion

5 · *The Indian Mutiny*
1857–1858

If Peace have its victories as well as War, like War it has its troubles, its perplexities, and its dangers. India at the present moment affords a striking illustration of this truth. From Cabul and Beloochistan to Birmah, and from the Himalayas to the Ocean, our arms have been victorious against all external foes. Our frontiers have neither assailants nor enemies sufficiently powerful and discontented to cause us anxiety. Internal enemies, as far as they exist in the shape of native potentates, with armies at their command, have ceased to trouble us. One by one their States have been 'annexed' and absorbed into the unity of our great Indian Empire. The ancient Sovereigns have become the pensioners upon our generosity or our justice, and their subjects have learned to appreciate the benefits of the more stable and less rapacious government which has superseded that of their own countrymen. Great Britain, while holding her own in India by the force of arms, and by the prestige of invincibility which the successive victories of a century have thrown around the British name, has begun to turn the immense natural resources of the country to account. But, amid all these realities of present, and prognostics of future, prosperity and peace, a sudden cause of alarm, has sprung up in an unexpected quarter. The native regiments, having nothing to do, and being, as it is alleged, vastly under-officered, have turned their enforced idleness to mischievous account. Rumours have been rapidly spread among them that the British Government had determined to interfere with their religious rites and ceremonies. These groundless rumours, not being sufficiently checked and contradicted, have passed from regiment to regiment, until open mutiny has been the result. In all cases the mutinies have been suppressed, and regiment after regiment has been disbanded; the native officers losing all claim to pay or pension from the Indian Government, but the same deprivation not being allowed to extend to the European officers. The question whether the insubordination and mutiny of the troops are not in some degree owing to the system, by which, for the sake, we suppose, of economy, the native regiments are not officered by Europeans to the full extent required by discipline and efficiency is one of very high importance. The good Captain, no less than the good General, ought to know his men, and sympathise with them, not only in the exercise of merely professional duty, but in their amusements and their comforts. He should study their character, and not despise their prejudices of race and creed, if he really wishes to command them, or would turn their valour to proper account. If unacquainted with them he cannot acquire their confidence, on the one hand; and on the other, with a peaceful people like the Hindoos, he may ignorantly offend their most cherished notions of propriety and dignity, and unconsciously goad them to mutiny and rebellion. Here, then, are the remedies for the evil: – a more intimate study of the character of the Hindoo, or Sepoy, soldiery on the part of the British officers already in the service, and an immediate increase of the number of such officers to the extent required by efficiency. With efficiency will come safety; and rumours of a character to awaken the religious prejudices, or to excite the fanatical fears, of the native troops will cease to exist. We do not believe that the Governor-General of India has lent himself to any project, great or small, for the Christianisation of the Hindoo people, attributed to him by an Indian journal, and brought under the notice of Parliament by Lord Ellenborough; neither do we believe that any political disaffection exists among the natives in any part of India; but, even without such sources of danger as either of these would be, a mutinous spirit among the troops is a danger sufficiently great to cause anxiety. Such a danger must be immediately confronted and removed. Unhesitating, inflexible severity to the actual mutineers, accompanied by politic consideration for the religious prejudices, habits, and education of the troops where no mutiny has shown itself, may, if immediately employed, prevent the extension of the mischief. Fires cannot be allowed near powder magazines, and mutinies in India must be suppressed at any cost.

ILLUSTRATED LONDON NEWS, *Saturday, 13 June 1857*

A CHRONOLOGICAL TABLE OF EVENTS IN INDIA
1857–8

1857.

Jan. 22. Cartridges disturbances began at Dumdum.

Feb. 6. Cartridge grievances inquired into at Barrackpore.

Feb. 11. General Hearsey warned government of disaffection.

Feb. 26. 19th Bengal N. I. riotous at Berhampore.

Mar. 26. Cartridge disturbances at Umballa.

Mar. 27. Proclamation explaining Cartridge question.

Mar. 29. 34th B. N. I. riotous at Barrackpore.

Mar. 31. 19th B. N. I. disbanded and dismissed.

Apr. 24. Cartridge disturbances at Meerut.

May 1. Cartridge disturbances at Lucknow.

May 3. 7th Oude Infantry mutinied at Lucknow.

May 5. 34th B. N. I. disbanded and dismissed.

May 9. 3rd B. N. C. punished at Meerut.

May 10. COMMENCEMENT OF THE GREAT REVOLT AT MEERUT.

May 10. Troops in Company's pay on this day – 38,000 Europeans, 200,000 Natives.

May 11. Meerut mutineers (11th and 20th B. N. L., and 3rd B. N. C.) marched to Delhi.

May 11. 38th, 54th, and 74th B. N. I., mutinied at Delhi.

May 13. 16th, 26th, and 49th B. N. I., and 8th B. N. C., disarmed at Meean Meer near Lahore.

May 14. General Anson departed from Simla, to head troops.

May 16. B. N. Sappers and Miners mutinied at Meerut.

May 17. 25th B. N. I. riotous at Calcutta.

May 19. Anson's Proclamation concerning cartridges.

May 20. 55th B. N. I. mutinied at Murdan.

May 20. 9th B. N. I. mutinied at Allygurh and vicinity.

May 21. First siege-column left Umballa for Delhi.

May 21. Europeans at Cawnpore began their intrenchment.

May 22. 24th, 27th, and 51st B. N. I., with 5th B. N. C., disarmed at Peshawur.

May 24. Colvin's proclamation – disapproved by Viscount Canning.

May 24. Portion of Gwalior Horse mutinied at Hattrass.

May 24. General Anson left Umballa for Delhi.

May 27. General Anson died at Kurnaul.

May 27. Wilson's Field-force left Meerut for Delhi.

May 28. Reed succeeded Anson provisionally.

May 28. 15th and 30th B. N. I. mutinied at Nuseerabad.

May 30. Portions of 13th, 48th, and 71st B. N. I., with 7th N. C., mutinied at Lucknow.

May 30. Wilson defeated Delhi rebels at Ghazeeoodeen Nuggur.

May 31. Wilson defeated Delhi rebels, near the Hindoun.

May 31. Barnard left Kurnaul to command army against Delhi.

May 31. 28th B. N. I. mutinied at Shahjehanpoor.

June 1. 44th and 67th B. N. I. disarmed at Agra.

June 3. 17th B. N. I. mutinied at Azimghur.

June 3. 41st B. N. I., 9th and 10th Oude Irreg. I., and 2d Oude Mil. Police, mutinied at Seetapoor.

June 3. 29th B. N. I. mutinied at Mooradabad.

June 3. 72nd B. N. I. and a wing of 1st B. N. C., mutinied at Neemuch.

June 4. 37th B. N. I., 13th Irreg. C., and Loodianah Sikhs, mutinied at Benares.

June 4. 12th B. N. I., and 14th Irreg. C., mutinied at Jhansi.

June 5. 1st, 53rd, and 56th B. N. I., and 2d B. N. C., mutinied at Cawnpore.

June 5. Wing of Loodianah Sikhs mutinied at Jounpoor.

June 6. Barnard and Wilson joined forces at Bhagput.

June 6. 6th B. N. I. mutinied at Allahabad.

June 6? Hurrianah Battalion mutinied at Hansi.

June 6? Bhurtpore Levies mutinied at Bhurtpore.

June 7. 36th and 61st. B. N. I., and 6th B. C., mutinied at Jullundur.

June 8. 22d B. N. I., and 6th Oude I., mutinied at Fyzabad.

June 8? Massacre of Europeans at Jhansi.

June 8. Barnard defeated Delhi rebels at Badulla Serai.

June 8. Barnard arrived with siege-army before Delhi.

June 9. 15th Irreg. C. mutinied at Sultanpore.

June 9. Europeans driven from Futtehpoor by rebels.

June 10. 1st Oude Irreg. I. mutinied at Pershadeepore.

June 11. Wing of 12th B. N. I., and 14th Irreg. C., mutinied at Nowgong.

June 10? Europeans driven from Neemuch by rebels.

June 11. Neill relieved Allahabad from the rebels.

June 11. 60th B. N. I. mutinied at Rohtuk.

June 12. First boat-party from Futteghur massacred by Nena Sahib.

June 13. Press 'Gagging' Act passed at Calcutta.

June 13. 45th and 57th B. N. I. mutinied at Ferozepore.

June 14. 43rd and 70th B. N. I. and 2d N. C. disarmed at Barrackpore.

June 14. Gwalior Contingent mutinied at Gwalior.

June 15. King of Oude under surveillance at Calcutta.

June 18. 10th B. N. I. mutinied at Futteghur.

June 19. Defeat of Nuseerabad rebels outside Delhi.

June 23. Nagpoor Irreg. C. disarmed at Nagpoor.

June 23. Severe Battle outside Delhi.

June 26. 33rd and 35th B. N. I. disarmed at Phillour.

June 27. First news of the Revolt reached England.

June 27. Boat-massacre at Cawnpore, by Nena Sahib.

June 30. Disastrous Battle of Chinhut, near Lucknow.

June 30. 4th Irreg. C. mutinied at Mozuffernugger.

June 30. Europeans at Saugor intrench themselves in fort.

July 1. Europeans driven out of Indore.

July 1. 23d B. N. I. mutinied at Mhow.

July 1. Siege of Europeans in Lucknow began.

July 2. Severe Battle outside Delhi.

July 2. Rohilcund mutineers entered Delhi.

July 3. Mussulman Conspiracy discovered at Patna.

July 4. Death of Sir H. Lawrence at Lucknow.

July 4. Kotah Contingent mutinied at Agra.

July 5. Death of Sir H. Barnard outside Delhi.

July 5. Reed took command of siege-army.

July 5. Disastrous Battle of Shahgunje, near Agra.

July 7. 14th B. N. L. mutinied at Jelum.

July 7. 58th B. N. I. disarmed at Rawul Pindee.

July 7. Havelock's column left Allahabad for Cawnpore.

July 7. 42nd B. N. I., and 3d Irreg. C., mutinied at Saugor.

July 9. 46th B. N. I., and 9th C., mutinied at Sealkote.

July 11. Second boat-party from Futteghur arrived at Bithoor.

July 12. Nicholson defeated Sealkote mutineers.

July 12. Havelock defeated rebels at Futtehpoor.

July 12. Sir Colin Campbell left England for India.

July 14. Severe Battle outside Delhi.

July 15. Havelock defeated rebels at Aong.

July 15. Havelock defeated rebels at Pandoo Nuddee.

July 15. Massacre at Cawnpore, by Nena Sahib.

July 16. Havelock defeated Nena Sahib at Aherwa.

July 17. Havelock entered Cawnpore victoriously.

July 17. Havelock defeated Nena Sahib near Bithoor.

July 17. Reed resigned command before Delhi – Wilson succeeded.

July 20. Fierce Attack by rebels on Lucknow Garrison.
July 24. 12th Irreg. C. mutinied at Segowlie.
July 25. Havelock crossed Ganges into Oude.
July 25. 7th, 8th, and 40th B. N. I. mutinied at Dinapoor.
July 26. Nearly 6,000 persons sheltered in Agra Fort, of whom 2,000 children.
July 27. Mr Wake's defence of Arrah commenced.
July 29. 26th B. N. I. mutinied at Lahore.
July 29. Havelock defeated rebels at Onao.
July 29. Havelock defeated rebels at Busherutgunje.
July 30. Captain Dunbar's disaster at Arrah.
July 31. Ramgurh Infantry mutinied at Ramgurh.
July 31. Siege-army before Delhi = 6,918 effectives, and 1,116 sick and wounded.
Aug. 1. 63rd B. N. I. and 11th Irreg. C. disarmed at Berhampore.
Aug. 1. Severe Battle outside Delhi.
Aug. 1. 27th Bombay N. I. mutinied at Kolapore.
Aug. 2. Vincent Eyre defeated Koer Singh near Arrah.
Aug. 8. 59th B. N. I. disarmed at Umritsir.
Aug. 8. Nicholson arrived with his Column at Delhi.
Aug. 10. Severe Battle outside Delhi.
Aug. 12. Havelock's second victory at Busherutgunje.
Aug. 12. Vincent Eyre defeated Koer Singh at Jugdispore.
Aug. 13. Havelock retreated across Ganges to Cawnpore.
Aug. 14. 5th Irregl C. mutinied at Berhampore.
Aug. 15–18. Hodson defeated rebels outside Delhi.
Aug. 16. Havelock defeated Nena Sahib at Bithoor.
Aug. 20. Fierce attack by the rebels on Lucknow Residency.
Aug. 22. Jhodpore Legion mutinied at Erinpoora.
Aug. 24. Montgomery defeated rebels at Allygurh.
Aug. 25. Nicholson won Battle of Nujuffghur near Delhi.
Aug. 25. Meeting in London at the Mansion-house, to establish Indian Mutiny Relief Fund.
Aug. 28. 51st B. N. I. mutinied at Peshawur.
Sept. 5. Outram's Column left Allahabad for Cawnpore.
Sept. 5. Fierce attack by rebels on Lucknow Residency.
Sept. 7. Indore mutineers captured Dholpore.
Sept 7. Siege-army before Delhi = 13,000 men.
Sept 9. Mr Colvin died at Agra.
Sept 11. Cannonading of Delhi commenced.
Sept 11. Viscount Eyre defeated rebels at Koondun Puttee.
Sept 14. Delhi entered by storm – death of Nicholson.
Sept. 15–20. Gradual Conquest of Delhi city and fortifications.
Sept. 15–20. Outram joined Havelock and Neill at Cawnpore.
Sept. 16. 60th B. N. I. mutinied at Nagode.
Sept. 18. 52nd B. N. I. mutinied at Jubbulpoor.
Sept. 19. Outram and Havelock crossed Ganges into Oude.
Sept. 20. Goorkhas defeated rebels at Mundoree.
Sept. 21. Hodson captured King and Princes of Delhi.
Sept. 23. Outram and Havelock captured the Alum Bagh.
Sept. 25. Outram and Havelock entered Lucknow Residency.
Sept. 25. Death of Neill at Lucknow.
Sept. 27. Outram and Havelock besieged in Residency.
Sept. 28. Greathed defeated Delhi rebels at Bolundshuhur.
Oct. 3. Peel's Naval Brigade arrived at Allahabad.
Oct. 5. Greathed defeated Delhi rebels at Allygurh.
Oct. 9. 32nd B. N. I. mutinied at Deoghur.
Oct. 10. Greathed defeated Indore rebels near Agra.
Oct. 15. Gwalior Contingent took the field, as a rebel army.
Oct. 15. Rajah of Kotah's troops mutinied.
Oct. 19. Greathed and Hope Grant retook Minpooree.
Oct. 26. Greathed and Hope Grant arrived at Cawnpore.
Oct. 28. Sir Colin Campbell started from Calcutta, for scene of hostilities.

Nov. 1. Peel's Naval Brigade defeated rebels at Kudjna.
Nov. 9. Mr Cavanagh's adventure at Lucknow.
Nov. 9. Europeans besieged in Fort of Neemuch.
Nov. 9. Sir Colin Campbell crossed Ganges into Oude.
Nov. 12. Sir Colin Campbell captured Jelalabad Fort.
Nov. 14–17. Sir Colin Campbell fought his way into Lucknow.
Nov. 18. Wing of 34th B. N. I. mutinied at Chittagong.
Nov. 20. 73rd B. N. I. mutinied at Dacca.
Nov. 23. British evacuated Lucknow.
Nov. 24. Stuart defeated Bundela rebels near Mundesoor.
Nov. 25. Death of Havelock, outside Lucknow.
Nov. 27, 28. Windham beaten by Gwalior rebels near Cawnpore.
Nov. 29. Lucknow Garrison recross Ganges to Cawnpore.
Dec. 6. Sir Colin defeated 25,000 rebels at Cawnpore.
Dec. 9. Hope Grant defeated rebels at Serai Ghât.
Dec. 14–17. Seaton defeated rebels in Minpooree district.
Dec. 19. Government announced to East India Company an approaching change in Company's powers.
Dec. 28. Osborne reconquered Myhere from Bundela rebels.
Dec. 30. Wood defeated rebels near Sumbhulpore.
Dec. 31. East India Company protested against the proposed legislation for India.

1858.

Jan. 1. Bareilly mutineers defeated at Huldwanee.
Jan 3. Sir Colin Campbell arrived at Futteghur.
Jan 6. Jung Bahadoor and his Goorkha army entered Goruckpore.
Jan 6. Raines defeated a body of rebels at Rowah.
Jan 12. Outram defeated 30,000 rebels outside Alum Bagh.
Jan 27. Adrian Hope defeated rebels at Shumshabad.
Jan 27. Trial of the King of Delhi commenced.
Jan 28. East India Company petitioned Parliament against government proceedings.
Feb. 3. Rose liberated the Europeans at Saugor.
Feb. 4. Sir Colin returned to Cawnpore from Futteghur.
Feb. 4. Maxwell repulsed Gwalior rebels at Chowra.
Feb. 9. Sir Colin and Canning met at Allahabad.
Feb. 9. Delhi and Meerut divisions placed under Punjaub government.
Feb. 10. M'Causland repulsed Bareilly rebels at Sunda.
Feb. 11. Great convoy of women and children left Agra.
Feb. 12. Lord Palmerston brought in India Bill No. 1.
Feb. 12–18. Debates thereon – government majority, 318 to 173.
Feb. 19. Franks defeated Bunda Hossein at Chundah.
Feb. 19. Franks defeated Mahomed Hossein at Humeerpoor.
Feb. 20. Palmerston Ministry resigned.
Feb. 21. Derby Ministry formed – Lord Ellenborough at the India Board.
Feb. 21. Outram repulsed 20,000 rebels at Alum Bagh.
Feb. 23. Hope Grant took Meeangunje from Oude rebels.
Feb. 26. Goorkhas captured fort of Mobarukhpoor in Oude.
Feb. 28. Sir Colin crossed Ganges, to head his army.
Mar. 2. Sir Colin advanced to the Alum Bagh.
Mar. 2–21. Gradual conquest of Lucknow from rebels.
Mar. 3. Viscount Canning's Proclamation to the Oudians.
Mar. 4. Rose defeated Bundelas at Mudenpore Pass.
Mar. 5. Rowcroft repulsed 12,000 rebels at Goruckpore.
Mar. 5. Goorkhas defeated Oude rebels at Kandoo Nuddee.
Mar. 10. Rose defeated rebel Rajah of Shagurh.
Mar. 10. Roberts headed the Rajpootana Field-force.
Mar. 11. Jung Bahadoor joined Sir Colin outside Lucknow.
Mar. 11. Showers defeated a body of rebels at Bah.
Mar. 16. Return of the Guide Corps to Peshawur.

Mar. 17. Stuart captured Chendaree from rebels.
Mar. 21. Rose with Siege-army arrived before Jhansi.
Mar. 21. Lucknow finally conquered by British.
Mar. 22. Millman repulsed by Azimghur rebels at Atrowlia.
Mar. 22. Roberts with Siege-army arrived before Kotah.
Mar. 25. Moncrieff routed a body of Coles at Chuckerderpore.
Mar. 26. Mr Disraeli brought in India Bill No. 2.
Mar. 29. Army of Oude broken up into separate columns.
Mar. 30. Roberts captured Kotah.
Apr. 1. Rose defeated Tanteea Topee outside Jhansi.
Apr. 2. Rose captured Jhansi – Ranee escaped.
Apr. 2. Kerr defeated Dinapoor rebels near Azimghur.
Apr. 2. Death of Captain Sir William Peel at Cawnpore.
Apr. 6. Seaton defeated Minpooree Rajah at Kankur.
Apr. 7. East India Company protested against both India Bills.
Apr. 12. House of Commons determined to proceed by Resolutions on India Bill.
Apr. 14. Disaster at Rhodamow under Walpole.
Apr. 14. Death of Adrian Hope at Rhodamow.
Apr. 17. Rowcroft defeated rebels at Amorah.
Apr. 17. Jones defeated Rohilcund rebels at Nagul.
Apr. 18. Sir Colin resumed operations from Cawnpore.
Apr. 18. Douglas defeated Koer Singh at Azimutgurh.
Apr. 18. Douglas defeated Koer Singh at Muneer Khas.
Apr. 19. Ellenborough's 'Secret Dispatch' written.
Apr. 19. Whitlock took Banda, and defeated Nawab.
Apr. 21. Le Grand's disaster at Jugdispore.
Apr. 21. Jones defeated Rohilcund rebels at Nageena.
Apr. 21. Koer Singh eluded Douglas, and crossed Ganges.
Apr. 22. Walpole defeated rebels at Sirsa.
Apr. 25. Jones recovered Mooradabad from Oude rebels.
Apr. 25. Sir Colin reached Futteghur.
Apr. 27. Sir Colin entered Rohilcund.
Apr. 28. Sir Colin joined Walpole at Ramgunga.
Apr. 30. Sir Colin entered Shahjehanpoor.
Apr. 30. Penny's Column won Battle of Kukerowlee.
Apr. 30. Death of Penny at Kukerowlee.
Apr. 30. Mr Disraeli brought in 'Resolutions' in House of Commons.
May 3. Lugard crossed Ganges in pursuit of Koer Singh.
May 3–11. Hall held fort of Shahjehanpoor against 8,000 rebels.
May 5. Sir Colin defeated rebels outside Bareilly.
May 7. Sir Colin captured Bareilly – rebel leaders escaped.
May 7. Corps of Bengal European Cavalry determined on.
May 9. Lugard defeated Koer Singh at Jugdispore – Koer Singh killed.
May 9. Rose marched in pursuit of Tanteea Topee and the Ranee.
May 11. Rose defeated them at Koonch.
May 11. Jones relieved Hall at Shahjehanpoor.
May 11. Ellenborough resigned – Lord Stanley appointed to Board of Control.
May 12. Lugard defeated Ummer Singh near Jugdispore.
May 12. Hope Grant defeated 16,000 Oude rebels at Sirsee.
May 14–21. Great debates in parliament, on Canning's Proclamation and Ellenborough's Dispatch.
May 15. Jones attacked in great force at Shahjehanpoor.
May 15–23. Rose in fierce conflict with Tanteea Topee in and near Calpee.
May 17. Jung Bahadoor returned to Nepaul.
May 18. Sir Colin repulsed rebels at Shahjehanpoor.
May 21. Light summer clothing ordered for troops.
May 22. Coke joined Sir Colin from Pileebheet.

May 23. Rose captured Calpee – Tanteea Topee, Ranee of Jhansi, and Nawab of Banda, fled towards Gwalior.
May 24. Incendiarism at Allahabad.
May 24. Sir Colin captured fort of Mohumdee.
May 26. Railway opened from Allahabad to Futtehpoor.
May 28. Sir Colin returned to Futteghur from Rohilcund and Oude.
May 28. Sir Colin thanked his army for past services.
May 30. Rebel leaders from Calpee arrived at Gwalior.
June 1. Scindia defeated by Tanteea Topee and Calpee rebels.
June 2. Rebels captured Gwalior – Scindia fled to Agra.
June 4. Lugard defeated rebels in Jugdispore jungle.
June 7. Lord Stanley resumed India debates in House of Commons.
June 9. Mahomed Hossein defeated at Amorah.
June 9–11. Moncrieff defeated rebels at Chuckerderpore.
June 13. Hope Grant defeated 16,000 rebels at Nawabgunge.
June 15. The Moulvie killed in action at Powayne.
June 16. Rose arrived near Gwalior.
June 16–19. Great Battle in and near Gwalior.
June 17. Death of the Ranee of Jhansi at Gwalior.
June 17. Lord Stanley brought in India Bill No. 3.
June 17. Canning's reply to Ellenborough's Secret Dispatch.
June 18. Mahomed Hossein defeated at Hurreah.
June 20. Rose recaptured Gwalior, and reinstated Scindia.
June 21. Napier left Gwalior in pursuit of Tanteea Topee.
June 23. East India Company's objections to Bill No. 3.
June 24. India Bill read second time in Commons.
June 29. Mr Manson murdered by Rajah of Nargoond.
End of month. 30th and 31st Bombay N. I. formed, to contain faithful men from mutinous 21st and 27th.
End of month. Faithful men of mutinous 3rd, 36th, and 61st Bengal N. I., formed into a new regiment in Punjaub.
July 2. Roberts with Rajpootana Field-force reach Jeypoor.
July 8. India Bill passed the Commons.
July 9. India Bill read a first time in Lords.
July 9. Tanteea Topee plundered Tonk – soon afterwards driven out by Holmes.
July 12. Rajah of Nargoond hanged at Belgaum.
July 13. India Bill read second time in the Lords.
July 14–20. Berkeley captured several small forts in Oude.
July 17. Rattray captured rebel chiefs at Dehree.
July 21. Hope Grant set out from Lucknow to confront rebels.
July 23. Roberts left Tonk in pursuit of Tanteea Topee.
July 28. Hope Grant relieved Maun Singh from siege at Shahgunje.
July 29. Hope Grant entered Fyzabad, and drove out rebels.
July 30. Cavanagh defeated a body of rebels in Muhiabad.
July 31. India Bill passed the Lords.
July 31. Outbreak of prisoners at Mymensing.
Aug. 1. Bundela rebels seized Jaloun – expelled by Macduff.
Aug. 2. India Bill (Act) received royal assent.
Aug. 3. Man Singh captured Paoree.
Aug. 7. Court of Directors elected seven members for new Council of India.
Aug. 8. Roberts defeated Tanteea Topee at Sunganeer.
Aug. 11. Parkes headed a column from Neemuch, to check Tanteea Topee.
Aug. 12. Tanteea Topee checked at Marwar frontier, by Erinpoora force.
Aug. 13. Horsford retook Sultanpore from Oude rebels.
Aug. 13. Carpenter defeated rebels near Kirwee.
Aug. 14. Roberts defeated Tanteea Topee at Kattara.
Aug. 20. Tanteea Topee crossed Chumbul to Julra Patteen.

Aug. 23. Napier drove Man Singh out of Paoree.
Aug. 25–29. Hope Grant fighting with Oude rebels outside
   Sultanpoor.
Aug. 29. Brahmin plot discovered at Gwalior.
Aug. 31. Disarmed 62nd and 69th B. N. I. mutinied at Moultan.
Aug. 31. Man Singh encamped at Sirsee, north of Goonah.
Sept. 1. Ashburner defeated rebels near Mahoni.
Sept. 1. Last day of E. I. Company's governing power.
Sept. 2. New Council of India commenced its sittings.
Sept. 5. Napier defeated Man Singh at Bujeepore.
Sept. 15. Michel defeated Tanteea Topee at Beora.
Sept. 16–30. Continuous chase after Tanteea Topee, by various
   British columns.
Oct. 3–8. Dawson besieged by Oude rebels at Sundeela.
Oct. 5. Eveleigh defeated rebels at Meeangunje.
Oct. 8. Barker and Dawson defeated rebels at Punno.
Oct. 19. Tanteea Topee defeated by Michel at Sindwah.
Oct. 25. Tanteea Topee defeated at Multhone.
Oct. 29. Beni Madhoo defeated at Poorwa.
Oct. 30. Mehndee Hossein defeated at Sufdergunje.
Oct. 31. Tanteea Topee crossed the Nerbudda.
Nov. 1. Queen's Proclamation issued.
Nov. 1. Sir Colin's final plans laid.
November. Gradual defeat and surrender of rebels in Oude
   and Behar.
November. Gradual defeat and surrender of rebels in Central
   India.

(The History of the Revolt in India)

The History of the Revolt in India, which was published in 1859, sets the scene:

'The magnificent India which began to revolt from England in the early months of 1857; which continued that Revolt until it spread to many thousands of square miles; which conducted the Revolt until it spread to many thousands of square miles; which conducted the Revolt in a manner that appalled all the civilised world by its unutterable horrors – this India was, after all, not really unsound at its core. It was not so much the PEOPLE who rebelled, as the SOLDIERS. Whatever grievances the hundred and seventy millions of human beings in that wonderful country may have had to bear; whatever complaints may have been justifiable on their parts against their native princes or the British Government; and whatever may have been the feelings of those native princes towards the British – all of which matters will have to be considered . . . still it remains incontestable that the outbreak was a military revolt rather than a national rebellion. The Hindu foot-soldier, fed and paid by the British, ran off with his arms and his uniform, and fought against those who had supported him; the Mohammedan trooper, with his glittering equipments and his fine horse, escaped with both in like manner, and became suddenly an enemy instead of a friend and servant. . . .

'The first week in May marked a crisis in the affairs of British India. It will ever remain an insoluble problem, whether the hideous atrocities that followed might have been prevented by any different policy at that date. The complainings and the disobedience had already presented themselves: the murders and mutilations had not yet

8th Hussars and sepoy, 1857.

commenced; and there are those who believe that if a Lawrence instead of a Hewett had been at Meerut, the last spark that ignited the inflammable materials might have been arrested. But this is a kind of cheap wisdom, a prophecy after the event, an easy mode of judgment, on which little reliance can be placed. Taking the British officers in India as a body, it is certain that they had not yet learned to distrust the sepoys, whom they regarded with much professional admiration for their external qualifications.

'But there was one fact which all these officers admitted, when it was too late to apply a remedy. Whether the Hindoo or the Mohammedan element was most disturbed, all agreed that the British forces were ill placed to cope with any difficulties arising out of a revolt. Doubt might be entertained how far the disloyalty among the native troops would extend; but there could be no doubt that European troops were scanty, just at the places where most likely to be needed. There were somewhat over twenty thousand Queen's troops at the time in India, with a few others on the way thither. Of these, as has been shewn in a former page, the larger proportion was with the Bengal troops.

'The complement of Queen's troops for the Bengal presidency, was two regiments of light cavalry, fifteen regiments of infantry, and one battalion of rifles; but it had been greatly reduced, and when the mutiny broke out, there were fewer European troops in the province than there had been for many years.

'But instead of being distributed in the various Bengal and Oude provinces, they were rather largely posted at

Non-commissioned officers of the native Bengal infantry.

two extreme points, certainly not less than two thousand miles apart. . . . Four regiments of the Queen's army were guarding the newly annexed country of the Punjaub, while three others were similarly holding the recent conquests in Pegu. What was the consequence, in relation to the twelve hundred miles between Calcutta and the Sutlej? An almost complete denudation of European troops: a surrendering of most of the strongholds to the mercy of the sepoys.

'At Allahabad, the great supply magazine of the province was left almost wholly to the guard of the sepoys. Lucknow had only one European regiment and one company of artillery, notwithstanding that, as the capital of Oude, it was in the midst of a warlike and

excited population; while the native army of the province, capable of soon assembling at the city, comprised no less than fourteen regiments of infantry, six of cavalry, and six companies of artillery. Cawnpore, a very important station with a large medical depôt, contained three regiments of native infantry, one of native cavalry, and two companies of native artillery with twelve guns; while the English force was only a company of infantry, and about sixty artillerymen with six guns. The large magazine of Delhi, the great storehouse of ammunition for the military stations all around it, was left to be guarded entirely by sepoys.

'In short, the Company's forces were almost as unfavourably distributed as they could possibly be, to stem the Revolt at its beginning; and there may not be much hazard in assuming that the natives were as well acquainted with this fact as the British.'

William Cooke Stafford, in *England's Battles by Sea and Land*, which was published soon after the Mutiny, describes how the revolt was triggered off:

'There had previously been several mutinies in the native army . . . but they had been suppressed with little difficulty. There is no doubt, however, that for several years dissatisfaction had been growing up in its ranks, from various causes. An order issued during the administration of Lord Dalhousie, to enlist the sepoys for general service only, had caused discontent; for the old soldiers were afraid, that, if men could be obtained on those terms, they would be obliged also to assent to them, or that they would be discharged without pension. The Bengal sepoys also complained greatly of the abolition of an extra allowance which had been made them for their services in Scinde. Both Hindoos and Mohammedans entertained vague apprehensions that their religious faith was to be in some way undermined; and the latter had never been the same men since the Affghan war [in] which they were previously. The annexation of Oude, whose king was the last independent Mohammedan sovereign in India, was a great "grievance" to the sepoys connected with that province; and shortly after the annexation, two mysterious circumstances took place. *Chupatties* – a species of unleavened cake, which forms the food of the lower classes and of the soldiers – were circulated amongst the people; and the lotus-flower – a Hindoo symbol – was passed from hand to hand amongst the troops. There is little doubt, that there were signs of a secret conspiracy amongst the men; which, on the introduction of the greased cartridges to use with the Enfield rifle, suddenly broke out.

'The Hindoo's abhorrence of those cartridges arises from his veneration for the cow; whilst the Mohammedan shrank from them because he detested the pig. The fat of these two animals was used in their manufacture; and the sepoys were taught to believe, that their introduction was intended to carry out the long-cherished design, which they had been told the "Feringhee" entertained, of subverting the religion of both the Hindoo and the Mohammedan. Those who were at the bottom of the conspiracy, and the movers of the secret organisation, intimated [according to the *Edinburgh Review*], that "it was determined to render their military service the means of their degradation, by compelling them to apply their lips to a cartridge saturated with animal grease – the fat of the swine being used for the one, and that of the cow for the degradation of the other. If the most astute emissaries of evil who could be employed for the corruption of the Bengal sepoy, had addressed themselves to the task of inventing a lie for the confirmation and support of all his fears and superstitions, they could have framed nothing more cunningly devised for their purposes."

'It appears, from the parliamentary papers, that the greased cartridges had been sent to India as early as

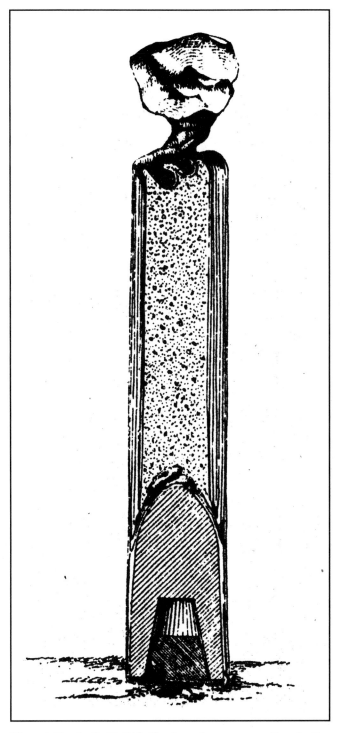

The cartridge for the Enfield rifle, shown here, was a cardboard cylinder containing gunpowder and a bullet. To open the cartridge, which was greased at its lower end, the twist of paper was torn or bitten off.

1853, for the purpose of being tested in that climate, as they were of four different kinds of manufacture; and the object was, to ascertain which would answer best in India. The commander-in-chief, however, aware of the native prejudices, distinctly stated, that "unless it was known that the grease employed in the cartridges was not of a nature to offend or interfere with the prejudices of caste, it would be expedient not to issue them for test to native corps, but to Europeans only." We hear nothing of the objection of natives to the cartridges till January, 1857; we may conclude, therefore, that this order was, up to that time, scrupulously observed. They were tested; and the consequence was, the adoption of a cartridge for India, manufactured according to a plan suggested by Captain Boxer, of the royal laboratory at Woolwich, where they were made up; but the greasing process was left to be gone through in India. Low-caste Hindoos were employed to perform it; and on the 22nd of January, one of these men, who was in the government service at Dumdum (a town a few miles from Calcutta, being half-way between that city and Barrackpore, where ordnance-works are established), asked a Brahmin, of the 2nd grenadiers, to give him a drink of water from his "lota," or bottle. The Brahmin was one of the high-caste, and he indignantly refused, as the touch of the workman would have defiled his utensil. The workman retorted, that he need not be so particular, as he would soon lose caste, for he would have to bite cartridges greased with the fat of cows. This alarmed the Brahmin, who spread the report among the sepoys, and the men also took alarm, as they were afraid the consequence would be, that their friends at home would refuse to eat with them, on account of their degradation. The officers soon learned what was passing among the privates, and they were paraded for the purpose of hearing their objection to the cartridges. This was stated; and the result was, that the men were allowed to use wax and oil; and it was also ordered, that no more cartridges should be imported from England, but that the materials being sent over, they should be entirely made up in India. It was thus hoped the difficulty was got over; but it was only a temporary calm before the storm.'

Towards the end of January there were disturbances at Barrackpore involving the 34th Native Infantry. A month later the same regiment so disaffected the 19th Native Infantry at Burhampore that they committed the first overt act of decided mutiny. Subsequently the Indian Government ordered from Rangoon Her Majesty's 84th Regiment of Foot, who arrived on 20 March and proceeded to the Barrackpore area, to which the 19th Native Infantry were being marched to be disarmed and disbanded. William Cooke Stafford tells of the dramatic events:

'While they were on the march, on the 29th, the first outrage on a European officer was committed. Mungul Pandy, a private of the 34th (from whom the mutineers were subsequently called "Pandies"), loaded his musket, and threatened to shoot the first European he came across. It was no idle threat. Lieutenant Baugh, the adjutant of his regiment, hearing of his conduct, rode towards the parade-ground, and, as he approached, Pandy fired at him, wounding his horse, bringing both horse and rider down; and although Lieutenant Baugh had loaded pistols with him, he would certainly have been killed, had not assistance come up. Sheikh Pultoo, a Mohammedan (an orderly), who had followed Lieutenant Baugh, in fact saved his life, by seizing the mutineer just as he had succeeded in reloading his musket, but not till the lieutenant was seriously wounded. A guard of the 34th, near the spot, had taken part with Mungul Pandy; they beat their officers, who came to assist Lieutenant Baugh; and did not disperse till Major-general Hearsey rode up, and threatened to shoot the first man who refused to obey orders. The major-general promoted Sheikh Pultoo to the rank of havildar (sergeant), for which act, not strictly en *règle*, he was rebuked by the governor-general in council. This outbreak was followed by the arrival, on the 30th, of the 19th at Barraset, eight miles from Barrackpore, where they were met by a deputation from the 34th, who proposed to them that they should "kill all their officers, march at night into Barrackpore, where the 2nd and 34th were prepared to join them; fire the bungalows, surprise and overwhelm the European force, secure the guns, and then march on to, and sack, Calcutta." The sepoys of the 19th, however, appear to have repented to their previous conduct, and refused. They marched quietly into Barrackpore the next morning, and – the 84th having been ordered up from Chinsurah on the 3rd of April – coolly gave up their arms, "many of them showing signs of deep contrition": they were then marched from the cantonments, and discharged. – This was the first native regiment disarmed and broke up on account of the mutiny.

'Mungal Pandy was tried and executed, as was a jemadar (native lieutenant) of the 34th, who had commanded the guard on the 29th of March. No steps were taken against the men who composed the guard, culpable as they were; and certainly, during the entire month of April, the government at Calcutta were either bewildered with their position, and did not *know* how to act; or they were in a state of ignorance of what was going on around them.

'It was in Oude that the next overt act took place. The 7th native irregulars quartered at Lucknow, on hearing of the disbanding of the 19th native infantry, showed signs of discontent.

'Fortunately, at that period, the late Sir Henry Lawrence was British commissioner at Lucknow. On the 3rd of May, he had a letter brought to him, addressed by the 7th irregulars to the 48th, of which the following was the purport: – "We are ready to obey the directions of our brothers of the 48th, in the matter of the cartridges, and to resist either actively or passively." The 7th had already threatened the lives of several of their officers, and Sir Henry resolved, on reading this letter, which had been brought to him by some native officers of the 48th, to disband them. He therefore ordered the 48th, with the 13th and 71st native infantry, the 7th native cavalry, her majesty's 32nd foot, and a battery of eight guns, manned by Europeans, to proceed to the lines of the mutineers, and form in front. The 7th were then summoned to lay down their arms: seeing the artillery with their portfires lighted, they obeyed at once; and the ringleaders were seized, to await their trial; the rest were discharged. Sir Henry followed up this act by rewarding the sepoys of the 48th (who had furnished information of the proceedings of the 7th), in the presence of all the troops then at Lucknow, whom he addressed in the most spirited terms. Thus, for the time, peace and order were preserved in Oude.'

James Grant describes the initial bursting of the dam:

'But a more eventful scene was at hand. Ninety men of the 3rd Light Cavalry, at Meerut, when ordered out for carbine practice with the new cartridge, all, save five, declined to use it. The eight-five malcontents were at once brought before a court-martial, and sentenced to ten years' imprisonment with hard labour. On the 9th of May their sentences were read out on parade. Their uniform was stripped off them, and iron shackles were fixed to their ankles. Many of these men were the flower of the regiment, who had done the Queen good service in many a battle, and they implored the general to have mercy, and not degrade them by a doom so ignominious; but they were marched off to gaol. On the following evening, while the Europeans were in church, the men of the 11th and 20th Bengal Native Infantry began to assemble tumultuously within their lines, and were evidently bent on mischief. The European officers at once hurried to the spot, in the hope of pacifying them. One of the first who arrived was Colonel Finnis (brother of the then Lord Mayor of London), who was shot in the back while in the act of haranguing the 20th. Choking in blood, he fell from his horse, and was hewn to pieces. The work of slaughter thus fairly inaugurated, the sepoys gave way to the most dreadful excesses; while the troopers of the 3rd, with yells, rushed to the gaol, burst in its gates, and released not only their comrades, but every felon and miscreant in the place. Joined by these wretches, and all those vagabonds who usually infest our Indian military stations, the European bungalows were sacked and given to the flames, while an indiscriminate massacre ensued of all Christians, without regard to sex or age. The women and children, who took refuge in the gardens, were all tracked out and shot down amid the most fiendish yells.

'None who witnessed the horrors of that Sunday night at Meerut ever forgot them. "On all sides [wrote one] there shot up into the heavens great pinnacles of waving fire, of all hues and colours, according to the fuel that fed them; huge volumes of smoke rolling suddenly off in the sultry night air, and the crackling and roar of the conflagration mingling with the shouts and riot of the mutineers.

'" . . . What spectacles of terror met the eye almost simultaneously with the return of day! The lifeless and mutilated corpses of men, women, and children were to be seen, some of them so frightfully disfigured, and so shamefully dishonoured in death, that the very recollection of such sights chills the blood."

'It is difficult to believe that there was at this time, in Meerut, an European force consisting of H.M. 60th Rifles, the 6th Dragoon Guards (only half-horsed, however), a troop of horse artillery, and 500 artillery recruits – about 2,000 men in all, and fully officered. But, unfortunately, the command was in the hands of General Hewitt, an old man, who, though he had done good service in his day, was now unfitted by age, enervated by long residence in India, and unable to act with proper promptitude at such a crisis.

'He pleased, in his report, that he did not think the result was premeditated, and that much valuable time was lost in calling out the Europeans, whose barracks were at some distance from the native lines. When the Queen's Carbineers were, at length, in their saddles, they dashed off at a brisk pace, through clouds of blinding dust and darkness, for it was then eight in the evening, and there is no twilight in India. Instead of riding straight for the scene of outrage, for some unknown reason they skirted it, and finally debouched on the left rear of the native infantry cantonments, which were then sheeted with fire.

'On reaching the parade-ground of the 11th, they found the 60th Rifles and artillery already there; but the mutineers and others were all off en masse for Delhi, horse and foot, where a sure welcome awaited them.

'Had the wretched General Hewitt at once set off with the Carbineers and horse-artillery guns, leaving the Rifles to follow, he would undoubtedly have overtaken and cut them to pieces, and thus prevented the horrors that took place at Delhi; but he contented himself with little more than a reconnaissance. An officer of the Carbineers volunteered to push on with a party, and possess himself of the bridge of the Jumna, but this was not permitted.

'The 60th Rifles contrived to pick off a few of the rearmost of the fugitives, and then the horse artillery galloped to the front, unlimbered, and opened a useless fire upon a copse, in which it was supposed many were concealed. The heavy discharges of grape crashed and tore among the trees, but did no other damage; and after this demonstration, on the plea of protecting the station against any other nocturnal attack, the force returned to Meerut, while, flushed with their partial success, the mutineers, without further molestation, pushed on for the city of the Moguls."

The inexorable march of events is recorded in *The History of the Revolt in India*:

'While these varied scenes were being presented; while sepoy regiments were revolting throughout the whole breadth of Northern India, and a handful of British troops was painfully toiling to control them; while Henry Lawrence was struggling, and struggling even to death, to maintain his position in Oude; while John Lawrence was sagaciously managing the half-wild Punjaub at a troublous time; while Wheeler at Cawnpore, and Colvin at Agra, were beset in the very thick of the mutineers; while Neill and Havelock were advancing up the Jumna; while Canning was doing his best at Calcutta, Harris and Elphinstone at Madras and Bombay, and the imperial government at home, to meet

Mutineers advancing on Delhi.

the trying difficulties with a determined front – while all this was doing, Delhi was the scene of a continuous series of operations. Every eye was turned towards that place. The British felt that there was no security for their power in India till Delhi was retaken; the insurgents knew that they had a rallying-point for all their disaffected countrymen, so long as the Mogul city was theirs; and hence bands of armed men were attracted thither by antagonistic motives. Although the real siege did not commence till many weary weeks had passed, the plan and preparations for it must be dated from the very day when the startling news spread over India that Delhi had been seized by rebellious sepoys, under the auspices of the decrepit, dethroned, debauched representative of the Moguls.

'It was, as we have already seen . . . on the morning of Monday the 11th of May, that the 11th and 20th regiments Bengal native infantry, and the 3rd Bengal cavalry, arrived at Delhi after a night-march from Meerut, where they had mutinied on the preceding evening. At Delhi, we have also seen, those mutineers were joined by the 38th, 54th, and 74th native infantry. It was on that same 11th of May that evening saw the six mutinous regiments masters of the imperial city; and the English officers and residents, their wives and children, wander-

ers through jungles and over streams and rivers. What occurred within Delhi on the subsequent days is imperfectly known; the few Europeans who could not or did not escape were in hiding; and scanty notices only have ever come to light from those or other sources. A Lahore newspaper, three or four months afterwards, gave a narrative prepared by a native, who was within Delhi from the 21st of May to the 23rd of June. Arriving ten days after the mutiny, he found the six regiments occupying the Selimgurh and Mohtabagh, but free to roam over the city; where the sepoys and sowars, aided by the rabble of the place, plundered the better houses and shops, stole horses from those who possessed them, "looted" the passengers who crossed the Jumna by the bridge of boats, and fought with each other for the property which the fleeing British families had left behind them. After a few days, something like order was restored, by leaders who assumed command in the name of the King of Delhi. This was all the more necessary when new arrivals of insurgent troops took place, from Allygurh, Minpooree, Agra, Muttra, Hansi, Hissar, Umballa, Jullundur, Nuseerabad, and other places. The mutineers did not, at any time, afford proof that they were really well commanded; but still there *was* command, and the defence of the city was arranged on a

Sir Henry Barnard.

definite plan. As at Sebastopol, so at Delhi; the longer the besiegers delayed their operations, the greater became the number of defenders within the place, and the stronger the defence-works.

'It must be remembered, in tracing the history of the siege of Delhi, that every soldier necessary for forming the siege-army had to be brought from distant spots. The cantonment outside the city was wholly in the hands of the rebels; and not a British soldier remained in arms in or near the place.

'Major-general Sir Henry Barnard was the medium of communication on this occasion. Being stationed at Umballa, in command of the Sirhind military division, he received telegraphic messages on the 11th of May from Meerut and Delhi, announcing the disasters at those places. He immediately despatched his aide-de-camp to Simla, to point out the urgent need for General Anson's presence on the plains instead of among the hills. . . . Hearing this news on the 12th, General Anson himself left Simla on the evening of the 14th, and arrived at Umballa early on the 15th.

'Anson and Barnard, when together at Umballa, had to measure well the forces available to them. The Umballa magazines were nearly empty of stores and ammunition; the artillery wagons were in the depôt, at Phillour; the medical officers dreaded the heat for troops to move in such a season; and the commissariat was ill supplied with vehicles and beasts of burden and draught. The only effectual course was found to be, that of bringing small detachments from many different stations; and this system was in active progress during the week following Anson's arrival at Umballa. Anson was greatly embarrassed by the distance between Umballa and the station where the siege-guns were parked; he knew that a besieging army would be of no use without those essential adjuncts; and it was on that account that he was unable to respond to Viscount Canning's urgent request that he would push on rapidly towards Delhi.

'On the 23rd of May, Anson sketched a plan of operations, which he communicated to the brigadiers whose services were more immediately at his disposal. Leaving Sir Henry Barnard in command at Umballa, he proposed to head the siege-army himself.'

William Cooke Stafford's *England's Battles by Sea and Land* tells of the adventures of Anson's small force as it marched on Delhi:

'The column marched in two brigades: the 1st, under Brigadier Halifax, comprised two squadrons of the 9th lancers, her majesty's 75th foot, the 1st Company's European regiment, and the 3rd troop of the 3rd brigade of horse artillery, with six guns. The 2nd, commanded by Brigadier Jones, comprised the 2nd European regiment, the 60th native infantry, two squadrons of the 9th lancers, one squadron of the 4th lancers, and the 2nd troop of the 3rd brigade of horse artillery, with six guns. Four companies of the 1st, and six of the 2nd, fusiliers, one squadron of the 9th lancers, and two guns, had preceded the column to Kurnaul. On the 25th, the

commander-in-chief reached Kurnaul, where, on the following day, he was attacked by cholera, and died on the 27th. Sir Henry Barnard, who had arrived on the 26th, assumed the command; and on the 6th of June, the little army reached Allipore, ten miles from Delhi, where it was joined on the 7th by a small force under Brigadier-general Wilson, who had left Meerut on the 27th of May, with 400 of the 60th rifles, 200 of the 6th carabiniers, one horse field battery, half a troop of horse artillery, two 18-pounder guns, and the head-quarters of the sappers and miners; the latter about 100 strong. On their route, at Guzeeoodeen Nugger, where the little river Hindun is crossed by an iron bridge, this force was attacked, on the 30th, by a body of the rebels with siege guns, sent to take possession of the bridge. It was the first time the mutineers had met the British in the open field, and the attack was very determined; the heavy guns opening upon Brigadier Wilson's force. They were replied to by the two 18-pounders; and a company of the 16th rifles being sent to occupy the disputed bridge, four guns of Major Tombs' horse artillery, supported by a squadron of carabiniers, moved along the river, to outflank the enemy: the remainder of the force attacked the centre of the rebels, the fire of whose artillery soon paled before that of the British guns. The rifles were then ordered to advance, which they did in dashing style; and the enemy fled, but not till they had actually crossed bayonets with our troops, leaving their guns, ammunition, and stores. The next day the rebels appeared again in force, on the ground from which they had been driven on the 30th: they were once more soundly beaten; but the British were so exhausted by the heat of the sun, that they could not, this time, prevent the enemy from carrying off their guns.

'When the forces of Sir H. Barnard and Brigadier Wilson were united, they scarcely amounted to 4,000 men; though the latter, before he arrived at Allipore, had been joined by the Sirmoor battalion of Ghoorkas, 600 strong. The first movement made by this force – so inadequate in numbers to the work it had to perform – was to attack, on the 8th of June, a position in which the rebels had intrenched themselves, at Badlee Serai, four miles from Delhi. They held the Serai (the Mohammedan name for a *chollry*, or rest-house – a place of refreshment for travellers), which was on the right of the trunk road to Delhi, as the British advanced; and their camp was grouped round it, on a natural elevation. About 150 yards in front of the serai, they had thrown up a sand-bag battery of four heavy guns and an 8-inch howitzer. The attack was made on three different points – the main attack being in front, where Brigadier Showers, with the 75th foot and 1st fusiliers, operated on the right; and Brigadier Graves, with the 60th rifles, 2nd fusiliers, and the Sirmoor battalion, on the left. Brigadier Grant, with ten horse artillery guns, under Major Turner, three squadrons of the 9th lancers, under Lieutenant-colonel Yule, and about fifty Jhind horsemen, under Lieutenant Hodson, was ordered to cross a canal which ran near the enemy's station, and attack it

Delhi from Flagstaff Tower.

in flank. The artillery, consisting of eight guns, was attached to the 1st and 2nd brigades. Those brigades started at the same time; but Brigadier Showers and the guns came first into action. They were received by a heavy fire from the enemy's battery. . . . The fire from the British guns made no impression upon those of the enemy, which were sheltered behind a parapet; and after witnessing the cannonade for a short time, Sir Henry Barnard ordered the 75th to charge, and take the battery. This they did "with heroic bravery," led by Brigadier Showers and Colonel Herbert, and supported by the 1st fusiliers. This gallant feat was just completed, when Brigadier Graves came up on the left, and Brigadier Grant in the rear. The rebels could not withstand this combined attack; and they retreated, leaving the camp and several guns in possession of the British.'

James Grant takes up the story:

'This . . . encounter took place five miles from Delhi, and Sir Henry Barnard, afraid to delay lest the enemy might form fresh works for him to storm, resolved, weary through his troops were, to push on at once. He formed his force in two great columns; one was led by Brigadier Wilson, with Shower's brigade in support, while he in person led the other, supported by Grove's brigade. Wilson marched along the Main Trunk Road, where he had to fight his whole way through gardens, high walls, and other obstacles, while the other, diverging to the left, proceeded straight through the cantonments, and came in sight of the magnificent city, with its vast marble palaces, its mosques and temples, its towering Koutab Minar, Houmayoun's tomb, and the vast extent of fortifications where, thick as bees, the armed rebels were clustered with all their cannon. But this point was not attained till the prowess of our troops had been sorely tested again.

'The intense excitement of our troops, as a general rule, enabled them to surmount everything; they had but one ardent and intense longing – for battle and vengeance. "Our blood is roused [wrote one of them at this time], we have seen friends, relations, mothers, wives, and children brutally murdered, and their bodies multilated frightfully. This alone, without the pluck that made us victorious over the Russians, would enable us, with God's assistance, to be victorious over these enemies. As the riflemen charge – ten to a hundred – the word is passed, "Remember the ladies! remember the babies!" and everything flies before them. Hundreds are shot down or bayoneted. The sepoys, it is true, fight like demons; but we are British, and they are natives."

'The rebels had constructed another line of defence from the Flagstaff Tower to the late Maharajah Hindoo Rao's house, and there – as men who fought with halters round their necks – disputed every inch of the ground. They knew their fate if beaten, and how the column that came on from Umballa had been hanging, flogging, and shooting, or blowing from the guns, every mutineer that hands could be laid on. By nine o'clock the Army of Retribution – as it was justly named – had forced the ground, driven the rebels from their guns and into the city, and finally sweeping the ridge, met upon it at Hindoo Rao's house, which from that time became the key of our position. The whole cantonments and parade-ground were ours again. Of the former, blackened walls alone remained.'

The ridge and cantonments were not left clear for the assaulting force, the enemy being completely driven from them. The day's fighting had cost four officers and 47 other ranks killed, and 13 European officers, one native officer and 118 other ranks wounded.

It did not take much reconnaissance to convince everyone that it would be futile to attempt to carry the city until considerable reinforcements and the siege-

Panoramic view of Delhi, 1857.

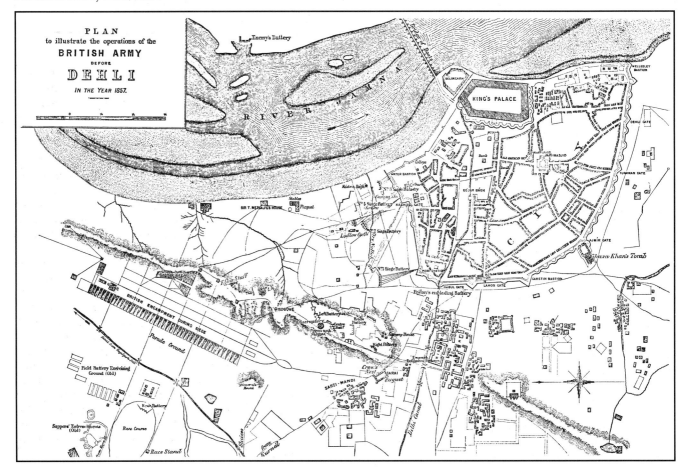

Hindoo Rao's house with a battery in front.

train arrived. General Barnard, with the backing of General Reed, the provincial commander-in-chief who had joined the force, resolved to maintain the position on the ridge.

The British dispositions are described in *The History of the Revolt in India*:

'The position taken up by the besiegers may be thus briefly described. The camp was pitched on the former parade-ground of the deserted encampment, at a spot about a mile and half from the northern wall of the city, with a rocky ridge acting as a screen between it and the city. This ridge was commanded by the rebels until the afternoon of the 8th; but from that time it was in the hands of the besiegers. The British line on this ridge rested on the left on an old tower used as a signal-post, often called the Flagstaff Tower; at its centre, upon an old mosque; and at its right, upon a house with enclosures strongly placed at the point where the ridge begins to slope down towards the plain. This house, formerly occupied by a Mahratta chief named Hindoo Rao, was generally known as Hindoo Rao's house. Owing to the ridge being very oblique in reference to the position of the city, the right of the line was of necessity thrown much forward, and hence Hindoo Rao's house became the most important post in the line. Near this house, owing to its commanding position, the British planted three batteries; and to protect these batteries, Rifles, Guides, and Sirmoor Goorkhas were posted within convenient distance. Luckily for the British, Hindoo Rao's house was "puckabuilt", that is, a substantial brick structure, and bore up well against the storm of shot aimed at it by the rebels.'

The defences of the city of Delhi facing them are detailed by William Cooke Stafford: 'little or nothing was known of the strength of the place. Its defences enclosed, before the work of destruction commenced, an area of three square miles. The fortifications consisted of a series of bastions, connected by long curtains, and the martello towers before-mentioned. The bastions rose sixteen feet from the ground; and the masonry was twelve feet thick. The curtains were also of masonry, and about the thickness and height of the bastion. Running round the base of the bastions and curtains was a berm or terrace, varying in width from fifteen to thirty feet, and having on its exterior edge a wall eight feet high, loopholed for musketry. That wall was a continuation of the escarp wall of the ditch, which was twenty feet deep, and twenty-five feet wide. The counterscarp was an earthern slope of easy incline; the glacis was about sixty yards wide, and covered scarcely half the walls. The river Jumna ran on the east side of the city; and on its banks stood the palace of the king, and the old fort of Selimghur. On each bastion eleven guns were mounted.'

James Grant gives details of the garrison of Delhi:

'One of the first measures of General Wilson was to discover the number and quality of the garrison there, and he reported it thus: – Bengal Native Infantry: 3rd, 9th, 11th, 12th, 15th, 20th, 28th; 29th, 30th, 36th, 38th, 44th, 45th, 54th, 57th, 60th; 61st, 67th, 68th, 72nd, 74th, and 78th; the 5th and 7th Gwalior Contingent, the Kotah Contingent, and Hurriana Battalion, with 2,600 other miscellaneous infantry. Native Cavalry: portions of five or six regiments, besides others of the Gwalior and Malwa Contingents. There arrived in the city mutinous regiments from sixteen different stations, all more or less stained with the crimes of murder and outrage, and estimated at 15,000 bayonets 12,000 of whom were veteran sepoys, with 4,000 cavalry, well horsed and disciplined. The artillery were numerous in proportion.' (The mutineers were deprived of a certain amount of ammunition and supplies by the blowing up of the main magazine in Delhi by Lieutenant Willoughby and other courageous officers and men, some of whom were able to escape the violent explosion, which occurred on 11 May – the day the mutineers entered the city.)

When General Wilson took over command, he and Brigadier Throwers were the only generals in perfect health; 101 officers had died in action, of wounds, and sunstroke, or were then on the list of sick or wounded. His total force at that time consisted of:

Infantry–		Officers and Men.
H.M. 8th foot, head-quarters,	..	198
H.M. 61st foot, head-quarters,	..	296
H.M. 75th foot, head-quarters,	..	513
H.M. 60th Rifles, head-quarters,	..	299
1st European Bengal Fusiliers,	..	520
2ds European Bengal Fusiliers,	..	556
Guide Infantry,	..	275
Sirmoor battalion, Goorkhas,	..	296
1st Punjaub Infantry,	..	725
4th Sikh Infantry,	..	345
	..	= 4,028

Cavalry –		
H.M. Carabiniers,	..	153
H.M. 9th Lancers,	..	428
Guide Cavalry,	..	338
1st Punjaub Cavalry,	..	148
2d Punjaub Cavalry,	..	110
5th Punjaub Cavalry (at Alipore)	..	116
		= 1,298

Artillery and Engineers –		
Artillery, European and Native,	..	1,129
Bengal Sappers and Miners,	..	209
Punjaub Sappers and Miners,	..	264
		= 1,602
		6,018

Besides these effectives, there were as non-effectives, 765 sick + 351 wounded = 1,116.

More besieged than besiegers, the small force clung doggedly to the ridge throughout June, July and August in the face of repeated attacks by the mutineers and rebels clustering around the shadowy representative of an extinct Mogul dynasty. In these numerous encounters the loss of the enemy was always greater than that of the British force, but being constantly reinforced, they could accept heavier casualties. A contemporary account tells of the manner of it all:

'The besieged, in every way stronger than the besiegers, continued their attacks on various sides of the heights. They gave annoyance, but at the same time excited contempt by the manner in which they avoided open hand-to-hand conflicts. An officer of engineers, commenting on this matter in a private letter, said: "At Delhi, they are five or six to one against us, and see the miserable attempts they make to turn us out of our position. They swam up the heights in front of our batteries by thousands; the ground is so broken and full of ravines and rocks, that they can come up the whole way unseen, or you may depend upon it they would never venture. If they had the pluck of a goose, their numbers might terrify us. It is in the Subzee Mundee that most of the hard fighting goes on; they get into and on the tops of the houses, and fire into our pickets there; this goes on until we send a force from camp to turn them out, which we invariably do, but not without loss. We have now cleared the ground all around of the trees, walls, and houses; as a consequence, there is a large clear space around our pickets, and Pandy will not venture out of cover; so we generally let him pop away from a distance until he is tired."'

The History of the Revolt in India describes the vicissitudes borne by the besiegers:

'In some of these numerous operations, when the rainy season commenced, the amount of fatigue borne by the troops was excessive. It was the special duty of the cavalry, not being immediately available for siege-services, to guard the rear of the camp from surprise; and to insure this result, they held themselves ready to "boot and saddle" at a few minutes' notice glad if they could insure only a few hours of sleep in the twenty-four. Many an officer, on picket or reconnoitring duty, would be in the saddle twelve hours together, in torrents of rain, without food or refreshment of any kind. Yet, with all their trials, they spoke and wrote cheerfully. An artillery-officer said: "Our position here is certainly by nature a wonderfully secure one; and if the Pandies could not have found a better place than Delhi as the headquarters of their mutiny, with an unlimited magazine at their disposal, I doubt if *we* could have been so well off anywhere else. Providence has assisted us in every way. From the beginning, the weather has been most propitious; and in cantonments I have never seen troops so healthy as they are here now. Cholera occasionally pays us a visit, but that must always be expected in a large standing camp. The river Jumna completely protects our left flank and front; while the large jheel (water-course) which runs away to the south-west is at this season quite impassable for miles, preventing any surprise on our right flank; so that a few cavalry are sufficient as a guard for three faces of our position" – that is, a few, if constantly on the alert,

Repelling a sepoy attack on the ridge at Delhi, 1857.

and never shirking a hard day's work in any weather.'

The British camp presented an assortment of nations, an officer writing from the ridge, described the picture it presented:

'What a sight our camp would be, even to those who visited Sebastopol! The long line of tents, the thatched hovels of the native servants, the rows of horses, the parks of artillery; the English soldier in his grey linen coat and trowsers (he has fought as bravely as ever without pipe-clay); the Sikhs, with their red and blue turbans; the Affghans, with their wild air, and their gay head-dresses and coloured saddle-cloths; and the little Ghoorkas, dressed up to the ugliness of demons, in black worsted Kilmarnock hats and woollen coats, the truest and bravest soldiers in our pay. There are scarcely any Porbeas (Hindoos) in our ranks, but of native servants many a score. In the rear are the booths of the native bazaars, and further out on the plain, the thousands of camels, bullocks, and horses, that carry our baggage. The soldiers are loitering through the lines, or in the bazaars. Suddenly the alarm is sounded, and every one rushes to his tent. The infantry soldier seizes his musket, and slings on his pouch; the artillerymen gets his guns harnessed; the Affghan rides out to explore; in a few minutes every one is in his place. If we go to the summit of the ridge of hills which separates us

from the city, we see the river winding along to the left, the bridge of boats, the towers of the palace, and the high roofs and minarets of the great mosque, the roofs and gardens of the doomed city, and the elegant-looking walls, with batteries here and there, the white smoke of which rises slowly up among the green foliage that clusters round the ramparts.'

Mid-August arrived with still no appearance of an impending assault on the city, nor was there any prospect of an effectual blockade by which the defenders might be starved into submission. At 1,500 yards from the walls, their batteries were too distant to achieve anything, the guns being too few and too light. Hearts were raised early in the month when General John Nicholson, preceding his movable column by a week, came into the camp 'to be welcomed with emotions of homage, as if he had been the very god of war!' A courageous soldier, intolerant of any of his officers who did not show his own high standards of bravery and leadership, his impetuous reactions were revealed in a magazine published in India: 'Seeing an English officer not so far forward in attack as he thought proper, our Irish paladin - who was over six feet two, and strong in proportion – caught the offender by the shoulders and literally kicked him into the hottest of the firing.'

His column, 4,200 strong, marched into camp on 14

Bengal sepoys (from the Illustrated London News, *22 August 1857).*

August, adding to Wilson's force:

'H.M.'s 52nd Light Infantry; H.M. 61st, one wing; No. 17 Field Battery; 2nd Punjaub Infantry; one wing 7th Punjaub Police; 4th Sikh Infantry; 250 Moultanee Horse, with guns, stores, and treasure. The 52nd, which Colonel Campbell had clothed in *karkee-rung*, native grey cloth, mustered 680 bayonets, but by the 14th of September, fever and cholera reduced the number to 240 of all ranks.' (*Historical Record of the 52nd Regiment*).

Meanwhile, the siege-train was moving slowly and ponderously on its way, its line of guns and limbers, carts and tumbrils, extending over 13 miles of the road from Ferozepore, and on 4 September it ground its way into the camp. Stafford tells that it consisted of: 'thirty-two pieces, 24 and 18-pounders, and 10 and 8-inch mortars and howitzers. By the 6th, more reinforcements of troops reached head-quarters, including detachments of artillery, of the 8th foot, and the 60th rifles; the 4th Punjab rifles, and a wing of the Beeloch battalion. Independent of 2,977 wounded and invalids in hospital, the number of "effective rank and file of all arms, artillery, sappers, cavalry, and infantry, and including lascars, drivers, newly-raised Sikh sappers and artillery, and recruits of Punjab corps, was 9,866. The strength of the British troops (the European corps being mere skeletons) was 580 artillery, 443 cavalry, and 2,294 infantry."'

The same writer describes the preparations made for the actual assault:

'Hitherto the British had been rather the besieged than the besiegers: but constant preparations had been carried on for taking the offensive part; and the engineers, assisted by some companies of Muzbee Sikhs, and a body of Coolies, had collected materials for, and made, 10,000 fascines, 10,000 gabions, and 100,000 sand-bags, besides scaling-ladders, and platforms. On the arrival of the siege-train, it was resolved that regular siege operations should be commenced; and ground may be said to have been first broken before Delhi on the 7th of September. In the night of that day, the first siege battery was commenced, and it was in two divisions; in one, four 24-pounders were directed against the Cashmere bastion, distant 850 yards; and in the other, five 18-pounders, and one 8-inch howitzer, were destined to demolish the Shah bastion, distant 200 yards. These guns were got into position by the morning of the 9th, when they opened a most destructive fire on the enemy's works. No. 2 battery was constructed in the night of the 10th, and opened its fire on the morning of the 11th, upon the curtain of the Cashmere bastion: and on the morning of the 12th, two more batteries, Nos. 3 and 4, came into play, the former being thrown up within 180 yards of the Water bastion. To arm these batteries, the heavy guns were withdrawn from the ridge, and added to the siege-train; and to work them, the horse artillery were united to the foot; and the carabiniers and 9th lancers furnished a quota of volunteers, "whose intelligence and good-will rendered their services most valuable". Some newly-raised Sikh artillerymen also took their share; and all did their work well; the "batteries opening fire with an efficiency and

vigour which excited the admiration of all who had the good fortune to witness it. Every object contemplated, was accomplished with a success even beyond expectation; and while there are many noble passages in the history of the Bengal artillery, none will be nobler than that which will tell of its work on this occasion."

'On the 13th two breaches near the Cashmere and Water bastions were reported. Lieutenants Medley and Lang, and Lieutenants Greathed and Home, examined them in the night, and, reporting them to be practicable, orders for an assault the next morning, at daybreak, were issued; and the arrangements for the storming were made. The force was divided into five columns; and the troops composing them, and the services to which they were destined, were as follows:–

'*1st Column.* – Brigadier-general Nicholson. Her majesty's 75th regiment, Lieutenant-colonel Herbert, 300 men; 1st Bengal fusiliers, Major Jacob, 250 men; and 2nd Punjab infantry, Captain Greer 450 men. – To storm the breach near the Cashmere bastion, and escalade the face of the bastion. – Engineer officers attached: Lieutenants Medley, Lang, and Bingham.

'*2nd Column.* – Brigadier Jones, C.B. Her majesty's 8th, Lieutenant-colonel Greathed, 250 men; 2nd fusiliers, Captain Boyd, 250 men; 4th Sikh infantry, Captain Rothney, 350 men. – To storm the breach in the Water bastion. – Engineer officers attached: Lieutenants Greathed, Hovenden, and Pemberton.

'*3rd Column.* – Colonel Campbell. Her majesty's 52nd, Major Vigors, 200 men; the Kumaon battalion, Captain Ramsay, 250 men; 1st Punjab infantry, Lieutenant Nicholson, 500 men. – To assault by the Cashmere gate, which was first to be blown open with powder-bags. – Engineers attached to this column: Lieutenants Home, Salkeld, and Tandy.

'*4th Column.* – Major Reed. The Sirmoor battalion, the Guide infantry, such pickets (European and native) as could be spared from the Hindoo Rao's ridge (860 men), and the Cashmere contingent, strength not known. – To attack the suburb Kissengunge, and enter the Lahore gate. – Engineer officers attached: Lieutenants Maunsell and Tennant.

'*5th Column.* – (The reserve), Brigadier Longfield. Her majesty's 61st, Lieutenant-colonel Deacon, 250 men; 4th Punjab infantry, Captain Wilde, 450 men; wing Beelooch battalion, Lieutenant-colonel Farquhar, 300 men; Jhind auxiliaries, Lieutenant-colonel Dunsford, 300 men. – Engineer officers attached: Lieutenants Ward and Thackeray.

'Two hundred of the 60th rifles, under Lieutenant-colonel Jones, were to cover the advance of the storming party, and then join the reserve.

'All these men were in their places at 4 a.m.; the head of columns 1, 2, and 3, being kept concealed till the moment for the actual assault arrived. The signal for the advance was to be the passing of the rifles, in skirmishing order, to the front. Then the explosion party was to blow in the Cashmere gate, and the assault was to commence.'

Blowing up the Cashmere Gate.

Grant tells of the epic blowing of the Cashmere Gate:
'It was a portal of vast strength, and a party of picked marksmen, stationed at a wicket, rendered all approach to it a matter of nearly certain death. This was the barrier to be forced by the Engineers, led by Lieutenants Home and Salkeld, with Sergeants Smith and Carmichael, and sappers carrying the powder-bags, which they laid against the gate. How they reached it alive seemed miraculous, as they had to clamber across a broken bridge in the clear light of a fine morning, under the eyes and rifles of the mutineers, who had long since lost all scruple about handling greased cartridges. As soon as the bags were laid, the party slid down into the ditch, to make way for the firing-party, led by the gallant Salkeld.

'The latter, according to the Engineers' Report, "while endeavouring to fire the charge, was shot through the arm and leg, but handed over the slowmatch to Corporal Burgess, who fell mortally wounded just as he had accomplished the onerous duty. Havildar Tilluk Sing, of the Sikhs, and Ramloll, sepoy of the same corps, were killed during this part of the operation. The demolition being most successful, Lieutenant Home, happily not wounded, caused the bugler (Hawthorn) to sound the regimental call, as a signal for the advancing columns. Fearing that amidst the noise of the assault the sound might not be heard, he had the call repeated three times."'

Stafford takes up the tale: 'the troops advanced, the gateway was stormed with a cheer, and triumphantly carried, the entire column entering the main-guard, where it re-formed, and clearing the Water bastion, St. James's church, and the "Gazette Press" compound, proceeded through the Cashmere-gate bazaar, and arrived within a hundred yards of the Jumma Musjid – the arches and gates of which had been bricked-up, and could not be forced without powder-bags of artillery. The houses in the vicinity were occupied by rebels, who poured an unintermitting fire upon the column, and Colonel Campbell retired to a large enclosure, called the Begum's Bagh, or garden, which he held for an hour and

Lieutenant Home of the Bengal Engineers.

a-half under a galling fire of both artillery and musketry. The Kumaon battalion, which had deviated from the other two corps, and held the Kotwallee for some time, then joined; and the column fell back on the church.'

The other columns advanced to their appointed places of attack, supported by a tremendous fire from the British batteries. Grant paints a colourful picture of the scene:

'In extended order, the Rifles opened a skirmishing fire, while the columns dashed on at the double quick, which speedily became a wild rush, Nicholson's first; but all suffered equally from the well-directed artillery and steady file-firing of the mutineers as they broke like a red blaze over tower and curtain wall. Seldom or never had assaulting troops such terrible impulses to inspire them as those of the four columns that hurled their strength at Delhi now; and no danger daunted, no obstacles remained unsurmounted by them; and if daring can win glory, then glory was won there.

'The breaches were entered, over stones, guns, corpses, and every ghastly *débris*, by both columns simultaneously, Nicholson leading.'

A letter from a participant printed in the *Lahore Chronicle* tells:

'Columns 1 and 2 made for the Cashmere and Water bastions; a perfect hail-storm of bullets met them from the front and both flanks, and officers and men fell fast on the crest of the glacis. For ten minutes it was impossible to get the ladders down into the ditch to ascend the escarp; but the determination of the British soldier carried all before it, and Pandy declined to meet the charge of the British bayonet. With a shout and a rush the breaches were both won, and the enemy fled in confusion.'

The 1st Column then re-formed and with great impetuosity swung rapidly to the right, carrying the batteries, the Cashmere and Moree bastions, clearing the way to the Kabul Gate. Pushing on along the Rampart Road, the column encountered heavy resistance and was checked by a deadly fire from two guns commanding the road, so narrow as to admit only four men abreast. Along this narrow lane, which led from Trevelgan Gunge, Nicholson led his men against the Lahore Gate, leading straight into the great thoroughfare of Chandnee Chowk.

James Grant describes what transpired:

'But that narrow lane was swept by concentrated grape and musketry – a veritable rain of death – and there the noble and enthusiastic young General [Nicholson] fell desperately wounded, adding grief to the fury that now filled his soldiers. Their efforts were fierce; but the lane was swept by bullets, as a tunnel by a fierce wind or a penetrating torrent.' The command now devolved upon Brigadier Jones who, aware that Nicholson's column had tried for nearly two hours to force the lane and finding the enemy in great force, 'prudently resolved on retaining the Cabul Gate . . . already won. Sandbags were thrown up for shelter, and the guns of the vanquished turned against the city, with such effect that their shot reached the Selinghur Fort and the Calcutta Gate, close by the Palace, whose cowering inmates now felt that Nemisis was at hand.' (Grant)

The Fourth Column's attack on the western suburbs failed, despite a gallant effort to carry the Kissengunge suburb and the Lahore Gate. The Cashmere contingent, overpowered by numbers and handled fiercely by the sepoys because of the contempt they held for foes of their own colour, were forced to fall back: 'it was not until after a dreadful conflict for possession of the Eedgah, that the Cashmerians, Sirmoor Ghoorkas, Guide infantry and European piquets gave way, the attack was abandoned and the column fell back on the camp.' (Grant). During this fighting, a party of Guide infantry were surrounded in an enclosure, but the wing of the Baluch battalion, detached from the reserve to support them, charged and dispersed the rebels, and led off the Guides.

James Grant writes of the final scenes of the capture of Delhi:

'Within the town we held all the captured posts, and when night closed over the sanguinary scene we had to enumerate (according to Marshman) a loss in killed and wounded of sixty-six officers and 1,104 men. The first and second columns held all the line of walls from the vicinity of the Cashmere Gate to the Cabul Gate; the

Major Hodson, Commandant of Hodson's Horse.

third column and the reserve held the Cashmere Gate, St. James's Church, Skinner's House, the Water Bastion, Ali Khan's House, the College Gardens, the Moora and Nusseer Bastions, the Killa Ghaut Gate, and many open spots in that part of Delhi. Next morning the bank and its extensive grounds were captured, and this enabled General Wilson to get his guns turned on the king's magnificent palace – a stately and royal castle indeed, but since June the scene of manifold crimes and cruelties. On the same day the Jumna Musjid, a splendid and enormous edifice built of red and white marble by Shah Jehan, was stormed, and the adjutant-general reported to Government the capture of 205 guns, with vast quantities of warlike stores.

'On the 17th, dawn came in upon both armies, eager still for battle and conquest, and a series of combats ensued which left all the northern defences almost entirely in our hands. On the 18th, Wilson hurled columns of attack against the southern portion of the city, capturing all the great buildings in succession; while the magazine supplied us with great mortars wherewith to shell the palace, and then the women and children began to fly, and with them the wounded were permitted to depart. On the 19th, the Burn Bastion was taken, and Hodson captured the cavalry camp. The palace was now attacked, and its gates were blown open, but save by the wounded and some Mohammedan fanatics, who died like tigers, fighting to the last, it was found deserted.'

The *Illustrated London News* of 21 November 1857

reprinted the report from the *Bombay Times* of the final death throes of Delhi:

'The Buree bastion, with six guns and one mortar, was captured on the morning of the 19th, without loss; and on the following morning the Lahore gate fell into our hands. The Ajmere gate and earthworks around it had ceased firing, and were supposed to be deserted. They were occupied immediately afterwards without opposition. A heavy mortar fire was meanwhile kept up uninterruptedly on the portion of the city still held by the enemy, and, as it appeared afterwards, with the most destructive effect. Post after post was carried in the course of the day, and by five p.m. on the evening of the 20th, the whole city, palace, and suburbs were in our possession. The enemy's camp still remained standing outside, but apparently empty. It was occupied next morning, when nearly the whole of their baggage was found to have been left behind them. The bridge of boats and the river were now under the command of our guns, so we had the power to prevent further escape in this direction, in which it had hitherto been made. A scene of carnage and desolation was presented by the guilty and devoted city. Women and children, rushing about in wild distraction everywhere were protected. The rebels had sown no mercy; they looked for and they met with none.'

'Delhi was now ours, but with the loss of 3,807 killed, wounded, and missing, nearly a half of the whole engaged; and in the palace of the Great Mogul, General Wilson (who here won a baronetcy) and the officers of his staff drained goblets of wine to the health of her Majesty as Empress of India, while a thousand triumphant voices shouted with fervour, "God save the Queen!"' (Grant)

Europeans	Killed	Wounded
Officers	46	140
Non-commissioned officers	50	113
Rank and file	476	1,313
Natives		
Officers	14	49
Non-commissioned officers	37	104
Rank and file	389	1,076
	1,012	2,795

There is no authentic knowledge of the number of insurgents who fell.

'LATEST FROM DELHI.

PALACE, DELHI, *Oct. 15.*

'The ex-King, who is living in a small house within the Palace walls, is to be brought to trial in a few days for aiding and abetting the mutineers. Living with him is his favourite wife, Zeenut Mahal, and her son, Jumma Bukht, a lad of about seventeen or eighteen years old. Two of the King's sons, the Princes Mirza Bucktwaur Shah and Mirza Mendhoo, were tried last week for aiding and abetting the mutineers. One of them had been appointed Colonel of the 11th Native Infantry, and the other of the 74th. They were tried by a military commission of five officers, with Brigadier-General Chamberlain as President. Evidence was produced before the Court, principally documentary, consisting of reports, returns, &c., bearing the prisoners' seals, showing that they exercised command of their regiments, and acted. In their defence they pleaded total ignorance.

'The Court, however, found the prisoners guilty, and sentenced them to death; and, accordingly, yesterday they were short by a party of the 60th Rifles. Detachments of Rifles, Artillery, Sappers, and Goorkahs were present, and a great number of spectators. The bodies were cast into the Jumna River.

'On the morning of the 21st, Captain Hodson, with a light flying detachment, went out in pursuit of the fugitives, when the King and Queen surrendered.

'On the morning of the 22nd, a strong party of cavalry, under Captain Hodson, surrounded the tomb of Homaioon, took prisoners Meerza Mogul, Mirza Khirza Sultan, the King's sons, and Mirza Aboo Buser, his grandson. The Royal scoundrels were known to have taken throughout the most active share in the rebellion; they were shot on the spot, and their bodies exposed to the public gaze.'

Illustrated London News

A grim but pertinent postscript can be found in *The History of the Revolt in India*:

'The official dispatches were nearly silent concerning the proceedings, except military, in the interval of six days between the first assault of the city and the final subjugation, and during the remaining ten days of September. General Wilson, shortly before the final attack was to be made, issued an address to his soldiers, from which it will be seen, they were instructed to give no quarter to the mutineers – that is, make no prisoners, but put all armed rebels to death. This was attended to; but something more was done, something darker and less justifiable. It is not customary for soldiers to stab wounded and sick men in an enemy's army; but such was done at Delhi. The sense of hatred towards the mutinous sepoys was so intense, the recollection of the atrocities at Cawnpore was so vivid, that vengeance took place of every other feeling. The troops did that which they would have scorned to do against the Russians in the Crimean war – they bayoneted men no longer capable of resistance. They refused to consider the rules of honourable warfare applicable to black-hearted traitors; their officers joined them in this refusal; and their general's address justified them up to a certain point. If the rule laid down by Wilson had been strictly adhered to, there would have been military precedence to sanction it; but the common soldiers did not discriminate in their passion; and many a dark-skinned inhabitant of Delhi fell under the bayonet.'

CAWNPORE

No events connected with the Mutiny excited so much horror and deep sympathy as the massacre in Cawnpore, capital city of the district of the same name

King of Delhi.

separated from Oude by the river Ganges, where General Hugh Wheeler with only 200 European soldiers opposed a strong brigade of the 1st, 53rd and 56th Bengal Native Infantry and the 2nd Cavalry, some 3,500 trained soldiers, backed by the rabble of the town. Wheeler's situation was made more distressing by the presence of some four or five hundred women, children and non-combatants. The mutineers were encouraged and led by a local potentate, the Nana Sahib of Bithoor, who had long been fomenting a spirit of rebellion among the troops.

'On the morning of the 5th of June the whole of the native troops mutinied, set fire to their lines, and marched to the treasury, where they were joined by the Nana's troops. £170,000 was packed on elephants or in carts, and they departed from Delhi; but, halting at the village of Nawabgunge, they were joined by the Nana, who put himself at their head; and as his object was not to revive a Mogul dynasty, but to raise a Mahratta throne for himself as Peishwa, he prevailed upon them to return and drive the Feringhees out of their entrenchment.' (Grant)

William Cooke Stafford states that:

'It appears to have been the original intention of the

The intrenchment at Cawnpore.

mutineers to have gone to Delhi; but Nana Sahib persuaded them to follow him. "You receive seven rupees from the British government," he said, "I will give you fourteen rupees; don't go to Delhi; stay here; and your name will be great. Kill all the English in Cawnpoor first, and I will give you each a golden bracelet." The rebels consented; and having made a native captain their commander, and he having promoted their sergeants and corporals to the rank of captains and lieutenants, the next morning they returned, and halted about two miles from the intrenchments. There Nana pitched his tent, and hoisted two standards – one to the honour of Mohammed, the other to the Hindoo deity; to which he ordered all the faithful to repair. He himself spent the greater part of the day in mounting some heavy guns, of which he had obtained possession, and in making preparations for the attack.

'From that day, till the 25th of June, the Europeans were beleaguered, and exposed to an almost constant bombardment. . . .

'The general was struck with his own insecurity, especially as the station occupied a dead level, and possessed no fort or place of refuge. Such a place it was necessary to provide; and Sir Hugh fixed upon the hospital barrack, in the centre of the grand parade, for the purpose. He intrenched this building, armed it with all the guns of the battery, removed there the ladies, their children and servants, and all the other females and children; and then prepared himself to act, on the first sound of alarm, as circumstances might demand. . . .

'It was totally unfitted to stand an investment of any duration, being completely commanded from various quarters, and, moreover, was simply a bank or breastwork. "The selection of such a place," it has been said, "was certainly a fatal error; and it is difficult to explain how an officer of so much experience and ability as Sir Hugh Wheeler could have fallen into it. He had a choice of other places. His entrenchment was at the south-east extremity of the cantonment, below the town of Cawnpore; whereas, at an equal distance above it, at the north-east extremity, stood the magazine, amply supplied with guns and military stores, and near it the treasury, which happened at that time to be well replenished. Ravines on one side, and the proximity of the river on the other, gave the magazine strong natural defences, while a high enclosing wall of masonry, with numerous substantial buildings, supplied at once the means of resistance and, what was equally wanted, adequate shelter. The only plausible account of the preference given to the entrenchment is that Sir Hugh, after having so long served with sepoys, clung to the belief that they would not mutiny at all, or would, at worst, after temporary outrage, quit the station, and hasten off to Delhi.'

'The whole number of persons crowded within the entrenchment amounted to more than 900. Of these not more than 200 were combatants, and 330 were women and children; but these numbers vary in the several accounts.

'Henry Lawrence, who had only 600 Europeans to control the entire province of Oude, sent a small detachment of the 32nd to Cawnpoor. About the end of May, another party of Europeans, partly belonging to the 84th, and partly to the Madras 1st fusiliers, arrived. Still, the force was most insignificant; and on the 31st, the general wrote to Calcutta describing his situation, and stating, that the utmost he could do would be to defend the intrenched hospital for two or three weeks, till reinforcements could arrive.'

Grant takes up the account: 'A position was taken up by the mutineers in front of the meagre entrenchment, which Sir Hugh Wheeler and his little band defended with the most heroic and romantic gallantry, hourly expecting help from whence no help could come. Various assaults were repelled at great cost to the mutineers, who at last cannonaded the place almost with impunity from twelve pieces of cannon, while Sir Hugh at times could only reply with one; hence the miseries of the besieged have seldom, if ever, been exceeded in the history of the world, while the dauntless courage and endurance they displayed have never been surpassed.'

William Cooke Stafford again:

'Captain John Moore, of the 32nd, who served at Moultan and Goojerat, wrote thus from Cawnpore on the 18th of June to Lawrence at Lucknow:– "Our troops, officers, and volunteers, have acted most nobly, and on several occasions a handful of men have driven hundreds before them. Our loss has been chiefly from the sun and their heavy guns. Our rations will last a fortnight, and we are well supplied with ammunition. Report says that troops are advancing from Allahabad, and any assistance might save our garrison. We are, of course, prepared to hold out to the last."

'Another letter, dated 24th June, after mentioning that the attack had been continued for eighteen days and nights without cessation, says, "The condition of misery experienced by all is utterly beyond description in this place. Death and mutilation in all forks have been daily before us. The numerical amount of casualties has been frightful, caused both by sickness and the implements of war."

'The effect may be conceived. The barracks were soon so perfectly riddled as to afford little or no shelter; and many made themselves retreats under the walls of the intrenchments, covered over with boxes, cots, &c. "In these, with their wives and children, they were secure from the shot and shell of the enemy, though not so from the effects of the heat; and the mortality from apoplexy was considerable. At night, however, every man had to take the watch in his turn." The women and children slept under the walls; and "the live shells kept them in perpetual dread; for nearly all night these shells were seen coming in the air, often doing mischief when they burst. Thus the existence of those who remained alive was spent in perpetual dread and fear." As time progressed, "the stench from the dead bodies of horses and other animals, that had been shot in the compound, and could not be removed, as also the unusually great influx of flies, rendered the place extremely disagreeable." So time went on – husbands dying from wounds, or lingering under their agony; wives sometimes receiving injuries from the flying missiles; and more, with their children, sinking from fatigue and anxiety; whilst food ran short, and there were no signs of relief. Amidst all, however, those who were blessed with health, and those who, though wounded or suffering from illness, could move about, bore up wonderfully. They annoyed the enemy all in their power; and so resolute was their fire, and so skilful their aim when any near approach was made, that the rebels never ventured upon an assault. But the individual and collective bravery and zeal were of little avail. It was impossible to escape; and every day the fate of the devoted garrison seemed to be approaching near a crisis.'

'On the 24th of June, an aged lady named Mrs. Greenway, who with her family had been taken prisoner, and only spared on the promise of paying a lac of rupees as a ransom, arrived at the intrenchment, bearer of a note from the Nana to the effect that all officers and soldiers who had nothing to do with Lord Dalhousie's government, would be sent in safety to Allahabad if they would lay down their arms. On this, provisions and conveyance would be amply furnished them. Sir Hugh Wheeler, ignorant of the fate of the Futtehghur fugitives, authorised Captain Moore to act in the matter as he should consider best; and on the following day a treaty was made, by which Sir Hugh, on the part of the British Government, agreed to give up all the money, stores, and guns in the intrenchment; the Nana, on his part, undertaking, and solemnly swearing "not only to allow all the inmates of the garrison to retire unmolested, but to provide means of conveyance for the wounded, and for the ladies and children." Hostilities at once ceased, and preparations for a departure were joyfully begun.

'On the morning of the 27th, the miserable remnant of the garrison, with the women and children, quitted the intrenchment, and were permitted quietly to embark in boats; but the river-bank was lined with sepoys, "and then was perpetrated one of the most diabolical acts of treachery and murder that the darkest page of human annals records."

'Acting for the Nana, Tantia Topee took his seat on a

platform and ordered a bugle to sound. Then two guns, that had been concealed, were run out, and opened with grape; while a fire of musketry was poured from both banks of the river. The thatch of some of the native boats was ignited by hot cinders; thus many of the sick, the wounded, and the helpless women were burned to death. The stronger women, many with children in their arms, sprang into the current, and were shot down in succession, or sabred by the troopers, who rode their horses into the stream. A number of both sexes, however, reached the shore, and then the Nana issued his orders that not a man should be permitted to live; but that the women and children should be taken to his residence.' (Grant)

'While the siege of Cawnpoor had been going on, the advance of reinforcements to the relief of the garrison had been arrested by the mutinies at Benares and Allahabad. These were put down, and order restored, by the prompt and effective measures of Colonel Neill; but before any troops could be dispatched, Brigadier-general Havelock arrived at Allahabad, having been sent by Lord Canning to take the command in the Cawnpoor and Oude districts, directly after his reaching Calcutta from Persia. He lost no time in advancing to Cawnpoor, not having more than 2,000 men under his command. With this small force he defeated the rebels on the 12th of July, about four miles from Futteypore (a town seventy miles north-west of Allahabad, and fifty south-east of Cawnpoor); and again on the 14th of July, at Aoung, a small village six miles from Futteypore, where they had intrenched themselves. There was a second engagement the same day, in which Major Renaud was killed; the total loss in both encounters, being twenty-five in killed and wounded. On the evening of the 15th, the detestable miscreant, Nana Sahib, hearing of these defeats, had all the prisoners, male and female, in his possession, barbarously murdered! His ruffians – apt villains to do his bidding – assaulted the English ladies confined, as already stated, in a brick building in his camp, "with every kind of weapon, from the bayonet to the butcher's knife, from the battle-axe to the club. They cut off their breasts, they lopped off their limbs, they beat them down with clubs, they trampled on them with their feet; their children they tossed upon bayonets: blood flowed like water; but they were not glutted, nor did they quit the building till they were satisfied that not a living soul remained behind them." Nana then, at the head of 7,000 men, prepared to oppose the advance of Brigadier Havelock into Cawnpoor.' (Stafford)

This engagement and what followed is described in the *Illustrated London News* of 11 September 1857:

'SUMMARY OF THE MUTINY IN INDIA. The news by this mail, if not of a cheering nature, is at any rate of a less dreary character than any received since the commencement of the mutiny. The tide has obviously turned; success is everywhere crowning the British arms, and the Reign of Justice has begun to supersede the Reign of Terror. For the following summary we are mainly indebted to the Bombay newspapers:

Major-General Sir Henry Havelock.

'GENERAL HAVELOCK'S SUCCESSES. The advance of General Havelock's column from Allahabad has been one series of victories. In our last we mentioned that General Havelock had reached Cawnpore, but we are unable to give details of its capture. The column marched from its encamping ground at daylight on the morning of the 16th July, and, after a thirteen miles journey, halted to breakfast within two miles of the enemy's position in front of Cawnpore. After resting three hours it advanced to the attack. General Havelock had with him 1,300 Europeans and about 7,000 or 8,000 Sikhs, against 13,000 mutinous sepoys armed and disciplined in every respect like his own soldiers, and commanded by the arch-fiend Nena Sahib in person.

'The following graphic account of the fight before Cawnpore is from an officer with General Havelock's force, dated July 17:

'"We marched on the 16th, and then learned that the enemy had come out from Cawnpore to make their last stand at the place where the grand trunk road forks to Cawnpore and Delhi; that they had there entrenched themselves in a very strong position, with heavy guns in front and flanks, to sweep the road; and that all the force, upwards of 4,000 men, had turned out to make their last stand. So it was determined to try and turn their flank. Accordingly we struck off the road at an angle, and then turned down towards them again. We

The charge of the Highlanders before Cawnpore, under General Havelock.

bivouacked under the trees, and started at 1½ p.m. The heat was fearful. Many men dropped from the effects of the sun. At last the enemy caught sight, and opened a very heavy and well-directed fire on us, which we had to pass till we got to the turning-point. Then we moved down in line upon them, and opened fire on their guns, which were in a very strong position in a village. We silenced two with our artillery, but all we could do we couldn't get at the third heavy gun, it was so well masked. The 78th were ordered to charge and take the gun. I never saw anything so fine. The men went on, with sloped arms, like a wall; till within a hundred yards not a shot was fired. At the word 'Charge,' they broke just like a eager pack of hounds, and the village was taken in an instant. I was up almost as soon as they, and one man told me, with a grin, he had just killed three men out of one house. The enemy were now in retreat, for we had turned their position; but the fight was still hard, for their cavalry came round down upon our rear, and the guns had to be halted and opened on them. After that we got so far forward towards Cawnpore that, without knowing it, one of their heavy guns in position was passed, and they managed to slew it round and open fire on our rear. So we had to turn, and go back and take it. This was done by the 64th. In fact, it was, in point of heavy fire and fatigue, a very hard fight; but the end was that we took eight guns in all, and utterly routed the enemy, who evacuated Cawnpore during the night, and blew up the arsenal and magazine. We bivouacked on the field, with little bed and supper, and marched into Cawnpore this morning." . . .

'On the evening of this engagement the column encamped outside the walls of Cawnpore, and on the morning of the 17th our soldiers entered the city.

'General Havelock's force, on the reoccupation of Cawnpore, had, in eight days, marched 126 miles, fought four actions with Nena Sahib's army against overwhelming odds in point of numbers, and taken twenty-four guns of light and heavy calibre – and that, too, in the month of July in India! On the morning of the 17th July the force marched into Cawnpore. The soul-harrowing spectacle which there presented itself to them beggars description. The extent of the frightful catastrophe now became known. A wholesale massacre had been perpretrated by the fiend Nena Sahib. 88 officers, 190 men of her Majesty's 84th Foot, 70 ladies, 120 women and children of her Majesty's 32nd Foot, and the whole European and Christian population of the place, including civilians, merchants, shopkeepers, engineers, pensioners and their families, to the number of about 400 persons, were the victims of this satanic deed. The courtyard in front of the Assembly Rooms, in which Nena Sahib had had his head quarters, and in which the women had been imprisoned, was swimming in blood.

The house in Nana Sahib's camp at Cawnpore in which the women and children were massacred on 15 July 1857.

The well at Cawnpore into which the bodies of the murdered women and children were thrown.

The scene of the massacres at Cawnpore.

'A large number of women and children, who had been "cruelly spared after the capitulation for a worse fate than instant death," had been barbarously slaughtered on the previous morning – the former having been stripped naked, beheaded, and thrown into a well; the latter having been hurled down alive upon their butchered mothers, whose blood yet reeked on their mangled bodies. We hear of only four who escaped – a Mrs. Greenway, wife of a merchant, and three Indo-Britons. The diary of a lady is said to have been found at Cawnpore, written up to the day on which she was killed and containing information of great importance, on which the General is acting. We shall eventually obtain full particulars of the horrible tragedy that has been witnessed there.'

Once within the city, officers went out in search of survivors, and were horrified to come upon the charnel-house where the massacre of the 15th had been committed. William Cooke Stafford describes the scene:

'It was a flat-roofed building containing two rooms, with a courtyard between, in the manner of native houses. The floor of the inner room was found two inches deep in blood; it came over the men's shoes as they stepped. Ladies' hair, back-combs, parts of religious books, children's shoes, hats, bonnets, lay scattered about the room; there were marks of sword-cuts on the walls low down, as if the women had been struck at as they crouched. From the well at the back of the house, the naked bodies, limb separated from limb, protruded out. It was a sight sickening, heartrending, maddening. It had a terrible effect on our soldiers; and those who had glanced upon death in every form, could not look down that well a second time. Christian men, who had hitherto spared a flying foe, came out, bearing a portion of a dress, or some such relic in their hands, and declaring that, whenever they might feel disposed for mercy, they would look upon *that*, and steel their hearts.'

In an issue of the *Illustrated London News* dated 11 November 1857, it was reported:

'The following has been communicated to the *Poonah Observer*: -

'By recent letters received from Brigadier Havelock's force, it appears that, on the arrival of the detachment of the 78th Highlanders at that "place of skulls." Cawnpore, after the massacre of our countrymen, women, and children, they by some means or other found the remains of one of General Wheeler's daughters. The sight was horrible, and aroused them to that pitch that, gathering around, they removed the hair from off the poor girl's head, a portion of which was

THE WELL AT CAWNPORE.

SACRED TO THE PERPETUAL MEMORY OF
A GREAT COMPANY OF CHRISTIAN PEOPLE,
(TWO HUNDRED AND EIGHT), CHIEFLY WOMEN AND CHILDREN,
WHO NEAR THIS SPOT WERE CRUELLY MASSACRED BY THE FOLLOWERS,
AND BY ORDER, OF THE REBEL NANA DHUNDER-PANT, OF BYTHOOR,
AND CAST (THE DYING WITH THE DEAD) INTO THE WELL BELOW,
ON THE 15TH JULY, 1857.

The memorial at the well at Cawnpore.

carefully selected and sent home to her surviving friends. The remainder they equally divided among themselves; and, on each man receiving his carefully served out portion, they all quietly and very patiently applied themselves to the tedious task of counting out the numbers of hairs contained in each individual's lot; and when this task was accomplished, they one and all swore more solemnly by Heaven and the God that made them, that for as many hairs as they held in their fingers, so many of the cruel and treacherous mutineers should die by their hands – an oath that they will no doubt most religiously keep. . . .

'Cawnpore was reoccupied on the 17th. The Nana Sahib fled from Bithor, which was taken possession of by the troops, his palace burnt, and magazine blown up; 13 guns were taken, and a number of animals. Brigadier-General Havelock's force effected the passage of the river by the 28th, having met with great difficulty on account of the want of boats. Brigadier-General Neill was left in command at Cawnpore, with a small force of 300 Europeans and some guns, and he had re-established the British authority in the city and the bazaar, and the neighbourhood was tranquil. General Havelock marched on the morning of the 29th, met the enemy at Oonou, defeated them, and took 3 guns. After resting he proceeded on, when the enemy advanced to meet him: an action took place, which resulted in the total defeat of the enemy, with the loss of 12 more guns. Brigadier-General Havelock proceeded on to Busheergunge, where he again met with opposition; but he took the place, driving out the enemy, and took four more guns – in all 19 guns.'

In another part of the journal were more details of Havelock's advance: 'LUCKNOW. – The column under Brigadier-General Havelock, which had advanced to the relief of Lucknow, as far as Busheergunge, was in consequence of the amount of sickness, cholera having broken out severely, obliged to fall back four miles, to enable the sick to be sent back to Cawnpore. Lucknow, by the last accounts, was holding out.'

LUCKNOW

'There were events that made a deeper impression on the minds of the English public; military exploits more grand and comprehensive; episodes more fatal, more harrowing; trains of operation in which well-known heroic names more frequently found place – but there was nothing in the whole history of the Indian mutiny more admirable or worthy of study than the defence of Lucknow by Brigadier Inglis and the British who were shut up with him in the Residency. Such a triumph over difficulties had not often been placed upon record. Nothing but the most resolute determination, the most complete soldierly obedience, the most untiring watchfulness, the most gentle care of those who from sex or age were unable to defend themselves, the most thorough reliance on himself and on those around him, could have enabled that gallant man to bear up against the overwhelming difficulties which pressed upon him

Sir Henry Lawrence.

throughout the months of July, August, and September. He occupied one corner of an enormous city, every other part of which was swarming with deadly enemies. No companion could leave him, without danger of instant death at the hands of the rebel sepoys and the Lucknow rabble; no friends could succour him, seeing that anything less than a considerable military force would have been cut off ere it reached the gates of the Residency; no food or drink, no medicines or comforts, no clothing, no ammunition, in addition to that which was actually within the place at the beginning of July, could be brought in. Great beyond expression were the responsibilities and anxieties of one placed in command during eighty-seven of such days – but there was also a moral grandeur in the situation, never to be forgotten.' (*History of the Revolt in India*)

As soon as he heard of the outbreaks in mid-May, Sir Henry Lawrence had taken steps to prepare Lucknow for emergencies, and after a flare up on 30 May, his small force capably resisted all rebel actions throughout the month of June. William Cooke Stafford sets the scene:

'Lucknow, the capital of Oude, is situated on the right, or south-west side of the Ghoomtee, distant 610 miles from Calcutta, 128 from Allahabad, and 53 from Cawnpoor. All the principal buildings of the city, and

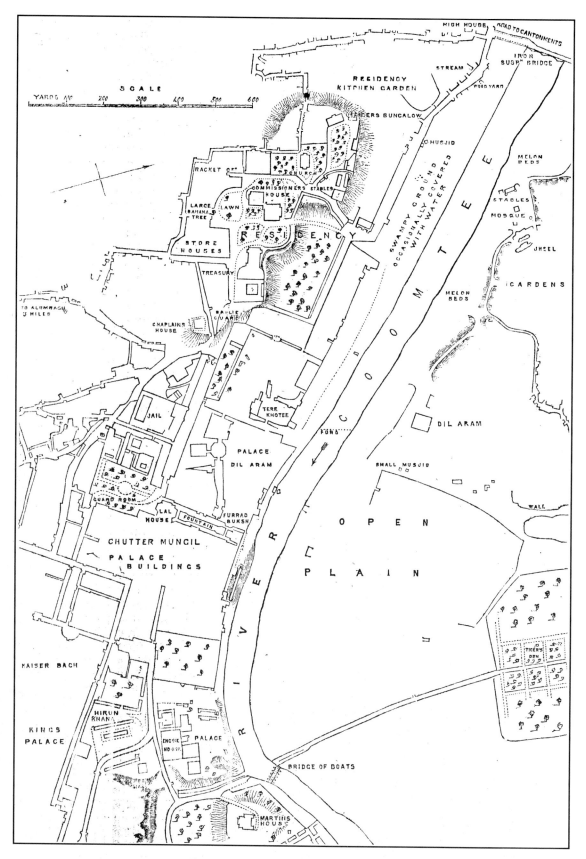

Plan of the residency and part of the city of Lucknow.

he British residency, were on the river's bank. The latter was a large inclosure, situated on higher ground than he rest of the town, which it may be said to have commanded. It contained the house of the resident, hose of the civil and military officers attached, all the necessary out-buildings, and many vaults, running underground to a considerable extent. To the west, between 800 and 900 yards from the residency, was a strong turreted, castellated fort, called the Muchee Bawn. The city lies to the south of the residency; and the cantonments on the other side of the Ghoomtee, to the north-east. Four miles from the residency, on the Cawnpoor road, is the Alumbagh, formerly a winter palace of the king of Oude, now a strongly-fortified post.'

This is an exact list of those who took up their quarters within the residency on 30 May, when the symptoms of mutiny rendered it no longer safe for the women and children to remain in the city or at the cantonment:

General staff,	9
Brigade staff,	5
Artillery,	9
Engineers,	3
H.M. 32nd foot,	22
H.M. 84th foot,	2
7th Bengal native cavalry,	13
13th Bengal native infantry,	10
41st Bengal native infantry,	11
48th Bengal native infantry,	14
71st Bengal native infantry,	11
Oude brigade,	26
Various officers,	9
Civil service,	9
Surgeons,	2
Chaplains,	2
Ladies,	69
Ladies, children of,	68
Other women,	171
Other women, children of,	196
Uncovenanted servants,	125
Martinière school,	8
	794

This list is taken from *The History of the Revolt in India*, as is the accompanying text:

'When the whole of the Europeans, officers and privates, had been hastily driven by the mutiny from the cantonment to the Residency; when all the native troops who remained faithful had been in like manner removed to the same place; and when the Muchee Bhowan and all the other buildings in Lucknow had been abandoned

Group of sepoys at Lucknow, from the Illustrated London News, *13 October 1857.*

by the British and their adherents – the intrenched position at and around the Residency became necessarily the home of a very much larger number of persons; comprising, in addition to the eight hundred or so just adverted to, many hundred British soldiers, and such of the sepoys as remained "true to their salt".'

On 29 June intelligence was received that about 600 rebels were in the area, and a force was sent out to intercept them. It was formed of 250 men of the 32nd Regiment, 100 Sikh cavalry; 35 Volunteer Horse, a party of Carnegie's native infantry, with an 8-inch howitzer, and 10 field-pieces drawn by elephants and horses and manned by native gunners. Sir Henry Lawrence took personal command. The outcome of the ensuing action is detailed in Brigadier Inglis's Account of the Siege of Lucknow, which was published in an Official Gazette Extraordinary:

'The troops, misled by the reports of wayfarers, who stated there were few or no men between Lucknow and Chinhut, proceeded somewhat farther than had been originally intended, and suddenly fell in with the enemy, who had up to that time eluded the vigilance of the advanced guard by concealing themselves behind a long line of trees in overwhelming numbers. The European force and howitzer, with the Native Infantry, held the foe in check for some time, and had the six guns of the Oude Artillery been faithful, and the Sikh Cavalry shown a better front, the day would have been won in spite of an immense disparity in numbers. But the Oude artillerymen and drivers were traitors. They overturned the guns into ditches, cut the traces of their horses, and abandoned them, regardless of the remonstrances and exertions of their own officers, of those of Sir Henry Lawrence's staff, headed by the Brigadier-General in person, who himself drew his sword upon these rebels. Every effort to induce them to stand having proved ineffectual, the force exposed to a vastly superior fire of artillery, and completely out-flanked on both sides by an overwhelming body of infantry and cavalry, which actually got into our rear, was compelled to retire with the loss of three pieces of artillery, which fell into the hands of the enemy in consequence of the rank treachery of the Oude gunners, and with a very grievous list of killed and wounded. The heat was dreadful, the gun ammunition was expended, and the almost total want of cavalry to protect our rear made our retreat most disastrous. All the officers behaved well, and the exertions of the small body of volunteer cavalry – only forty in number – under Captain Radcliffe, 7th Light Cavalry, were most praiseworthy.

'It remains to report the siege operations.

'It will be in the recollection of his Lordship in Council that it was the original intention of Sir Henry Lawrence to occupy not only the Residency but also the fort called Muchhee Bhowan, an old dilapidated edifice, which had been hastily repaired for the occasion, though the defences were even at the last moment very far from complete, and were moreover commanded by many houses in the city.

'The untoward event to the 30th June so far diminished the whole available force, that we had not a sufficient number of men remaining to occupy both positions. The Brigadier-General, therefore, on the evening of the 1st of July, signalled to the garrison of the Muchhee Bhowun to evacuate and blow up that fortress in the course of the night. The orders were ably carried out, and at twelve p.m. the force marched into the Residency with their guns and treasure, without the loss of a man; and shortly afterwards the explosion of 240 barrels of gunpowder and 6,000,000 bail cartridges, which were lying in the magazine, announced to Sir Henry Lawrence and his officers who were anxiously waiting the report, the complete destruction of that post and all that it contained. If it had not been for this wise and strategic measure, no member of the Lucknow garrison, in all probability, would have survived to tell the tale; for, as had been already stated, the Muchhee Bhowun was commanded from other parts of the town, and was moreover indifferently provided with heavy artillery ammunition, while the difficulty, suffering, and loss which the Residency garrison, even with the reinforcement thus obtained from the Muchhee Bhowun, has undergone in holding the position, is sufficient to show that, if the original intention of holding both posts had been adhered to, both would have inevitably fallen.

'It is now my very painful duty to relate the calamity which befel us at the commencement of the siege. On the 1st July an 8-inch shell burst in the room in the Residency in which Sir H. Lawrence was sitting. The missile burst between him and Mr Couper, close to both; but without injury to either. The whole of his staff implored Sir Henry to take up other quarters, as the Residency had then become the special target for the round shot and shell of the enemy. This, however, he jestingly declined to do, observing that another shell would certainly never be pitched into that small room. But Providence had ordained otherwise, for on the very next day he was mortally wounded by the fragment of another shell which burst in the same room, exactly at the same spot.

'When the blockade was commenced only two of our batteries were completed; part of the defences were yet in an unfinished condition, and the buildings in the immediate vicinity, which gave cover to the enemy, were only very partially cleared away. Indeed, our heaviest losses have been caused by the fire from the enemy's sharpshooters, stationed in the adjoining mosques and houses of the native nobility, the necessity of destroying which had been repeatedly drawn to the attention of Sir Henry by the staff of engineers. But his invariable reply was – "Spare the holy places, and private property too, as far as possible." And we have consequently suffered severely from our very tenderness to the religious prejudices, and respect to the right of our rebellious citizens and soldiery. As soon as the enemy had thoroughly completed the investment of the Residency they occupied these houses, some of which were within easy pistol-shot of our barricades, in

Defenders of Lucknow under fire from close-range rebel artillery.

General Sir Henry Havelock, KCB ('the Christian Soldier').

immense force, and rapidly made loopholes on those sides which bore on our post, from which they kept up a terrific and incessant fire, day and night, which caused many daily casualties, as there could not have been less than 8,000 men firing at one time into our position. Moreover, there was no place in the whole of our works that could be considered safe, for several of the sick and wounded, who were lying in the banqueting-hall, which had been turned into a hospital, were killed in the very centre of the building. . . . Neither were the enemy idle in erecting batteries. They soon had from twenty to twenty-five guns in position, some of them of very large calibre. These were planted all round our post at small distances, some being actually within fifty yards of our defences, but in places where our own heavy guns could not reply to them, while the perseverance and ingenuity of the enemy in erecting barricades in front of and around their guns in a very short time, rendered all attempts to silence them by musketry entirely unavailing. Neither could they be effectually silenced by shells, by reason of their extreme proximity to our position, and because, moreover, the enemy had recourse to digging very narrow trenches, about eight feet in depth, in rear of each gun, in which the men lay while our shells were flying, and which so effectually concealed them, even while working the gun, that our baffled sharpshooters could only see their heads while in the act of loading.

'The enemy contented themselves with keeping up this incessant fire of cannon and musketry until the 20th of July, on which day, at ten a.m., they assembled in very great force all around our position, and exploded a heavy mine inside our outer line of defences at the Water Gate. The mine, however, which was close to the Redan, and apparently sprung with the intention of destroying that battery, did no harm. But as soon as the smoke had cleared away, the enemy boldly advanced under cover of a tremendous fire of cannon and musketry, with the object of storming the Redan. But they were received with such a heavy fire, that after a short struggle they fell back with much loss. A strong column advanced at the same time to attack Innes' post, and came on to within ten yards of the pallisades, affording to Lieut. Loughnan, 13th N.I., who commanded the position, and his brave garrison, composed of gentlemen of the uncovenanted service, a few of her Majesty's 32nd Foot, and of the 13th N.I., an opportunity of distinguishing themselves, which they were not slow to avail themselves of, and the enemy were driven back with great slaughter. The insurgents made minor attacks at almost every outpost, but were invariably defeated, and at two p.m. they ceased their attempts to storm the place, although their musketry fire and cannonading continued to harass us unceasingly as usual.

'Matters proceeded in this manner until the 10th August, when the enemy made another assault, having previously sprung a mine close to the brigade mess, which entirely destroyed our defences for the space of twenty feet, and blew in a great portion of the outside wall of the house occupied by Mr Schilling's garrison.

On the dust clearing away, a breach appeared, through which a regiment could have advanced in perfect order, and a few of the enemy came on with the utmost determination, but were met with such a withering flank fire of musketry from the officers and men holding the top of the brigade mess, that they beat a speedy retreat, leaving the more adventurous of their numbers lying on the crest of the breach.'

Havelock's relief column fought their way into Lucknow on 25 September. The *Illustrated London News* of 21 November reported that and subsequent events:

'RELIEF OF LUCKNOW. General Havelock commenced crossing the Ganges at Cawnpore on the 19th September, and he completed that operation on the 20th. He had been previously joined by Sir James Outram, his senior; but that officer, influenced by a feeling of delicacy, declined to assume the command, or in any way to interfere with General Havelock's arrangements. He expressed, however, his intention of accompanying the force as a volunteer, and in that capacity attached himself to the Volunteer Cavalry.

'General Outram, on joining Brigadier-General Havelock's force, just previous to starting for Lucknow, issued an Order concluding thus:–

'The Major-General, in gratitude for, and admiration of, the brilliant deeds of arms achieved by General

Sir James Outram.

Major Vincent Eyre.

Havelock and his gallant troops, will cheerfully waive his rank on the occasion, and will accompany the force to Lucknow in his civil capacity as Chief Commissioner of Oude, and tendering his military services to General Havelock as a volunteer. On the relief of Lucknow the Major-General will resume his position at the head of the forces.

'The following order was issued on the same evening by General Havelock to the force about to proceed to the relief of the garrison at Lucknow:–

'Brigadier-General Havelock, in making known to the column the kind and generous determination of General Sir James Outram, K.C.B., to leave to him the task of relieving Lucknow, and rescuing its gallant and enduring garrison, has only to express his hope that the troops will strive, by their exemplary and gallant conduct in the field, to justify the confidence thus reposed in them.

'The heavy guns and baggage attached to the force were crossed over on the 20th, and on the 21st the General prepared to attack the enemy, entrenched a little beyond the old post of Oonae. He had with him about 2,500 men of all arms – a force which he divided into three brigades, two of infantry under Brigadiers Neill and Campbell, and one of artillery under Vincent Eyre. The Volunteer Cavalry, about 150 in number, nominally under the command of Major Barrow, were actually led by Sir James Outram. The attack was made on the enemy's front, whilst his right was turned: he

very soon fled in confusion, abandoning four guns. The rout was completed by a gallant charge led by Sir James Outram, in which 150 of the enemy were sabred. General Havelock did not allow his force an instant's rest, but pushed on in pursuit of the enemy, marching twenty miles after defeating them on the 21st, and fourteen on the following day, the enemy abandoning their guns and wounded in their flight. On the 25th he came up to the enemy, strongly posted within five miles of Lucknow, in number about 14,000; their position seemed impregnable, but Havelock went at it at once, and, after a desperate engagement, our troops, to the cry "Remember Cawnpore!" carried it. Our loss was severe, numbering 400 men, amongst whom, deeply regretted by all, was the gallant General Neill; Major Cooper, of the Artillery; Lieutenant Webster, 78th Foot; Lieut. Pakenham, 84th; Lieut. Bateman, 64th; and Lieut. Warren, 12th Irregular Cavalry.

'That Lucknow was relieved at all is due to the vigour and promptitude with which Havelock followed up his first success, and improved every advantage. A fact which shows in a strong light the indomitable pluck and courage of the English soldier may here be noted. No sooner had the rebels received information that Havelock was again crossing the Ganges than they determined to make a tremendous effort to overpower the garrison. They detached a large body to oppose Havelock near Oonao, and with the remainder of the force attacked our people. They were on the verge of success; some of them were actually penetrating into the entrenchment, when a sudden inspiration seized our men; there were plenty of shells, but no mortars; our men, reckless of life, and resolved to conquer or perish, seized the shells, lighted the fuses, and taking them in their hands hurled them with all their force at the enemy. It is not easy to conquer men who would dare such an action as this. So at least the enemy thought; they fell back awed and cowed, and did not resume the attack that day. Upon Havelock reaching the entrenchment it was found that two mines had been dug underneath it, both ready for the reception of powder. Another days' delay, and the fate of our garrison would have been sealed.'

The Bombay Gazette of 17 October, quoted in the *Illustrated London News*, reported:

'We have yet but vague and imperfect accounts from Lucknow, and are waiting further particulars with great anxiety. There is a report, strongly requiring confirmation, which we trust it may not receive, that the place is again besieged, our force having been surrounded by Nana Sahib with fifty thousand men. It has, on the other hand, been stated that the arch-ruffian of Bithoor has been betrayed by one of his own followers, and is now a captive; but this report also needs confirmation.'

Unfortunately, the report was correct: Lucknow was still under siege, confirmed by General Outram's report in the *Illustrated London News* of 21 November 1857:

'General Outram telegraphed on the 2nd inst. to Calcutta that the insurgents were too strong to admit to withdrawal from Lucknow. The sick and wounded, women and children, numbered more than 1,000. After making disposition for the safety of the garrison, General Outram proposes to retire on Cawnpore. He adds that two additional brigades, with powerful field artillery, will be required to withdraw the garrison or reduce the city.'

The following summary of events comes from the *Overland Bombay Times* of 2 November, again quoted in the *Illustrated London News*:

'The force at Lucknow, believed, when they left Cawnpore, to be too weak to maintain themselves at the capital, and intended to have rescued and brought back the inmates of the Residency, have been able to maintain their position, without material loss, since the 29th of September. They were expected to be reinforced about the 24th by her Majesty's 53rd and 93rd Regiments, and about the 30th by the whole of Colonel Greathed's column, pursuing its career of victory from Delhi, and so raised to the strength of some 7,000.

'Colonel Greathed obtained a brilliant victory over the rebels, of whom 2,000 were slain, at Agra, on the 10th of October. Moving his way downward to join Havelock.'

Appointed Commander-in-Chief, Sir Colin Campbell had remained in Calcutta for some weeks. According to Grant:

'He was called upon to remodel the whole military machinery, and to arrange with the Governor-General the system of strategy which would be the most desirable under the actual state of affairs. [At last,] learning that the intended retreat of the original garrison at Lucknow had been abandoned as impracticable, now hastened to place himself at the head of a force more adequate than that which had marched under Havelock and Outram and, fortunately, means were not wanting. From Europe, reinforcements had been pouring into India, and, in addition to these there was . . . the Naval Brigade under Captain Peel.'

No better account can be given than that provided by Campbell's official despatch:

'THE RELIEF OF LUCKNOW.
From His Excellency the Commander-in Chief to the Right Honourable the Governor-General.
HEAD-QUARTERS, SHAH NUJJEEF,
LUCKNOW, *Nov. 18, 1857.*

'My Lord, – I have the honour to apprise your Lordship that I left Cawnpore on the 9th November, and joined the troops under the command of Brigadier-General Hope Grant, C.B., the same day, at Camp Buntara, about six miles from Alumbagh.

'There being a few detachments on the road, I deemed it expedient to wait till the 12th before commencing my advance.

'On the day I marched early for Alumbagh.

'The advanced guard was attacked by two guns and a body of about 2,000 infantry. After a smart skirmish the guns were taken; Lieut. Gough, commanding Hodson's

Sir Colin Campbell who later became Lord Clyde.

Irregular Horse, having distinguished himself very much in a brilliant charge by which this object was effected.

'The camp was pitched on that evening at Alumbagh. This place I found to be annoyed to a certain extent by guns placed in different positions in the neighbourhood.

'I caused the post to be cleared of lumber and cattle, and placed all my tents in it.

'I made my arrangements for marching without baggage when I should reach the park of Dilkoosha, and the men were directed to have three days' food in their haversacks. I changed the garrison at Alumbagh, taking fresh men from it, and leaving her Majesty's 75th Regiment there, which had been so much harassed by its late exertions.

'On the 14th, I expected a further reinforcement of 600 of 700 men, who joined my rear guard after my march had commenced in the morning of that day.

'As I approached the park of Dilkoosha, the leading troops were met by a long line of musketry fire.

'The advance guard was quickly reinforced by a field battery and more infantry, composed of companies of her Majesty's 5th, 64th, and 78th Foot, under the

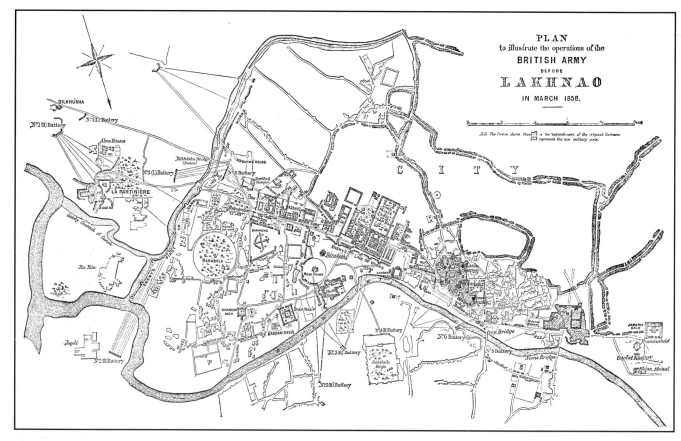

Plan to illustrate the operation of the British Army before Lucknow in March 1858.

command of Lieut.-Col. Hamilton, her Majesty's 78th Highlanders, supported by the 8th Foot. After a running fight of about two hours, in which our loss was very inconsiderable, the enemy was driven down the hill to the Martinière, across the garden and park of the Martinière, and far beyond the canal. His loss was trifling, owing to the suddenness of the retreat.

'The Dilkoosha and Martinière were both occupied Brigadier Hope's brigade being then brought up and arranged in position in the wood of the Martinère at the end and opposite the canal, being flanked to the left by Captain Bourchier's field battery and two of Captain Peel's heavy guns.

'Shortly after these arrangements had been made the enemy drew out a good many people and attacked our position in front. He was quickly driven off, some of our troops crossing the canal in pursuit. On this occasion the 53rd, 93rd, and a body of the 4th Punjaub Sikhs, distinguished themselves.

'With the exception of my tents, all my heavy baggage, including provisions for fourteen days for my own force and that in Lucknow, accompanied me on my march across country to Dilkoosha, covered by a strong rearguard under Lieutenant-Colonel Ewart, of her Majesty's 93rd Highlanders. This officer distinguished himself very much in this difficult command, his artillery, under Captain Blunt, Bengal Horse Artillery,

assisted by the Royal Artillery, under Colonel Crawford, R.A., having been in action for the greater part of the day. The rearguard did not close up to the column until late next day, the enemy having hung on it until dark on the 14th. Every description of baggage having been left at Dilkoosha, which was occupied by her Majesty's 8th Regiment, I advanced direct on Secunderbagh early on the 16th. This place is a high-walled inclosure of strong masonry of 120 yards square, and was carefully loopholed all round. It was held very strongly by the enemy. Opposite to it was a village at a distance of a hundred yards, which was also loopholed and filled with men.

'On the head of the column advancing up the lane to the left of the Secunderbagh, fire was opened on us. The infantry of the advance guard was quickly thrown in skirmishing order, to line a bank to the right. The guns were pushed rapidly onwards, viz., Captain Blunt's troop, Bengal Horse Artillery, and Captain Traver's, Royal Artillery, heavy field battery. The troop passed at a gallop through a cross-fire from the village and Secunderbagh, and opened fire within easy musketry range in a most daring number. As soon as they could be pushed up a stiff bank, two 18-pounder guns, under Captain Travers, were also brought to bear on the building. Whilst this was being effected, the leading brigade of infantry, under Brigadier the Hon. Adrian Hope, coming rapidly into action, caused the loopholed village

138

to be abandoned; the whole fire of the brigade being then directed on the Secunderbagh. After a time a large body of the enemy, who were holding ground on the left of our advance, were driven in by parties of the 53rd and 93rd, two of Captain Blunt's guns aiding the movement. The Highlanders pursued their advantage and seized the barracks, and immediately converted them into a military post, the 53rd stretching in a long line of skirmishers in the open plain, and driving the enemy before them.

'The attack on Secunderbagh had now been proceeding for about an hour and half, when it was determined to take the place by storm through a small opening which had been made. This was done in the most brilliant manner by the remainder of the Highlanders and the 53rd and the 4th Punjaub Infantry, supported by a battalion of detachments under Major Barnston. There never was a bolder feat of arms, and the loss inflicted on the enemy, after the entrance of the Secunderbagh was effected, was immense – more than 2,000 of the enemy were afterwards carried out. The officers who led these regiments were Lieutenant-Colonel Leith Hay, her Majesty's 93rd Highlanders; Lieutenant-Colonel Gordon, her Majesty's 93rd Highlanders; Captain Walton, her Majesty's 53rd Foot; Lieutenant Paul, 4th Punjaub Infantry (since dead); and Major Barnston, her Majesty's 90th Foot.

'Captain Peel's Royal Naval Siege Train then went to the front and advanced towards the Shah Nujjeef, together with the field battery and some mortars, the village to the left having been cleared by Brigadier Hope and Lieutenant-Colonel Gordon.

'The Shah Nujjeef is a domed mosque with a garden, of which the most had been made by the enemy. The wall of the inclosure of the mosque was loopholed with great care. The entrance to it had been covered by a regular work in masonry, and the top of the building was crowned with a parapet. From this, and from the defences in the garden, an unceasing fire of musketry was kept up from the commencement of the attack. This position was defended with great resolution against a heavy cannonade of three hours. It was then stormed in the boldest manner by the 93rd Highlanders, under Brigadier Hope, supported by a battalion of detachments under Major Barnston, who was, I regret to say, severely wounded; Captain Peel leading up his heavy guns with extraordinary gallantry within a few yards of the building, to batter the massive stone walls. The withering fire of the Highlanders effectually covered the Naval Brigade from great loss, but it was an action almost unexampled in war. Captain Peel behaved very much as if he had been laying the *Shannon* alongside an enemy's frigate. This brought the day's operations to a close.

'On the next day communications were opened, to the left rear of the barracks, to the canal, after overcoming considerable difficulty. Capt. Peel kept up a steady cannonade on the building called the mess-house. This building, of considerable size, was defended by a ditch

Captain Peel.

about twelve feet broad and scarped with masonry, and beyond that a loopholed mud wall. I determined to use the guns as much as possible in taking it. About three p.m., when it was considered that men might be sent to storm it without much risk, it was taken by a company of the 90th Foot, under Captain Wolseley, and a picket of her Majesty's 53rd, under Captain Hopkins, supported by Major Barnston's battalion of detachments under Captain Guise, her Majesty's 90th Foot, and some of the Punjaub Infantry under Lieutenant Powlett. The mess-house was carried immediately with a rush. The troops then pressed forward with great vigour, and lined the wall separating the mess-house from the Motee Mahal, which consists of a wide inclosure and many buildings. The enemy here made a last stand, which was overcome after an hour, openings having been broken in the wall, through which the troops poured, with a body of Sappers, and accomplished our communications with the Residency. I had the inexpressible satisfaction, shortly afterwards, of greeting Sir James Outram and Sir Henry Havelock, who came out to meet me before the action was at an end. The relief of the besieged garrison had been accomplished. The troops, including all ranks of officers and men, had worked strenuously and persevered boldly in following up the advantages gained in the various attacks. Every man in the force had exerted himself to the utmost, and now met with his reward.

'It should not be forgotten that these exertions did not date merely from the day that I joined the camp; the various bodies of which the relieving force was composed having made the longest forced marches from

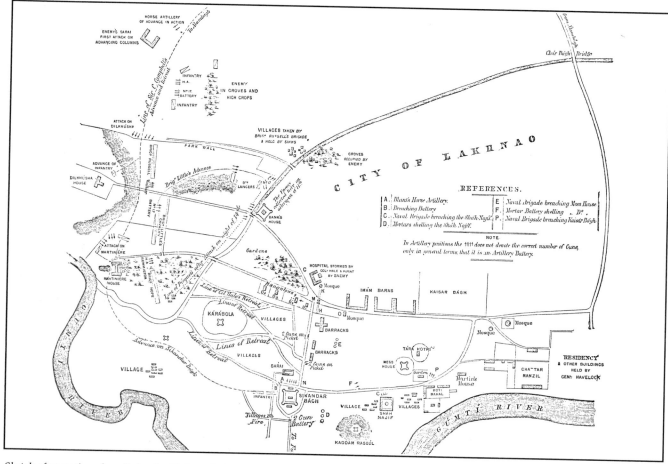

Sketch of operations for relief and withdrawal of the Lucknow garrison.

various directions to enable the Government of India to save the garrison of Lucknow. Some from Agra, some from Allahabad – all had alike undergone the same fatigues in pressing forward for the attainment of this great object. Of their conduct in the field of battle the facts narrated in this despatch are sufficient evidence, which I will not weaken by any eulogy of mine.'

In a subsequent report, dated 'Alumbagh, Nov. 25', Sir Colin Campbell records the incidents connected with the evacuation of the Lucknow Residency. After giving an account of three days' skirmishes with the enemy, he continues:

'Having led the enemy to believe that immediate assault was contemplated, orders were issued for the retreat of the garrison through the lines of our pickets at midnight on the 22nd.

'The ladies and families, the wounded, the treasure, the guns it was thought worth while to keep, the ordnance stores, the grain still possessed by the commissariat of the garrison, and the state prisoners, had all been previously removed.

'Sir James Outram had received orders to burst the guns, which it was thought undesirable to take away; and he was finally directed silently to evacuate the Residency of Lucknow at the hour indicated.

'The dispositions to cover their retreat and to resist

the enemy, should he pursue, were ably carried out by Brigadier the Hon. Adrian Hope; but I am happy to say the enemy was completely deceived, and he did not attempt to follow. On the contrary, he began firing on our old positions many hours after we had left them. The movement of retreat was admirably executed, and was a perfect lesson in such combinations.

'Each exterior line came gradually retiring through its supports, still at length nothing remained but the last line of infantry and guns, with which I was myself to crush the enemy if he had dared to follow up the pickets.

'The only line of retreat through a long and tortuous lane, and all these precautions were absolutely necessary to insure the safety of the force.

'During all these operations, from the 16th inst., Brigadier Greathed's brigade closed in the rear, and now again formed the rear-guard as we retired to Dilkoosha.

'Dilkoosha was reached at 4 a.m. on the 23rd inst. by the whole force.

'On the 22nd the enemy attacked at Dilkoosha, but was speedily driven off, under Brigadier Little's orders.

'I moved with General Grant's division to Alumbagh on the afternoon of the 24th, leaving Sir James Outram's division in position at Dilkoosha, to prevent molestation of the immense convoy of the women and wounded,

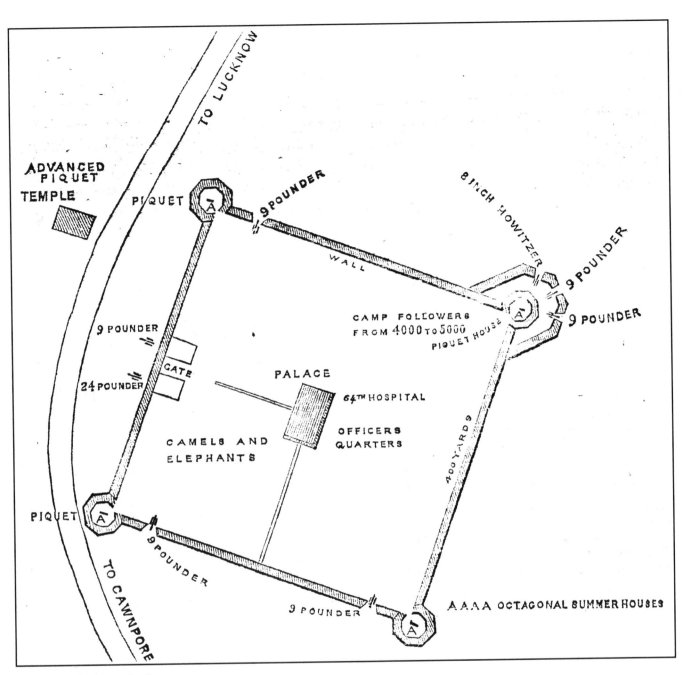

Fort of Alumbagh, near Lucknow.

which it was necessary to transport with us. Sir James Outram closed up this day without annoyance from the enemy.'

'I have the honour to be, my Lord, your Lordship's most obedient humble servant. C. CAMPBELL, General, Commander-in-Chief.'

Sir Henry Havelock, worn out with fatigue and anxiety, died at Alumbagh on 25 November 1857.

A supplement to the *Illustrated London News* of 16 January 1858 contained the following:

'SUMMARY OF EVENTS. The Commander-in-Chief, having relieved the Lucknow garrison, returned to

Cawnpore with the women and children, the wounded, and the State prisoners, twenty-three lacs of rupees, and the King's jewels; also, all the guns worth taking away. Sir James Outram had been left with a strong division at Alumbagh, in the vicinity of Lucknow. All the women and children from Lucknow, and most of the wounded, have safely reached Allahabad.

'On the 26th General Windham attacked and routed the first division of the Gwalior Contingent, 3,000 in number, which had arrived near Cawnpore, after crossing the Jumna at Calpee, taking all their guns except one light field-piece.

'On the 27th November, the main body of the Gwalior

The attack on the Alumbagh.

Contingent entered the civil station of Cawnpore and burnt down the tents of three of our regiments. They were repulsed with severe loss in an attack they made on our entrenchments on the 28th November. The Rifles captured two of their 18-pounders. The 64th Regiment suffered severely. Brigadier Wilson was killed.

'Sir Colin Campbell reached Cawnpore on the evening of the 28th of November. He dispatched the women and wounded towards Allahabad on the 3rd of December, and on the 6th he attacked and completely routed the Gwalior Contingent, pursuing them for fourteen miles along the Calpee road, and capturing their camp, sixteen guns, and an immense quantity of ammunition, park stores, grain, bullocks, &c. Our loss was insignificant.

'General Hope Grant pursued the fugitives of the Gwalior Contingent, and came up with them as they were beginning to cross their guns over the Ganges at Sera Ghaut. He attacked and totally routed them, capturing fifteen guns, and all their remaining stores and ammunition, without himself losing a man.'

In other parts of India British arms were equally successful, with punitive columns proceeding far and wide, pacifying districts 'by the lash and the musket'. Grant tells how, reinforced by some 9,000 Gurkhas under Jung Bahadoor:

'Campbell's whole force at this time amounted to 18,277 men of all arms – infantry, 12,498; cavalry, 3,169; artillery, 1,745; engineers, 865; but these numbers included the column of Outram, who, in addition to holding his post desperately and gallantly at the Alumbagh, had on two different occasions put to total rout two large bodies of the enemy who had attacked them. Though confronted by at least 50,000 trained sepoys, he never experienced the slightest check, but kept open his communications throughout with Campbell's camp at Cawnpore.'

Since the evacuation of Lucknow the rebels had not been idle. Animated by the Begum of Oude, a woman of indomitable energy and charisma, and incited by the Moulvie, a Moslem fanatic, there were now in Lucknow

Jung Bahadoor of Nepal, commander of the Gurkha contingent who fought with the British during the Mutiny.

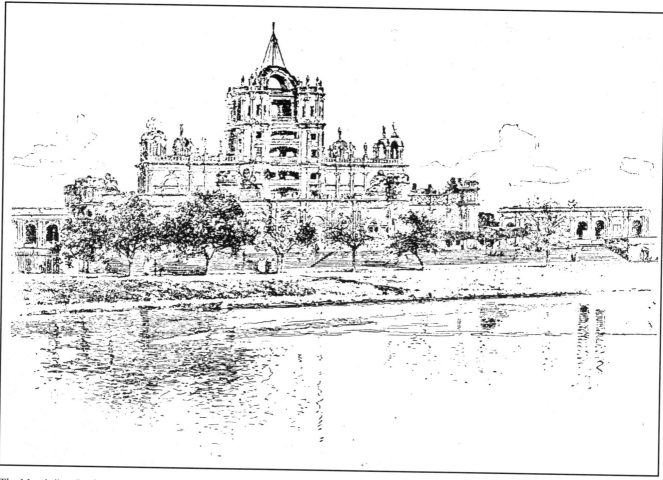

The Martinière, Lucknow.

forces said to exceed 50,000. Grant reveals their determination:

'They had left nothing undone to strengthen the city; and the extraordinary industry displayed by them had seldom been equalled, and never surpassed, in India. Every outlet had been covered by a work, and strong barricades and loopholed parapets had been constructed in every direction. The various buildings formed a range of most massive palaces and walled courts of vast extent, and they had been fortified with the greatest skill. Guns swept the long streets and narrow lanes, and others were mounted even on the domes of mosques and royal palaces; but our troops knew the perils of the task before them, and these served but to increase their noble ardour.

'The first portion of our army crossed the Ganges on the 4th of February, 1858, but the whole were not over until the 28th, when the head-quarters were established at Buntara; but operations did not actually commence till the 2nd of March, when Sir Colin, starting in the grey dawn with the second division of infantry, a strong force of artillery and cavalry, marched eastward of the Alumbagh, and menaced the Dilkhoosa palace, which the enemy abandoned on the following morning when our guns opened on it, and it was seized and occupied

by the 42nd Royal Highlanders; and then a battery was erected to play upon the Secunderbagh. On the 5th, Brigadier Franks came in with his conquering column, and scouts announced that the Ghoorkas of Jung Bahadoor were now near at hand.

'On the preceding day the last guns of the siege-train came up, when the right of our position rested on the Goomtee and Bibrapore, situated within an angle formed by the river, while the left stretched away in the direction of the Alumbagh, about two miles distant. The communication between these two extreme points was kept open by Hodson's Horse; and now the plan of the attack developed itself rapidly. Two floating bridges had been constructed across the Goomtee by means of porter casks lashed to cross-pieces of wood, and covered with planking. By means of these, 6,000 men, with thirty guns, under Sir James Outram, passed over to the other side on the 6th, and took up a position on the Fyzabad road, to close some of the great avenues of supply for the besieged, though it was impossible for Sir Colin to invest completely a city of twenty miles in circumference.'

In his official despatch, Campbell described the task facing his force:

'The series of courts and buildings called the

Ruins of the residency at Lucknow.

Kaiserbagh, considered as a citadel by the rebels, was shut in by three lines of defence towards the Goomtee, of which the line of the canal was the outer one. The second line circled round the large building called the Mess House and the Motee Mahal; and the first, or interior one, was the principal rampart of the Kaiserbagh, the rear of the enclosures of the latter being closed in by the city, through which approach would have been dangerous to an assailant. These lines were flanked by numerous bastions, and rested at one end on the Goomtee, and the other on the great buildings of the street called the Huzratgunge, all of which were strongly fortified, and flanked the streets in every direction. Extraordinary care had been expended on the defence of the houses and bastions to enfilade the streets.

'During the next two days the operations were almost entirely monopolised by the artillery; for as soon as it became apparent that Sir James Outram had turned the first line of defence by pushing boldly forward to the Chukkur Walla Kotee, every gun at the Dilkhoosa opened on the Martinière, and with such splendid effect that it was breached at one of the angles, and was

successfully stormed by the Black Watch, the 53rd, and Perthshire Light Infantry, led by Brigadiers Sir Edward Lugard, C.B. (of the 29th Foot), an officer of great experience, and by Adrian Hope. This achievement was immediately followed by a greater, when the Black Watch and 4th Punjaub Rifles rushed over the intrenchment that abutted on the Goomtee, and, strewing the whole ground with dead and dying, swept like a whirlwind the whole line of works forming the outer line of defence, so far as a building known as Banks's House.'

Grant takes up the narrative:

'Sir Colin now ordered the Naval Brigade with their ponderous guns to open fire on the garrisoned buildings within the college enclosure, in order to drive out the enemy's riflemen; and it was here that, while encouraging his blue-jackets, the gallant Sir William Peel was shot through the thigh, and borne to the rear; he died at Cawnpore. "No seaman of this time appeared to inherit in so large a proportion the calculated daring and the felicitous enthusiasm which gave Nelson the instinct of victory. If his contempt of danger was excessive, he never overlooked the minutest detail which could tend

145

to the safety or success of his undertakings." (*The Times*, 1858)

'As the rebels, who now found they were fighting with the gallows before them, withstood alike the musketry fire and that from six mortars and ten heavy guns, Sir Colin determined to try the bayonet; and then "as the stern and unbending line of Highlanders and Sikhs came on in grim silence, the sepoys fired a few hurried shots and fled from the works. In a few minutes later the Martinière was won, and with it fell the Secunderbagh and the Residency."

'During the night of the 12th Sir James Outram, who was reinforced by a number of heavy guns and mortars, directed his fire on the Kaiserbagh, while at the same time mortars in position a the Begum's house never ceased to play upon the lofty Imambara, the next large palace which it was necessary to storm between the Begum Kotee, and the spacious Kaiserbagh. Eventually the Begum's palace was stormed by the Sutherland Highlanders, who made terrible use of their bayonets, and by the Ghoorkas and Punjaub Rifles; while at the same time Sir James Outram captured the iron bridge of the Goomtee, and made a dreadful slaughter of the flying enemy.

'On the 19th the Moosabagh, which was occupied by 7,000 of the rebels, and was their last stronghold, fell to the British. It was a large palace, with gardens and enclosures situated at some distance to the westward, near the right bank of the river. It was under the immediate care of the ex-queen of Oude, Begum Hazarat-Mahal.

'Marching on the Moosabagh, Sir James Outram attacked it direct by the right bank of the river, while Brigadier Hope Grant cannonaded it from the left, and Brigadier Campbell took post westward from the Alumbagh to cut off all fugitives. Most complete was the rout, and ample the slaughter of the enemy.

'Two days subsequently the Moulvie, after a desperate resistance, was driven out of his post by Sir Edward Lugard, and his followers were pursued by Brigadier Campbell's cavalry, who cut and slashed them down on every hand for six miles along the highway. Resistance everywhere was at an end in Lucknow. . . .

'The plunder of the palaces followed their capture: costly garments, Indian jewellery, precious stones, gold and silver, lace and specie, were the prizes of the conquerors. Luxuriant viands also gratified the hungry and refreshed the weary.

'Sir Colin lost nineteen officers killed, and forty-eight wounded, and more than eleven hundred men. The loss of the enemy was many thousands, but the great majority escaped from indifferent pursuit. An earlier flight than could have been expected, according to the rules of war, baffled the general. Lucknow was taken, but the rebel army was in the field.

'Though with the fall of Lucknow it must have been apparent to the well-trained desperadoes who had defended it that all hope of successful resistance elsewhere was at an end, the struggle in Oude continued

still. Save the capital and the road to Cawnpore, the whole kingdom was still in the possession of the rebels and of those who adhered to them; while they were strong in Behar under the banner of Koer Sing; in Rohilcund, on the northwest, where, on being reinforced by fugitive mutineers from every point, Khan Bahadoor was in such strength as to make it doubtful whether a campaign against him should prelude the reduction of Lucknow; and in the south and south-west, where, throughout the most of Central India, the authority of the Governor-General and of Scindia and Holkar, native princes who had been faithful to us, was quite extinguished.

'Severe fighting was still in prospect before our troops, and as there was but a slender prospect of achieving much before the setting in of the rainy season, all that the Commander-in-chief could do was to provide for the security of shattered and half-desolate Lucknow by entrusting it to the care of Sir Hope Grant, with a force sufficient to garrison it and to overcome the adjacent country; and then prepare for the final crushing of the revolt by marching into Rohilcund, forming a junction with Sir Hugh Rose, who had been moving victoriously through Central India, and lastly to return once more into Oude, and from thence sweep the rebels.'

In *The Illustrated History of the British Empire in India and the East*, E. H. Nolan describes the events at Rohilcund:

'Rohilcund continued in arms; the great cities and towns, such as Bareilly, Shahjehanpore, and Moor-shedabad, were in the hands of the rebels. Khan Bahadoor Khan ruled at Bareilly, and his force was not to be despised. It became apparent to everybody how serious the consequences of the bad generalship which allowed the rebels and mutineers to escape from Lucknow. The plan of the commander-in-chief now was to scour the borders of the province with two columns, which setting out in opposite directions, should meet at Bareilly, the capital, where two of the Delhi princes had taken shelter with Bahadoor Khan. Brigadier Jones was ordered to advance from Roorkee with what was designated the Roorkee field-force, and to take a direction south-east. The other column was to leave Lucknow, under Brigadier Walpole, and was called the Rohilcund field-force.'

Jones succeeded in taking and occupying Moor-shedabad, where he remained awaiting further orders from Lucknow. Walpole marched out of Lucknow on 10 April with 6,000 men and 14 guns, moving along the left bank of the Ganges towards Rohilcund. Encountering a fort at Ruhya, he attacked it in a tactically inept manner, taking heavy losses, and then halted to await the arrival of the Commander-in-Chief. Nolan again:

'The month of April wore away: Bareilly was not captured, Rohilcund was not conquered, although it had been invaded from all quarters by four different armies, numerous, and perfectly equipped. The rebellion proved itself possessed of a vitality for which neither the governor-general nor the commander-in-chief were prepared. In Rohilcund, and all around it, people and chiefs were in arms, and no less than ten distinct columns of British were kept in harassing marches, beneath a burning sun, without being able to produce any decisive effect upon the insurrection. . . .

'The commander-in-chief marched direct into Rohilcund. On the 27th, the junction with Walpole was effected at Zingree, near the Ramgunga. They at once marched to Jellalabad. The moulvie occupied Shahjehanpore with a strong force. Sir Colin's dispositions were made to shut him up there, which he might have done, had he been as active or acute as the moulvie, who completely out-generaled the general, and departed with his troops to Oude, doubling upon the commander-in-chief. This was most disheartening to his excellency, and to the whole British army. Nana Sahib had been with the moulvie; before retreating, he unroofed all the buildings. He thus deprived the English of shade in the midst of the hot season. Sir Colin found a deserted town of dilapidated houses where he had hoped to pen up powerful enemies, and bring them to decisive battle, or immediate surrender. His plans so far were costly, cumbrous, slow, and abortive.'

Grant takes up the story:

'On the 2nd of May, he began to advance northwards on Bareilly, against which two other columns were moving – one under General Penny, by the way of Budaon, from the south-west; and another under General Jones, by Moradabad, from the north-west; but when the sequel came, it was found that Khan Bahadoor was only formidable while he was unmolested.

'On the 3rd, Sir Colin was joined by the column of Penny, who, *en route*, by some carelessness, allowed his troops to be entangled in an ambush and with difficulty saved them from destruction. By sheer dint of hard fighting they beat the foe, and resumed their march; but in the conflict Penny was slain by a body of fanatics, who made a rush at him, and then the beaten rebels hurried to Bareilly, where they strengthened the garrison. Colonel Richmond Jones, of the 6th Dragoon Guards, brought on the brigade to Sir Colin; while his namesake, Brigadier John Jones, *en route* from Moradabad, met also with resistance in his march; but drove the rebels headlong before him, while Campbell was advancing from an opposite direction.

'Reaching Bareilly, Jones carried the bridge, which the rebels were stoutly defending, when the boom of Sir Colin's cannon was heard on the other side of the city. The rebel cavalry contrived to make a sudden attack upon the head-quarter baggage, and created such confusion in Campbell's column as to make further operations for that day impossible. From fatigue, weakness, and sun-stroke, many, on the march, had sunk by the wayside. On the 7th, the attack was resumed. Khan Bahadoor, after making little more than a show of resistance, took to precipitate flight, and left the British in undisputed possession of Bareilly. But it happened that about the same time the Moulvie of Fyzabad, taking advantage of Campbell's march from Shahjehanpore,

made a dash at that town, seized, and pillaged it, driving the slender garrison into the gaol, where they had to defend themselves till succoured by a detachment sent by General Jones from Bareilly. With the capture of the latter, the campaign in Rohilcund was deemed at an end. Some desultory warfare was essayed by the rebels, who were otherwise unable to keep the field, while the operations on the part of the Europeans impracticable. In consequence, Sir Colin Campbell established his head-quarters at Futtehghur, to await the return of the dry and cold season, when he might once more take the field.'

According to Nolan, Campbell now broke up the Rohilcund Field Force and considered the rebellion in that province and in Oude to be subdued. Grant states:

'Leaving Sir Colin Campbell encamped at Futteghur, we shall, in the meanwhile, turn to another quarter, and notice briefly the progress of events in Central India. To check the revolt in its earlier stages had been impossible, as the mutineers were, in more than one instance, headed by the native princes; but their temporary triumph, amid cruelty and bloodshed, was not of long duration. When it was found that the troops of Bombay and Madras could be relied on, columns of them were organised to advance into Central India by the south-east and south-west. [Eventually] . . . the whole were to assume the name of the Central India Field Force, under General Sir Hugh Rose, G.C.B.'

The triumphant progress of Sir Hugh and his force is recorded by Nolan: 'with this, as a flying column, he proceeded to restore order in those provinces where, in a former chapter, mutiny was described as having gained ascendancy. He was ordered to fight his way northward to Jhansi, and subdue the rebel garrison of that place. His force was divided into two brigades, which sometimes acted far apart. The actions fought were generally in the open field, or in the vicinity of jungles and passes; and everywhere Sir Hugh rolled away, or cut through the living ramparts that obstructed his progress. The Rajah of Shagur, an independent district, joined the rebels. Rose and Sir Robert Hamilton, seized and confiscated his territory. Nana Sahib's brother, at the head of a vast mob of looters, was plundering various districts, and threatening the flanks of Sir Hugh's division. Brigadier Stuart, with one of Sir Hugh's brigades, operated to the south of Jhansi, and swept through Malwa, beating the rebels everywhere.

'A body of troops, called the Rajpootana field-force, was collected in the Bombay presidency. It was strong in European cavalry, infantry, and artillery, as well as in good native troops. General Roberts commanded it, and Brigadier General Lawrence attended it as political agent. On the 10th of March, this force marched from Nusserabad against Kotah. The rajah was faithful; the contingent had mutinied. The rajah held a portion of the city, and co-operated with General Roberts, who, by skilful generalship, captured the place without the loss of an officer, and losing only a few men; fifty guns were captured. The rebels, as usual, got away with no loss

The Ranee of Jhansi.

after that which they suffered in the bombardment and advance.

'General Whitlock, in a direction east of Jhansi, pursued wandering bands of rebels with such celerity as to leave them no rest, cutting up and dispering them in every direction.

'Sir Hugh Rose, having laid siege to Jhansi, maintained it with vigour.'

The epic story of the siege, the abortive relief attempt and the assault, is told by Grant:

'Jhansi, the little state which Lord Dalhousie had annexed five years before – a deed which the ranee so terribly revenged when the Mutiny took place. She had now assembled 10,000 men for the defence of the town, and was a woman who had given such proof of her talents that they would have excited admiration but for the horror she caused by her dreadful massacre of our people. On the 21st of March, Sir Hugh Rose was before Jhansi, a city of four miles and a half in circuit, surrounded by luxuriant and extensive woods, and girt by a wall of solid masonry, varying from six to twelve feet thick, and from eighteen to thirty feet in height, flanked by strong gun-bastions, and closely loopholed for musketry. Within the town, and enclosed by it on all sides except the west, where the rock on which it stands terminates in an abrupt and lofty precipice, rises the citadel, completely commanding both the town and the roads leading to it, and strongly fortified by nature and art. Its walls, constructed of solid granite, from sixteen to twenty feet thick, were flanked by elaborate outworks of the same solid construction; while the interior, partly occupied by the massive buildings of the palace, contained several lofty towers mounting heavy ordnance, and in some places pierced with five tiers of loopholes.

'The south appearing its weakest side, the concentrated fire of Sir Hugh's guns silenced many of those of the enemy; the great ramparts began to crumble, and all looked forward to the hour of assault with an ardour that was suddenly damped on the 31st of March, when tidings came that a body of 20,000 men, including that portion of the Gwalior Contingent which had escaped the vengeance of Sir Colin Campbell at Cawnpore, were advancing under the command of Nana Sahib's lieutenant, Tantia Topee, to the relief of the ranee. The odds were fearful now; but on the 1st of April, without slackening his fire against Jhansi, Sir Hugh moved out to meet the enemy with only 1,200 men, of whom 500 were British soldiers.'

(It was claimed at the time that Tantia Topee, a Mahratta chief, showed himself to be a braver man and a better general than his kinsman, the Nana, fighting with courage, manœuvring with skill and revealing expertise in choosing his field of battle.)

Grant's account continues:

'A battle which took place near the bank of the Betwa proved the utter inability of any native force to cope with our troops when handled as Rose handled them on that day. After a fire from his field-guns, which made dreadful havoc among the unwieldy masses of the enemy, both their wings were simultaneously charged by a handful of cavalry, then a wild cry arose in front – a shout of rage and vengeance, and through the smoke there flashed before the eyes of the rebels a slender line of white caps, red coats, and a hedge of steel, as our tiny force of infantry rushed, cheering, on with the bayonet, and then – huddled together, rolled into themselves as it were – the rebels were hurled in confusion and dismay across the river, leaving 1,500 dead behind them, and all the guns they had brought from Calpee. From the ramparts the cruel ranee saw the signal defeat of her confederates, and with a heart that began to shrink at last.

'On the 3rd of April, the town was assaulted by two columns of attack; one, composed of the 3rd Europeans, the Bombay and Madras Sappers, with the Hyderabad Contingent, entered on the left by escalade; the other, composed of some Royal Engineers, H.M. 86th (County Down), and the 25th Bombay Native Infantry, clad in scarlet, faced with pale yellow, stormed the breach direct; and both columns, after hewing a passage through the streets, met at the palace, which was stormed and sacked, but not till every avenue had been fiercely contested, "and no quarter was asked or given".

'The fighting did not finally cease till the 6th, when the ranee, after making a last desperate stand, escaped; she was seen in full flight mounted on a grey horse, and though attended by only a few followers, could not be overtaken.'

Nolan writes of Rose's advance on Kalpi (Calpee):

'Possessed of Jhansi Sir Hugh found his difficulties great. The Kotah rebel contingent infested the roads, the country people were in arms, and Tantia Topee was recruiting his forces at Calpee. The number of sick and wounded was great. While he remained at Jhansi settling affairs in that city, and reorganizing, he threw out parties in every direction, which scoured the country, dispersing bands, chastising rebel rajahs, razing forts, and defeating mutineers.

'The Rajpootana field-force performed numerous desultory exploits, and dispersed many bands of Rajpoot and Mahratta rebels. The Gujerat field-force disarmed the country, and hung or blew away from guns rajahs and native officers of the Bombay army detected in treasonable correspondence with Tantia Topee, Nana Sahib, and other rebel leaders.

'The rebels now became exceedingly anxious for Calpee. Ram Rao Gohind, a Mahratta, had collected three thousand men of his race, and three guns. Tantia Topee had made up his force to ten thousand men, composed of mutinous sepoys and sowars, about one thousand Mahratta horse, and not much less than seven thousand Ghazees, or fanatics. Calpee is on the right bank of the Jumna, and derived importance from being a place of support for the insurrection, and from being on the main road from Jhansi to Cawnpore.

'On the 9th of May Sir Hugh Rose, on his way to Calpee, had arrived at Kooneh, where Tantia Topee and the Ranee of Jhansi intercepted his march. The enemy was intrenched; Rose beat them out of their intrenchments, captured the town and several guns, and made much havoc, especially in the pursuit. The British, and the general himself, principally suffered from exposure to the sun. His advance to Calpee was resisted perpetually, but in vain: as the torrent bears away the branch which falls across its course, so the forces of the rebels were swept away in his progress. Maxwell, from Cawnpore, Whitlock, from the south, Riddell, from Etawah, were all acting in a combined system of operation with Sir Hugh Rose. As he approached Calpee, skirmishes were frequent, occurring daily, almost hourly. A nephew of Nana Sahib was the most active chief in obstructing Sir Hugh's approach. On the 18th Rose shelled the earthworks which had been constructed by Nana Sahib some time before. On the opposite bank of the Jumna Maxwell opened fire next day.'

Grant writes of a sortie by the rebels, which indicates how, throughout the Mutiny, British forces were encountering trained and disciplined soldiers, not irregular native bands:

'On the 20th, they made a sortie with force and skill; but were hopelessly repulsed; yet on the 22nd, after Golowlee, six miles from Calpee, had been reached, they were seen marching along the road in strength and in order of battle. An encounter at once took place, and for some time the conflict was maintained by the enemy with so much resolution, and with numbers so overwhelming, that the issue looked doubtful, till Rose resorted to the bayonet. Then hurled headlong from the field, the enemy's columns of infantry were broken up and scattered in every direction, after which Calpee was captured, with all their ammunition, stores, and the accumulated plunder of every station from which they had come.'

Believing that the rebellion in that part of India was subdued, on 1 June 1858 Sir Hugh Rose issued a general order:

'Soldiers! you have marched more than a thousand miles, and taken more than a hundred guns; you have forced your way through mountain passes and intricate jungles, and over rivers; you have captured the strongest forts, and beat the enemy, no matter what the odds, wherever you met him; you have restored extensive districts to the Government, and peace and order now reign where before, for twelve months, were tyranny and rebellion; you have done all this, and you have never had a check. I thank you with all my sincerity for your bravery, your devotion, and your discipline.'

The eloquent farewell address was a little premature, for on the very day it was delivered the fugitives from Kalpi entered Gwalior, drove Scindia from his throne and convulsed all central India by their success. Grant recorded the course of events:

'The . . . rebels entered Gwalior under Tantia Topee, who drove Scindia from his throne, and within a week was at the head of 18,000 men cantoned beside the capital. Scindia sent to Agra for succour; but none could be

given. He was then compelled to fly there for shelter, after appealing in vain to his troops, of whom 3,000 cavalry and 6,000 infantry, with eight guns, went over to Rao Sahib, the infamous Nana's nephew. The bodyguard fought till cut to pieces, and a remnant escorted their sovereign to Agra. On this the Nana was proclaimed Peishwa of the Mahrattas, the title he had assumed at Cawnpore. Rao Sahib was declared sovereign of Gwalior; the vast treasures of Scindia were seized, and the rich citizens were plundered, the flight from Calpee proved the ruin of Gwalior, to which the adjacent rajahs flocked with their retainers; thus a large army was organised, with plenty of stores and treasure to supply it.

'When he conquered at Calpee, Sir Hugh Rose was in ill-health, and probably it was owing to that circumstance, and the slenderness of his cavalry, that any escaped thence; but when tidings reached him of these events at Gwalior, he at once marched against the rebels, who were now led, less by Tantia Topee and others, than by the warlike Ranee of Jhansi, who, clad in male attire, mounted on a beautiful charger, and accompanied by a select staff, kept moving about where her presence was required, displaying a skill, energy, and enthusiasm worthy of a better cause. On the 16th of June, Rose was near the old cantonments at Gwalior, and reconnoitred the position at a time when the heat was 130° in the shade; and in the morning, though the troops were exhausted after a night march, he attacked instantly, and did so victoriously. The slaughter of the fugitives was frightful, some of the trenches that lay beyond the cantonments being filled to the brim with corpses. Sir Hugh then encamped within the captured lines.

'The ranee organised a fresh force to intercept a reinforcement that was coming up under Brigadier Smith from the westward. On the 17th of June, that officer drove the rebels before him, and it was in his last charge that the ranee, who had been in every engagement since she left Jhansi, was killed by one of our hussars, who was ignorant of her sex. Her body was borne away by her attendants to be burned.'

Nolan tells of the last days of the Mutiny:

'Tantia Topee assumed the direction of those opinions which she had guided, and fought with skill and energy. Smith, however, was victorious. His contingent was joined by the general-in-chief, who effected a flank movement to that side of the city. The next day he stormed the chief of the fortified heights held by the enemy, who, finding that no obstacles impeded the English, became panic-struck, and fled out of the place. The British cavalry pursued the broken fugitives, cutting them down in vast numbers, until the plains were strewn with their dead. Scindiah was reinstated upon his throne.

'The main body of the rebels had retreated to Kurawlee. Thither Rose sent light troops in pursuit, Brigadier Napier took the command. On arriving at Jowla Alipore, he observed the enemy in great force with twenty-five guns. After all their signal defeats an losses, they had an ample command of *matériel* of war. Napier had not a thousand men; the enemy counted ten times that number. The gallant brigadier, worthy of his name, achieved a swift, glorious, and complete victory, capturing all their guns. After a vain pursuit of the nimble fugitives, the conqueror returned to Gwalior.

'Tantia Topee, with another body of about eight thousand in number, directed his way to Geypore, the chief of the Rajpoot states. He carried with him the crown jewels, and the treasure of Scindiah. This daring and active chief now kept Central India in agitation.

'Sir Hugh Rose, worn out with toil, retired from his command, and the Central India field-force was broken up. Sir Edward Lugard soon after also retired, worn out with fatigue and anxiety. In this way almost all the eminent men which the mutiny had called forth as able commanders dropped away gradually, and gave place to others who followed up with success the work of pacification. The neck of the Indian rebellion was now broken. Proclamations of amnesty and pardon were issued by the government to all who would seek mercy – exceptions in cases of actual murder, and of the great ringleaders of insurrection, being of course made. These proclamations told upon vast numbers, but many remained contumacious to the last.

'After the hot season of 1858, the rebellion became a guerilla war, and a pursuit of bandits. The great leaders were discomfited, the minor rajahs and chiefs were captured, hung, blown away from guns, or, submitting, were pardoned. The moulvie was killed in an encounter with one of the Rohilcund rajahs, who deemed it his

Sir Hugh Rose.

'Blowing the Mutineers from the guns.'

interest to side with the English. The moulvie was a sincere zealot, and was probably the man who devised the scheme of the revolt, and created the rebellion. Nana Sahib's cowardice kept him from the path of danger, and he escaped capture. He ultimately fled into the Nepal dominions, with a band of followers. The Nana's nephew fell in one of the combats in Central India, after the flight of the rebels from Gwalior. Tantia Topee for some time eluded pursuit, and wandered about, a wretched, but gallant fugitive, until at last he became a prisoner, and paid with his life the penalty of his misdeeds. With the removal of that remarkable man from the scene of so many horrors, so great struggles, and so much bloodshed, the last spark of rebellion expired.

'In the summer of 1859, thanksgiving was offered for the entire suppression of the insurrection, but it was in fact subdued at the close of the campaign of 1858, with the exception of roving bands of marauders, for the suppression of which the police were adequate.'

BATTLE HONOURS – INDIAN MUTINY 1857–8

DELHI, 1857

6th Dragoon Guards (Carabiniers)
9th (The Queen's Royal) Regt. of (Light) Dragoons (Lancers)
8th (The King's) Regt. of Foot
61st (South Gloucestershire) Regt. of Foot
52nd (Oxfordshire) Regt. of Foot (Light Infantry)
1st Bn. 60th (The King's Royal Rifle Corps)
75th Regt. of Foot
H.E.I.C. 1st Bengal (European) Regt. (Fusiliers)
H.E.I.C. 2nd Bengal (European) Regt. (Fusiliers)

Indian Army

Hodson's Horse 1st Regt.
Hodson's Horse 2nd Regt.
1st Regt. of Cavalry, Punjab Irregular Force
2nd Regt. of Cavalry, Punjab Irregular Force
5th Regt. of Cavalry, Punjab Irregular Force
The Corps of Guides
Corps of Bengal Sappers & Miners
Punjab Sappers (Punjab Pioneers)
4th Regt. Sikh Infantry, Punjab Irregular Force
1st Regt. Punjab Infantry, Punjab Irregular Force
2nd Regt. Punjab Infantry, Punjab Irregular Force
4th Regt. Punjab Infantry, Punjab Irregular Force
1st Belooch Battalion, Bombay Native Infantry
The Sirmoor Battalion
7th (or Kamaon) Local Battalion

LUCKNOW, DEFENCE OF

5th Regt. of Foot (Northumberland Fusiliers)
32nd (Cornwall) Regt. of Foot
64th (2nd Staffordshire) Regt. of Foot
78th (Highland) Regt. of Foot (or Ross-shire Buffs)
84th (York & Lancaster) Regt. of Foot
90th Regt. of Foot (Perthshire Volunteers) (Light Infantry)
H.E.I.C. 1st Madras (European) Regt. (Fusiliers)

Indian Army

The Regiment of Ferozepore
The Regiment of Lucknow

LUCKNOW, RELIEF OF

9th (The Queen's Royal) Regt. of (Light) Dragoons (Lancers)
5th Regt. of Foot (Northumberland Fusiliers)
8th (The King's) Regt. of Foot
23rd (Royal Welch Fusiliers) Regt. of Foot
53rd (Shropshire) Regt. of Foot
75th Regt. of Foot
82nd Regt. of Foot (The Prince of Wales's Volunteers)
84th (York & Lancaster) Regt. of Foot
93rd (Highland) Regt. of Foot

Indian Army

Hodson's Horse 1st Regt.
Hodson's Horse 2nd Regt.
1st Regt. Sikh Irregular Cavalry
1st Regt. of Cavalry, Punjab Irregular Force
2nd Regt. of Cavalry, Punjab Irregular Force
5th Regt. of Cavalry, Punjab Irregular Force
Corps of Bengal Sappers & Miners
Punjab Sappers (Punjab Pioneers)
2nd Regt. Punjab Infantry, Punjab Irregular Force
4th Regt. Punjab Infantry, Punjab Irregular Force

LUCKNOW, CAPTURE OF

2nd (The Queen's) Regt. of Dragoon Guards
7th (The Queen's Own) Regt. of (Light) Dragoons (Hussars)
9th (The Queens' Royal) Regt. of (Light) Dragoons (Lancers)
5th Regt. of Foot (Northumberland Fusiliers)
10th (North Lincolnshire) Regt. of Foot
20th (East Devonshire) Regt. of Foot
23rd (Royal Welch Fusiliers) Regt. of Foot
90th Regt. of Foot (Perthshire Volunteers) (Light Infantry)
34th (Cumberland) Regt. of Foot
38th (1st Staffordshire) Regt. of Foot
42nd (Royal Highland) Regt. of Foot
97th (Earl of Ulster's) Regt. of Foot
53rd (Shropshire) Regt. of Foot
78th (Highland) Regt. of Foot (or Ross-shire Buffs)
79th Regt. of Foot (Cameron Highlanders)
84th (York & Lancaster) Regt. of Foot
93rd (Highland) Regt. of Foot
H.E.I.C. 1st Bengal (European) Regt. Fusiliers
H.E.I.C. 1st Madras (European) Regt. Fusiliers
The Rifle Brigade

Indian Army

The Regiment of Ferozepore
Punjab Sappers (Punjab Pioneers)
2nd Regt. Punjab Infantry, Punjab Irregular Force
4th Regt. Punjab Infantry, Punjab Irregular Force
27th Regt. Madras Native Infantry

CENTRAL INDIA

8th (The King's Royal Irish) Regt. of (Light) Dragoons (Hussars)
12th (The Prince of Wales's Royal) Regt. of Lancers
14th (The King's) Regt. of (Light) Dragoons
17th Regt. of (Light) Dragoons (Lancers)
H.E.I.C. 3rd Madras (European) Regt.
80th Regt. of Foot (Staffordshire Volunteers)
95th (Derbyshire) Regt. of Foot
71st (Highland) Regt. of Foot (Light Infantry)
72nd (Duke of Albany's Own Highlanders) Regt. of Foot
83rd Regt. of Foot
86th (Royal County Down) Regt. of Foot
88th Regt. of Foot (Connaught Rangers)
H.E.I.C. 3rd Bombay (European) Regt.

Indian Army

1st Cavalry Regt. Hyderabad Contingent
4th Cavalry Regt. Hyderabad Contingent

1st Regt. Bombay Light Cavalry (Lancers)
2nd Regt. Bombay Light Cavalry
3rd Regt. Bombay Light Cavalry
1st Regt. Scinde Irregular Horse
Corps of Madras Sappers & Miners
Corps of Bombay Sappers & Miners
31st Regt. Bengal Native Infantry
The Meena Battalion
The Mhairwara Battalion
1st Regt. Madras Native Infantry

19th Regt. Madras Native Infantry
3rd Infantry Regt. Hyderabad Contingent
5th Infantry Regt. Hyderabad Contingent
4th Regt. Bombay Native Infantry or Rifle Corps
10th Regt. Bombay Native Infantry
12th Regt. Bombay Native Infantry
13th Regt. Bombay Native Infantry
24th Regt. Bombay Native Infantry
25th Regt. Bombay Native Infantry

In Conclusion

These last pages, a fascinating blend of obituary and prophesy compiled by an anonymous journalist and published in the *Illustrated London News* more than 130 years ago, might be an appropriate consummation to this saga of 15 turbulent years of Anglo-Indian wars. The prize was the 'Jewel in the Crown' – India, which, in the event, was to be governed by the British for less than the century that followed. With that awareness and with hindsight, the seeming presumption and smugness of our Victorian great-great-grandfathers might be viewed with cynicism. However, this should not be allowed to temper our admiration and respect – even if given grudgingly – for that legion of British administrators and commanders who, in India and Britain, acted in a manner true to their beliefs and the age in which they lived. Nor should that timeless virtue, Courage, be over-looked; it was displayed constantly by British soldiers who were invariably fighting superior numbers of trained and disciplined native soldiers, themselves equally brave, sometimes to the point of fanaticism.

'What India may be made in the way of benefit of herself and to the whole British empire has been strikingly exemplified in the annexation of the Punjaub. That fertile province has become still richer; her people prosperous, peaceable, and loyal; her revenues a source of advantage to herself and to the government of India: and all this has resulted from a complete, instead of a partial conquest, a thorough disarming of the seditious and suspected, the impartial administration of justice, and adoption of laws and a financial system based upon correct principles of political economy. The Blue-books which have been issued respecting the government of the Punjaub, and the reports of trustworthy travellers and residents, place the prosperity of the whole Sikh districts beyond doubt, and prove that since the entire destruction of the Khalsa army, and the organisation of a separate, efficient, and economical government, the whole country of the five rivers has become a source of strength to the government of India. The readiness with which Sikh volunteers were formed, from Ferozepore to Peshawur, during the recent terrible revolt of the Bengal sepoys, and the efficiency with which the old soldiers of the maharajah served in our ranks, impose the conviction that, notwithstanding the impracticable nature of Brahminism and Mohammedanism, all India may in time be governed as well as the Punjaub, and made even more productive of advantage to its own people as well as to its rulers. As already remarked, the great revolt of the sepoys seems providentially to hasten and facilitate such results. So long as a native army constituted as was that of Bengal, and two other native armies so far similarly constituted as those of Bombay and Madras, dictated to the government, or were as much a source of apprehension as power, it was impossible to carry out those improvements of which India is susceptible, and which the British people desire. Even in the Punjaub it was the Bengal army that created our only danger. Should the armies of Bombay and Madras be permitted to remain as they are, or a Bengal army similar in any great degree to the former, be re-constructed, the perils which have so long hung over English rule in India will still impend. Present events, however, have determined the future for us, and the military and civil *régime* will henceforth guarantee the solidity of our dominions, its more thorough usefulness, and its greater honour and renown. The words of Sir Henry Russell, written in 1842, are strikingly appropriate to such considerations:– "Our tenure of India must, under all circumstances, be a military one. If we do not hold it by the exercise of our arms, at least we do by the impression of them. If ever we are thought to have lost our military supremacy, am afraid no other will remain to us; by our army w must either stand or fall. The most fearful of all disaste that we can dread, therefore, is disaffection among native troops. When it does occur, and occur it w unless it be preceded and anticipated by some othe will be the work of some one bold, able man of th selves, who obtains influence among them. Su

154

person has never yet appeared, it is true, but it would be a delusion for us to assume that no such person will appear. The natives of India are not an unlikely stock for such a shoot to spring from, nor is the mass ill-suited to the rising of such a leaven. The event, if ever it do come, will be abrupt. It will be an explosion. It will give no warning, but will be upon us before there is time to arrest it. The mischief will have been done before its approach has been discovered. It is only by being fore-seen that such a danger can be averted. . . . The more busily the troops are employed, the more they may be relied upon. In our own territory, as well as in the terri-tory of our allies, we must be provided against every emergency. Forces equipped for rapid movement and effective service must be maintained within reach of each other. No point on our border, no quarter of our territory, must be suffered to feel itself at liberty. No incursion will be attempted from abroad, no rising will be adventured at home, if it is not encouraged by the appearance of impunity. Even if these preparations should not be required to repel attack or suppress insur-rection, the very appearance of them will serve the purpose of preventing it." The recent revolt fulfilled the predictions of Sir Henry, except in the particular of a man of eminent military parts arising among the sepoys, which, however, he regarded as a possible or not very improbable event rather than one likely. The danger he depicted as existing in 1842 will exist in 1862, or at any other time, if we continue the old military system of absolute confidence in the sepoy; the preventive care, pointed out in the above quotation as essential, must be the policy of our future rule. The explosion has occurred, and the occasion is furnished not only of test-ing such predictions, but of profiting by such counsels. If we do take up the government of India with a resolute and just hand, the day will not be so distant as some imagine when over her vast area rich cities shall flour-ish; fertile fields bloom with the beauty and luxuriance of her glorious clime; peace smile within her borders over many millions of contented people; surrounding nations look upon our power as a beauty and a glory; and the grandeur of empire appear as the consequence and accompaniment not merely of our heroism or our skill, but of our virtue.'

Select Bibliography

The sources consulted when compiling this book are listed below; all were written at the time of, or soon after, the events described. This was deliberate to ensure that all the descriptions and opinions included in these pages are first-hand and, often, verbatim reports. Undoubtedly, and mentioned here with sincere gratitude, the single greatest source of information and on-the-spot accounts were issues of the Illustrated London News, which providentially began publication on 14 May 1842, the year before the first of the wars described in this book.

It is beyond the scope of this Bibliography to enumerate the literally countless books that have been written during the last century and more about the wars and armies in and of India. In the past, the author has avidly read many of them, but none has been used as a source of reference in the writing of this book.

Callwell, C. E., *Small Wars: Their Principles and Practice*, H.M.S.O., 1906

Fortescue, Sir John, *A History of the British Army*, Macmillan, 1912

Grant, James, *British Battles on Land and Sea*, Cassell, Petter, Galpin & Co.

Grant, James, *Illustrated History of India*, Cassell, Petter, Galpin & Co.

The History of the Revolt in India, W. & R. Chambers, 1859

Moore-Smith, G. C. (editor), *The Autobiography of Lieutenant-General Sir Harry Smith*, John Murray, 1902

Nolan, E. H., *The Illustrated History of the British Empire in India and the East*, James S. Virtue

Rait, Robert S., *The Life and Campaigns of Hugh, First Viscount Gough, Field Marshal*, Archibald Constable, 1903

Stafford, William Cooke, *England's Battles by Sea and Land*, The London Printing & Publishing Co.

The War in India: Despatches of Lieutenant-General Viscount Hardinge, General Lord Gough, Sir Harry Smith and other documents, John Ollivier, 1846

Wylly, H. C., *The Military Memoirs of Lieutenant-General Sir Joseph Thackwell*, John Murray, 1908

Periodicals and journals

Illustrated London News 1843–59

The Journal of the Society for Army Historical Research

Picture Credits

The illustrations on pages 14, 15, 17, 28, 45, 52, 55, 69, 71, 75, 76, 81, 82, 84, 91, 96, 97, 104, 116, 122, 126 and 131 are all reproduced by kind permission of *The Illustrated London News*. The remainder of the illustrations in this book are taken exclusively from those contemporary books listed in the bibliography.

Index

Napier, General Sir Charles 12,
    13, 15–18, 20–6, 31, 86, 90, 97
Nicholson, John 12, 115, 119

Omerkote fortress 25
Outram, Sir James 12, 16, 18,
    135–6, 139, 141, 145–6

Peel, Captain, Royal Navy and
    Naval siege train 139, 145
Pennycuick, Brigadier 87
Punch, magazine (on Gough) 96
Punniar, battle of 27, 30, 36–7

Queen's troops, distribution in
    India (1857) 103–4

Ramnuggur, battle of 78–81, 82–3
Ranjit Singh, ruler of Punjab 39
Ranjur Singh, Sikh leader 57–8
Robertson, Lieutenant J.P. (letter
    from Mudki) 43–5
Rohilcund 146–7
Rose, General Sir Hugh 12,
    146–7, 149, 150–1

Secunderbagh, at Lucknow 138–9
Sepoys 21–2
    Indian Mutiny 11
    at Mudki 44, 49

Shere Mohammed 23–6
Shere Singh, Rajah 76–8, 85, 91
Sikhs 11, 12, 28
    army (khalsa) 39, 41, 96–7
    1st Sikh War 39–73
    2nd Sikh War 74–98
    British casualties by regiments
        (1st Sikh War) 73
Sind (Scinde) Campaign 13–26
Sind, Amirs of 15, 16, 18
Smith, General Sir Harry 12,
    30–1, 39, 57–63, 67–8
Sobraon, battle of 65–71

casualties, British 69–70
casualties, Sikh 70
Gough's despatch 65–70
Sikh guns captured at 68–9

Tantia Topee 149, 150, 151, 152
Tej Singh, Sikh leader 53
Thackwell, General Sir John 35,
    81–2, 86–7, 88–9, 92, 95–7

Wheeler, General Hugh 121–3
Whish, General 75–7, 83, 91
Wilson, Brigadier 110